Helping Doctoral Students Write

Helping Doctoral Students Write offers a new approach to doctoral writing. By treating research *as* writing and writing *as* research, the authors offer pedagogical strategies for doctoral supervisors that will assist the production of well-argued and lively dissertations.

It is clear that many doctoral candidates find research writing complicated and difficult, but the advice they receive often glosses over the complexities of writing and/or locates the problem in the writer. Rejecting the DIY websites and manuals that promote a privatized, skills-based approach to writing research, Kamler and Thomson provide a new framework for scholarly work that is located in personal, institutional and cultural contexts. Their discussion of the complexities of forming a scholarly identity is illustrated by stories and writings of actual doctoral students.

The pedagogical approach developed in the book is based on the notion of writing as a social practice. This approach allows supervisors to think of doctoral writers as novices who need to learn new ways with words as they enter the discursive practices of scholarly communities. This involves learning sophisticated writing practices with specific sets of conventions and textual characteristics. The authors offer supervisors practical advice on helping with commonly encountered writing tasks such as the proposal, the journal abstract, the literature review and constructing the dissertation argument.

In conclusion, they present a persuasive argument that universities must move away from simply auditing supervision to supporting the development of scholarly research communities. Any doctoral supervisor keen to help their students develop as academics will find the new ideas presented in this book fascinating and insightful reading

Barbara Kamler is Professor of Education at Deakin University, Australia.
Pat Thomson is Professor of Education at the University of Nottingham, UK and an Adjunct Professor at the University of South Australia.

This is an exceptionally wise and useful book. Kamler and Thomson draw on a wide range of scholarship and insider knowledge to offer superb advice about scholarly writing in general and the doctoral dissertation in particular. A gem of a resource.

Mike Rose, the University of California Los Angeles
and author of The Mind at Work *and* An Open Language:
Selected Writing on Literacy, Language, and Opportunity.

This unique book dispenses more thoughtful and useful advice than a whole shelf full of currently available how-to books on dissertation writing. Kamler and Thomson do a superb job of demystifying the dissertation process – from initial questions through literature review to manuscript preparation – without ever reducing it to a step-by-step procedure. On one hand, the book shows the dissertation to be a profound rhetorical achievement; on the other hand, the authors' pragmatic and commonsense approach makes it seem quite attainable. They see doctoral students as disciplinary newcomers and offer eminently practical advice to supervisors on how to introduce students to their discipline's knowledge-making practices. Although their analysis is sharp and critical, their tone throughout is reassuring, collegial, and humane. Anyone who supervises doctoral students will benefit from this book.

Dr Anthony Paré, Director, Centre for the Study and Teaching of Writing,
McGill University, Montreal, Canada

This thoughtful and well-crafted book addresses writing-centered supervision. Using straightforward language, the authors suggest a number of strategies to help doctoral researchers write with authority. By exploring ways of using metaphors, showing how arguments are developed, and creating a scholarly persona in the text, they demonstrate and model a range of writing and textual strategies that might be used in a dialogue-based supervision. I highly recommend it, not only for doctoral courses, but also as a framework for the textual practices of scholarship. The examples used within each chapter are excellent. This book can indeed inspire thinking about our own writing as researchers, as well as our social practice as supervisors of doctoral researchers. As such, it is both timely and powerful.

Professor Jorun Møller, University of Oslo,
Department of Teacher Education and School Development.

This is a brilliant book. It is clear, engaging and based on impressive practical experience and scholarship. I immediately wanted to share it with colleagues and students. The authors show how the development of doctoral writing – a topic generally absent from doctoral education or reduced to a subsidiary 'skills' agenda – can and should be integral to learning to do research itself. With their guidance, supervisors and doctoral (and other) researchers can develop writing practices which 'combine aesthetic judgments, technical virtuosity, epistemologies and …. research sensibility'.

Professor Diana Leonard, author of A Women's Guide to Doctoral Studies,
Institute of Education, London, UK

Helping Doctoral Students Write is a must-read for students and academics who are serious about academic writing and postgraduate education. Kamler and Thomson model, in the reader-friendly way they have written their book, that it is possible to make even difficult ideas fascinating and accessible. The many examples in the text support their position that students can learn to exploit the meaning potential of grammar to adopt more authoritative scholarly identities. They convincingly make the case that text work is identity work.

Professor Hilary Janks, Applied English Language Studies
University of the Witwatersrand, South Africa

Helping Doctoral Students Write

Pedagogies for supervision

Barbara Kamler and Pat Thomson

Routledge
Taylor & Francis Group

LONDON AND NEW YORK

First published 2006
by Routledge
2 Park Square, Milton Park, Abingdon, Oxon, OX14 4RN

Simultaneously published in the USA and Canada
by Routledge
270 Madison Ave, New York NY 10016

Routledge is an imprint of the Taylor & Francis Group, an informa business

Transferred to Digital Printing 2010

© 2006 Barbara Kamler and Pat Thomson

Typeset in Times by
HWA Text and Data Management, Tunbridge Wells

British Library Cataloguing in Publication Data
A catalogue record for this book is available from the British Library

Library of Congress Cataloging-in-Publication Data
A catalog record for this book has been requested

ISBN 10: 0–415–34683–5 (hbk)
ISBN 10: 0–415–34684–3 (pbk)
ISBN 10: 0–203–96981–2 (ebk)

ISBN 13: 978–0–415–34683–2 (hbk)
ISBN 13: 978–0–415–34684–9 (pbk)
ISBN 13: 978–0–203–96981–6 (ebk)

For our children
Simon, Shaun, Susan and Jeremy

Contents

Figures

Tables

Foreword

We did not intend to write this book. We began having a conversation about doctoral writing as a result of a presentation Pat gave to a doctoral summer school at which Barbara was present as a university staff member. Pat's discussion of the writing decisions she had made in her PhD thesis sparked lively conversation.

We discovered that we thought in similar ways about writing, despite the differences in our backgrounds and professional training. Barbara was trained as an educational linguist and after her PhD moved to combine this with critical discourse analysis in a range of research projects on gender and school literacy. She describes herself as a teacher and researcher of writing across the lifespan, most recently focusing on cultural narratives of aging and cross-generational literacy pedagogies. Her interest in writing is deeply connected to issues of social justice, identity and representation. Pat is a late career academic, having spent most of her life as a school principal and school system policy maker; she combined journalism teaching with extra-curricular activities in print and radio media. She describes herself as a scholar committed to social justice and her research focuses on policy, questions of power, place and identity, and democratizing education. Her interest in writing stems from being a compulsive writer herself.

We came together in a serendipitous manner, but our mutual concerns about the relative scarcity of well-theorized material about doctoral supervision and writing has kept us in dialogue.

We began writing this book after giving a performance at a conference about 'writing up'. We explain our exasperation with this term in the first chapter. But sometime during the writing of the paper, we realized we had the makings of a book. We gave a series of workshops in Canada, Australia and South Africa to help us sort out key moves in the production of a doctoral thesis – working with literatures, writing abstracts, constructing arguments, and writing conference papers. At every workshop there were more people than we expected, and this affirmed our belief that doctoral writing was a kind of present absence in the landscape of doctoral education. It was something that everybody worried about, but about which there was too little systematic debate and discussion.

We interviewed our colleagues and our students as well as workshop participants, and their voices appear in the text in semi-fictionalized accounts. We have adopted a convention of combining actual words and events drawn from actual interviews with fictional characters. We also use the writing of students, both exemplary and problematic texts, but modify these so that they are not identifiable. This is partly about ensuring confidentiality but it is also about trying to capture the patterns, emotions and experiences at issue rather than anything specific. For that reason we have not given citations for any of the student writings. Rather, we focus on the way in which they have written and argued. Fictionalizing accounts has also given us more licence to write imaginatively in ways that we hope will resonate with readers (see Clough, 2002). We thank our students and colleagues for the gift of their words and hope that they agree with the ways we have represented them.

We want to acknowledge from the outset that actually getting words on the page is difficult. Anxiety about how to begin a piece of writing is not confined to doctoral students, nor does it necessarily go away once the doctorate is completed. We have separately and together made several starts on various parts of this book accompanied by much pacing, tea drinking and cleaning. Since one of us lives in England and the other in Australia, we have worked through these periods by simply following our own advice – just sit and write anything! When we have worked together it has become obvious that one of us takes more time considering each section of text, while the other tends to write furiously and then spends time reflecting on it. Nevertheless, each of us has made several false starts and we have ultimately written ourselves into the production of this text, just as doctoral students do.

A major challenge we have faced in the writing of this book arises from the difficulty of speaking across diversity. We have set ourselves the task of writing something that speaks to supervisors in different disciplines, in different countries and in different institutions. Indeed, the doctorate itself is diversifying, with multiple versions of the award, and what is an acceptable 'product' for examination. However, we suggest that, despite these differences, questions of writing are too often reduced to grammatical and stylistic problems, rather than, as we argue, a matter of text work/identity work. We hope that readers will find things in the text that do speak to their contexts.

We have assumed that busy supervisors will be pleased to have a book that is based in scholarship and research, but which is, for the most part, written with a light touch. By this we mean that we have not heavily referenced the text, nor have we elaborated the nuances of the various arguments we make. We have provided some signposts to the broader literatures that underpin our position, but we do not assume that readers will necessarily share our views.

We see this book as useable, but it is not a manual, a how-to text. It is possible, we think, to dip in and out of the chapters, rather than read the book from cover to cover, but we do suggest that it is worth looking at chapters one and two. These are where we spell out our theoretical premises and set the framework for our approach to doctoral writing and supervision pedagogies. In the third and fourth chapters we come to grips with work on literatures, while in chapter five we get up close and personal with the pronoun 'I'. We consider how students can construct their dissertation as an argument in chapter six, and in chapter seven we provide a set of linguistic tools supervisors can use to help students make their texts more readable and logical. Chapter eight focuses on the important question of becoming writerly. In our final chapter we examine ways in which doctoral writing can become part of an institutional culture and practice.

We have people to thank. We have already acknowledged how important our students have been to this book. Without them we would literally have had nothing to learn and say. But other people have helped us too. We would like to put on record our intellectual debt to Alison Lee and Bill Green whose work has so firmly written doctoral pedagogies and academic literacies onto the scholarly map in Australia. We would also like to thank Philip Mudd at Routledge for his early enthusiasm, energetic support and patience – not to mention drinks. We have also been helped by some critical friends along the way who ensured we could find our way through some argumentative fog we created for ourselves: thank you to Lesley Farrell and Rod Maclean for their close reading and productive suggestions. Rosemary Luke helped out with last-minute proofreading and indexing. Then of course there are our families who, having heard more than enough about the intricacies of this book, then watched despairingly as we turned into the Grinch who stole Christmas in order to finish the manuscript.

We are pleased/relieved to be finally finished with this text. We know that the pleasure of completion is common to writers everywhere – be they doctoral researchers or their supervisors. But we actually don't want to be finished with the topic. We would be delighted to hear from others about their supervision experiences and pedagogic strategies: we see this as part of an ongoing dialogue about how to help doctoral students write.

Chapter 1

Putting doctoral writing centre stage

Whole sections in academic catalogues and entire shelves in bookshops are now devoted to a new kind of self-help book – the how-to-write-your-dissertation manual. These invite doctoral researchers to buy advice from experienced scholars to supplement the assistance given by their own supervisors.

The proliferation of such guidebooks is not simply a savvy niche-marketing strategy by publishing companies, nor should it be theorized away as an example of the democratization of expertise that is characteristic of high modernity (Giddens, 1991). Rather, as everyone involved with doctoral education knows, doctoral work is associated with a number of anxieties. Students have numerous questions. Will the work be good enough? How can all of the relevant literatures be read in time? What brings all of the data together? How can the research be organized into 100,000 words? These dissertation primers address these concerns, and more.

Our every day academic conversations with colleagues inside and outside our own institutions suggest that the issue of getting the dissertation written is as problematic for supervisors as it is for doctoral students. Supervisors often describe students as either 'being able to write' – or not. Frustrations over turgid prose, badly structured arguments and laboured literature reviews are common. So, supervisors too have numerous questions. Why can't my students write an argument? How can I help them say things more simply? What can I do to get my students to write more logically? Why is their writing so tentative? There are few places to which supervisors can refer for discussion specifically about doctoral writing, few places which might assist them to think differently about the textual practices of scholarship.

This book begins to address this gap. It is written primarily for supervisors, although doctoral researchers might also find it of use. But it is not a self-help manual. It is not a how-to-do-writing-supervision compendium. We avoid the direct address – the 'you can/must/ought/will benefit' of the advice mode. Tempting as it is to tell people what to do, we try instead to talk about things that we have done that we found useful, and we provide sufficient detail for readers to imagine how they might use or remake strategies for their own supervision contexts. We write about pedagogy, the work of teaching and learning. We draw on: our reading in socio-linguistics, critical discourse analysis, policy sociology and pedagogical theory; our experiences in doctoral supervision (not all of them easy); our research into academic writing practices; and our own writing biographies.

In this book, we foreground issues related to language and texts. We object to the ubiquitous term 'writing up' as the dominant way to think about writing the dissertation. Instead, we work with notions of 'research as writing'. We attend closely to the language used to describe doctoral writing because we believe it shapes not only how writing is produced, but also the writers themselves.

We therefore offer new metaphors and ways of understanding the labour and craft of doctoral writing. We foreground writing and writing strategies. We pay attention to the field of scholarly writing, its genres and conventions. We explore the connections between academic writing practices and the formation of 'the doctoral scholar'.

We use the British and Australian nomenclature of *supervision* and *supervisor* to describe the doctoral 'teacher' and we refer to the person undertaking the doctorate as the *doctoral researcher*. We also use the term 'student' to signify the institutional power relations at work in the supervisory relationship. But our preference is to define doctoral candidates in terms of their work (research) and to acknowledge the increasing diversity of ages, experience and professional status they bring to doctoral study. We use the terms *thesis* and *dissertation* interchangeably to describe the summative research text presented for examination. In doing so, we recognize that there are cultural differences in the ways different countries organize their doctorates. In Britain and Australia, for example, the dominant pedagogical relationship is with a supervisor and a co- or associate supervisor with whom students meet on a regular basis in tutorials. The new preferred model in Britain, however, also involves a first year of intensive research training coursework and, increasingly, Australian students are taking some compulsory studies. In North America, by contrast, students must pass a range of coursework subjects as part of the degree; the dissertation research is overseen by a committee who act as both examiner and guide, with one adviser providing more intense support. Examination in Britain is most often conducted by one internal and one external examiner and a viva (a confidential oral examination). In Australia, two examiners external to the university provide a written report, with a third being called in if there is a dispute. There is no viva.

These differences are not insignificant. The kind of audience and the kind of critical scrutiny the dissertation receives in examination will influence how students write. It clearly matters if judgments are made by academics inside the university (US) or outside (Australia) or a combination of the two (UK); whether a doctoral defence occurs in the private context of a viva (UK, New Zealand) or committee defence (US), or in a more public, adversarial forum as in Scandinavian and northern European countries. Our argument in this book, however, is that whatever the form of examination and whatever the form of supervision – whether by a committee of advisers or individual/multiple supervisors – greater attention to *writing* the doctorate is required.

In this book we place the scholarly practice of writing centre stage. We recognize it as one of the major sites of anxiety for students and, we contend, their supervisors. We understand that the absence of discussion is why supervisors and doctoral researchers alike turn to advice books. And we seek to offer an alternative, more theorized approach based on current understandings of writing, identity and social practice. To begin, we first interrogate some taken-for-granted assumptions about 'writing up' and the way these have marginalized serious attention to the practices of doctoral writing.

Talking down 'writing up'

When students talk about the writing they do in the doctorate, it is common for them to say 'Oh, I'm just writing up'. The phrase 'writing up' is ubiquitous in the various advice manuals on the market and on websites which proffer advice about writing. Even some of the most useful books on research writing, such as Wolcott's (2001) *Writing Up Qualitative Research*, embed the phrase in their title. We object to this way of talking about writing, primarily because it suggests that writing is ancillary or marginal to the real work of research. First we do the research, then we 'write it up', as if that were a fairly straightforward and mechanical act of reportage.

Writing, however, is a vital part of the research process. The activity of research is one that, from the outset, involves writing. Researchers keep notes, jot down ideas, record observations, summarize readings, transcribe interviews and develop pieces of writing about specific aspects of their investigation. These writings are not simply getting things down on paper, but are making meaning and advancing understandings through these various writings. Then there are public texts – conference papers, articles, and the thesis itself – all of which do productive work. It is through these writings that researchers produce knowledge and become members of their various scholarly communities.

The phrase 'writing up' actually obliterates all this labour and complexity. And we are not just being picky about words. Our concern is that such ways of speaking have effects. They can actually mislead students about what is entailed in writing the doctorate. A pivotal study by Torrance and Thomas (1994) noted that students who delay completion, or fail to complete their dissertation, often do so because of writing-related issues. These students see a 'strict demarcation between collecting data, or doing research, and the writing of this material as a dissertation' (Torrance and Thomas, 1994: 107); and it is this perception that produces problems for student writers. Other research findings about the connections between writing and academic 'success' (Hendricks and Quinn, 2000; Leibowitz and Goodman, 1997; Lillis, 2001; Lillis and Turner, 2001) suggest we need to address the writing issues that actually prevent students from developing productive research writing practices (see Mullen, 2001).

For us, one of these issues is reconceptualizing research writing so that it is not reduced to 'writing up'. This ubiquitous metaphor is most commonly used to denote a distinct phase of post-fieldwork activity. But like Lee (1998), we contend that the metaphor does important work in making doctoral writing both natural and invisible. We can state our objections as three propositions:

'Writing up' obscures the fact that doctoral writing is thinking. We write to work out what we think. It's not that we do the research and then know. It's that we write our way to understanding through analysis. We put words on the page, try them out, see how they look and sound, and in the writing we see things we had no idea were there before we started writing. If the goal of research is to make sense of the data we have produced, and to theorize it in order to develop understanding, then writing the research is central to the process of inquiry itself.

'Writing up' obscures the fact that producing a dissertation text is hard work. Writing is physical, emotional and aesthetic labour. Sitting at a keyboard for hours on end is hard on nerves and bodies. Many scholars carry their scholarship deep in their psyche, bones and muscles. But the dissertation is also about the craft of word-play. Choosing words that encapsulate an idea, selecting quotations that effectively summarize an important point, and making decisions about syntax and subheadings are all important to how the final text flows and is read. In no way are these ideas of labour and craft captured in the matter-of-factness of 'writing up'. Rather the phrase evokes a glibness: 'Oh I've done the hard work, now I'm doing the easy bit, I'm just "writing it up"'.

'Writing up' obscures the fact that doctoral writing is not transparent. Researchers do not simply write up 'the truth' and language is not a transparent medium through which we capture and communicate findings. Facts are not already there, waiting for the researcher to discover and grab. What writing creates is a particular representation of reality. Data is produced in writing, not found. And the data and subsequent texts that are written are shaped and crafted by the researcher through a multitude of selections about what to include and exclude, foreground and background, cite and not cite. These choices often have profound ethical dimensions and raise issues that need conscious attention by doctoral writers. Such issues are not even imaginable in the oversimplifying, apparently neutral term 'writing up'.

So why do we say 'writing up'? Tradition, bad habit, misconception? Why not writing down? Writing over? Writing around? Better yet, why don't we say 'I'm writing my research', where the present continuous verb *writing* implies a continuous process of inquiry through writing? We agree with Laurel Richardson (1990; 1994) when she says that researching *is* writing. It is not separate from the act of researching. Later in the chapter we offer principles that underpin this alternative to 'writing up'. But first, we expand our discussion of research writing by interrogating another misconception about doctoral writing: namely that it is a set of *skills* rather than a situated social *practice*.

Doctoral writing – a question of skills or a social practice?

Rather than simply talking down 'writing up', we want to 'talk up' the notion of writing as a social practice.

We see research writing as an institutionally-constrained social practice. It is about meaning making and learning to produce knowledge in particular disciplines and discourse communities. It is not simply about skills and techniques that can be learned in a mechanical way. This distinction between *skill* and *practice* is central to our pedagogies for supervision. While we argue that there is a startling lack of explicit attention given to *writing* the doctoral dissertation, the attention which *is* given is diminished when it treats writing as a discrete set of decontextualized skills, rather than as a social practice.

In using the term practice, we are connecting to a scholarly tradition that regards writing as social action. Here, language is understood as being in use, bound up with what people actually do in the social and material world. Thus, ways of using language are not simply idiosyncratic or unique attributes of individual writers. They are repeated and practised and so become part of the patterned routines of both individuals and institutions. Lillis (2001) captures well what this shift to writing as social practice means:

> In broad terms, what this entails is that student academic writing, like all writing, is a social act. That is, student writing takes place within a particular institution, which has a particular history, culture, values, practices. It involves a shift away from thinking of language or writing skills as individual possession, towards the notion of an individual engaged in socially situated action; from an individual student having writing skills, to a student doing writing in specific contexts.
>
> (Lillis, 2001: 31)

The problem with a skills-based orientation is that it is founded in a notion that language is transparent, a straightforward conduit for thought. The process of writing is thus simplified into a linear process, where students are exhorted to think first, then write. They need to plan, get the chapter outline clear, and proceed, bit by bit, chapter by chapter, as if the meaning was already formed prior to the writing. When a draft is produced, it is treated as more or less finished in terms of meaning. What is required is simply tidying and polishing, as if writing were somehow like setting a table – once the cutlery and plates are all out of the drawers and cupboards it is just a matter of setting them straight.

And problems with writing are most often seen in skill-deficit terms. They are located in individual students who don't get it or don't have it, rather than say, in broader disciplinary and institutional contexts in which students write, or in misconceptions or confusions about how to proceed. And the advice given to solve writing problems often focuses on the surface features of writing. Spelling, punctuation, grammar, or simplified models of text structure or citation rules are offered to students because these are the more tangible aspects of academic writing.

Implicit in the plethora of advice appearing on university websites and advice books is the assumption that the problems and their solutions are fairly straightforward, easy to identify and resolve. When we searched research writing websites, we mostly found handy tips and oversimplified guidelines for writing. This advice indicated not even the most basic understandings of writing developed in genre-based (Derewianka, 1990) or process approaches (Graves, 1983; Murray, 1982) in the 1980s and 1990s. Here is a typical, reductive tidbit:

> Ask yourself what would have been the perfect paper for you to have read in order to understand everything you need to know. Then write it …
>
> Papers must be understandable and meaningful. Papers are for replication and understanding … Each sentence must be as informative as possible. Include all relevant information. Never use anything you do not know is absolutely and totally real. Outline the paper until it is perfectly clear, then write it …
>
> The following list of questions steps you through the major issues which must be addressed in a research paper. After each question is answered the construction of the research paper is simply developing transitions between items.
>
> (http://www.jsu.edu.depart/psychology/sebac/fac-sch/rm/Ch4–5.html.
> Accessed October 2001)

Skills-based books on doctoral writing are also abundant. The absurdity of some of these approaches is evident in titles such as *Completing Your Doctoral Dissertation or Master's Thesis in Two Semesters or Less* (Ogden, 1993) or *Writing Your Dissertation in Fifteen Minutes a Day* (Bolker, 1998). *The Research Student's Guide to Success* (Cryer, 2001) typifies one version of the genre. The topics covered include: liaising with an institution, settling in as a new student, keeping records, producing reports, developing skills for creative thinking, producing your thesis and afterwards. Writing is discussed at various points throughout the text but always in terms of technique, and the emphasis is on tips 'that work'.

Writing the Winning Dissertation (Glatthorn, 1998) approaches dissertation writing as more than formulaic, but its skills orientation oversimplifies the text work involved in constructing a dissertation. For example, in a chapter titled 'Mastering the academic style' students are exhorted first to use the recommended style guide, then to use the writing process (as if it were a singular thing) by following this illuminating procedure:

> Write a paragraph.
> Stop and read what was written.
> Revise that paragraph.

Write another paragraph – and start the cycle all over again.

(Glatthorn, 1998: 109)

Further on, students are offered suggestions for achieving the persona of a scholar who is informed and knowledgeable: 'strive for clarity', 'project maturity', 'project a sense of formality', 'strike an appropriate balance between confidence and tentativeness' (Glatthorn 1998: 112–13). While supervisors might agree with these assertions, they are presented as commands and the examples provided are framed as correct and incorrect options. Thus under the heading 'write clear mature sentences' we find:

> 3. Reduce the number of ands. Excessive use of the conjunction *and* suggests a childish style. Consider these two examples:
> TOO MANY ANDS: The teacher put the assignment on the board, and then she checked the roll and found that three students were absent.
> BETTER: After putting the assignment on the board, the teacher found by checking the roll that three students were absent.
>
> (Glatthorn, 1998: 117)

We linger over this text because it highlights the way so many skills-based books either labour the banal or reduce writing to a set of arbitrary rules and matters of etiquette. By following their seemingly arbitrary advice, rather than more informed research-based strategies, doctoral researchers are lured into believing that the winning dissertation will emerge, as if by magic.

There *is*, however, a rich literature that does treat academic writing as a social practice and meaning making as a social phenomenon. And it is to these texts we now turn.

Doctoral writing as a social practice

There are numerous texts which address academic writing (but not necessarily research or doctoral writing) as social practice. Lea and Street (2000), for example, argue the importance of moving away from skills-based, deficit models of student writing in order to engage the complexity of writing practices that are taking place at degree level in universities. Notable in this tradition, are those texts which explore academic writing as discipline-specific practice. Bazerman (1981; 1988) and Myers (1985), for example, explore rhetorical differences across academic disciplines: Bazerman focuses on writing in the academic fields of literature, sociology and biochemistry, Myers in biology. Some have studied the way graduate students learn to appropriate discourse conventions in a variety of disciplinary communities (Berkenkotter and Huckin, 1985; Dias and Paré, 2000; Kamler and Maclean, 1997; Prior, 1998). Others, mostly UK based, conduct tutor-led investigations with writers in higher education. Clark and Ivanic (1997), for example, explore the politics of writing and identity while

Lillis (2001) examines essayist writing in higher education from the perspective of non-traditional writers.

Other texts look more explicitly at research writing and explicate the kind of writing that researchers do. *Writing Up Qualitative Research* (Wolcott, 2001) is typical of narratives produced by experienced researchers attempting to make clear the processes that they use when writing. Again the emphasis is on technique, so chapters focus on how to make a writing plan, and problems of sorting and organizing data. But importantly, Wolcott doesn't just talk about producing the final text, he talks about writing all the way through the research process. Other chapters discuss keeping track of references, doing the literature review, making the link to theory and method, theory as narrative, revising and editing, running out of space, crowding more in, and getting published. A lot of this is undoubtedly very useful. Doing research *does* involve being organized, paying attention to scholarly conventions, and being able to see the production of a thesis or book as a series of steps. We do recommend this book to students, even though we blanch at the title 'writing up', because it is a largely unpretentious demystification of some technical aspects of the research writing process.

Dissertation writing has also been investigated by qualitative researchers who research their own writing. Ely *et al.* (1997), for example, specifically address the practice of composition. They focus on a variety of types of writing that might be developed as research texts. They discuss the differences between descriptive and analytic memos, two different kinds of texts students write in response to field data or a piece of scholarly reading (Ely *et al.* 1994, Chapter 4). Their use of theory to tell a research story rather than the researcher's narrative being weighed down by theory (Ely *et al.* 1994, Chapter 5) is very helpful to doctoral researchers early in their candidature. Ely and her colleagues present a combination of theory, handy hints, and feminist politics. They discuss support groups for critically reading each other's work, getting work published, and writing as self-development. This is another book that we recommend to our students for its readability and practicality.

Our thinking has also been informed by theorizing about the ethics and epistemologies of writing in the social sciences. Sociologists, cultural studies scholars and anthropologists have, since the 'crisis in the humanities', focused on writing as a social practice which takes place in a particular time/place/tradition. They situate their arguments both in terms of knowledge (epistemology) and ways of being in the academy (ontology). They do not eschew technique, nor handy hints, nor literacy sensibility, but place these within a wider/deeper frame. Laurel Richardson (1997), in particular, has inspired us to think beyond 'sociological vérité', the presentation of data as if style and voice were unimportant. She also encouraged us to eschew 'the self-centred reflexive style, where the people studied are treated as garnishes and condiments, tasty only in relationship to the main course, the sociologist' (Richardson, 1997: 20).

As well as a proliferation of books on research writing, supervisors will be aware of an explosion of texts in recent years on supervision (Bartlett and Mercer,

2001; Delamont *et al.* 1997; 2000; Phillips and Pugh, 1987; Wisker, 2004). Very few of these, however, address what we might call a writing-centred supervision; nor do they provide any meaningful discussion of dissertation writing as social practice. A scan of their tables of contents reveals either no mention of writing or a nod to the ubiquitous 'writing up'.

Writing, diversity and doctoral supervision

The need for assistance with writing is greater than ever given the growth in doctoral studies and the diversity of doctoral candidates (Pearson, 1999). The image of the social science doctoral student as a young person, able to devote themselves to full-time study in order to progress into an academic career, is outdated. In the social sciences in particular, doctoral candidates are now equally likely to be mid-career professionals as young students straight from undergraduate work. They are joined by increasing numbers of older candidates who may be seeking a career change, a post-retirement option, or simply to further an area of interest (Leonard *et al.* 2004). Those who arrive mid-career come with a wide range of work and life experiences and more than half now study part-time (Evans, 2002). Increasing numbers study at a distance (Evans and Pearson, 1999; McWilliam *et al.*, 2002; Smyth *et al.* 2001). Doctoral researchers also have various motivations for undertaking doctoral study and they include members of university staff in both academic and administrative positions seeking to increase their qualifications.

In addition, many universities in Western countries now actively seek large numbers of students from developing countries for income generation, rather than aid, purposes. The addition of students with English language demands, various histories of undergraduate and postgraduate experience and different cultural norms and expectations creates new pressures on supervision. Amongst these are questions of writing the doctorate and guiding students to develop a scholarly identity – made more complicated by the fact that the genre of the dissertation is also diversifying. There is now considerable experimentation with length of doctoral candidature and length of dissertation. There is more variety in the nature of texts presented as research with arts-informed and artefact-based dissertations growing in popularity.

Many universities are becoming aware of the need to support supervisors in their work, but this concern is generally couched in terms of quality assurance and training. Supervisor workshops are the most common form of intervention, combined with mentoring schemes. Universities also require supervisors to keep detailed audit trails of their interactions with students, but this is primarily to avoid student complaints and litigation. The inclusion of PhD completion rates in government measures of performance has placed a new emphasis, in countries such as Australia and the UK, on 'getting students through'. But the press by universities for documentation and smooth passage from enrolment to graduation does not necessarily enhance what actually happens in pedagogical practice.

Thus supervision remains an intensely private affair. Very few universities offer the kind of continuous professional development taken for granted by school teachers in some education systems, and opportunities to discuss diverse methods of working with doctoral writers are rare. Writing and language, while a significant issue, is something for supervisors and their students to deal with by themselves.

When assistance is provided for writing, it most often occurs outside the supervisory relationship. In Australia and the UK, for example, assistance is offered through specialist support units, which are often located outside academic faculties (there is further discussion of these writing initiatives in Chapter 9). In the best scenario, learning support personnel are connected to specific disciplines. Academic writing assistance is framed as discipline-specific practice and overt links are made between the teaching of writing and the contexts in which students write (see for example Cadman, 2000). But such assistance is not readily available to most doctoral researchers, and the help which is available is often framed as remedial work (such as foundation courses for overseas students) and removed from other forms of research education.

Even in the United States, where there is a long tradition of English composition for all undergraduate students, there is very little teaching of writing in graduate education. Rose and McClafferty (2001) argue, further, that there is too little professional discussion of what we as supervisors can do to help our graduate students write more effectively. While it's common to bemoan the quality of scholarly writing both inside and outside the university, little is done to 'address the quality of writing in a systematic way at the very point where scholarly style and identity is being shaped' (Rose and McClafferty, 2001: 27). (See Chapter 9 for a discussion of the writing course developed by Rose at UCLA.)

Universities could certainly do more by offering social practice oriented instruction in high-level writing for doctoral researchers. We think writing groups and workshops can be very helpful and we recommend that our doctoral researchers take advantage of any such opportunities.

Our major emphasis in this book, however, is to explore how we might create pedagogic spaces within the supervisory relationship. To conclude the chapter, we therefore articulate the principles of writing that underpin this pedagogical work.

Principles of doctoral writing

We have already foreshadowed the understandings about language and writing that underpin our approach to doctoral writing throughout this chapter. We now consolidate them as a set of principles which inform our approach in the book. In doing so, we bring to bear our own epistemological position as post-critical researchers. We are informed by a view of language and knowledge which is culturally bound and imbued with power relations. We don't hold that there are absolute meanings, but we do have a value position, informed by feminist work.

Research is writing

Right from the time we begin to think about the research questions we are interested in pursuing, we begin to write. We record the books we have read, we take notes from them, we keep a journal of our ideas; we have a folder full of jottings. As the research progresses, we write summaries and short papers that compile some of the ideas with which we are working. We make notes to discuss with others and write conference papers where we put our ideas into the public arena for the first time. Researching cannot be separated from writing.

Making meaning through language is a discursive activity

Knowledge is always constructed by language, and by the historical circumstances and specific environment in which it arises. We think of knowledge as discursive. A discourse is a particular formation of stories and practices, which constructs both knowledge and power relations. A discourse defines and produces what we know, what and how we talk about an object of knowledge, and it influences how ideas are put into practice. We live in a world where there are many discourses, many different, overlapping, intersecting and competing sets of stories and practices. Foucault (1991) argues that nothing has *meaning* outside discourse. For any given period of time there are socially constructed discursive formations which limit and form:

- What is sayable – what it is possible to speak about
- What is conserved – what disappears and what is repeated and circulated
- What is remembered – what is recognized and validated, what is regarded as able to be dismissed
- What is reactivated – what is transformed from foreign cultures or past epochs and what is done with them
- What is appropriated – which individuals and groups have access to which discourses, the institutionalization of discourses and the struggles for control over them.

What is produced in research writing is a representation

What we write is not what actually happened, but a written approximation. This representation is not a 'reflection' of something that is out there. Our writing does not function as a mirror. Rather, the writer imposes her view of reality through the writing process. When we choose what to include and exclude, what to foreground and what to critique, we are engaging in a discursive activity. As noted, we construct meaning through language systems which are based in our culture, place and time and through prevailing discourses, as well as through our own particular biography. Research writing is not a private activity, but is social, since meanings and therefore representations are socially produced through us as researchers.

The written representation is a text

The process of writing allows us to put our words out onto a page and thus to see them as separate from our 'self'. They are no longer just thoughts, but available as *text*, a stretch of meaningful language which we can look at critically. By asking the questions Foucault poses around discourse, for example, we can begin to see how our own work has blind spots and taken-for-granted assumptions, phrases and terms. Because our choices, experiences and positioning are inevitably involved in the research texts we write, we need to interrogate them as rigorously as we can and understand that they can be written differently. Putting ideas onto a page is an important part of that process. We can see the texts that we produce in the same light as any other text.

Research writing is a particular genre

Research writing such as field notes, articles, literature reviews, conference papers and the dissertation itself are particular kinds of texts, or genres, which are constructed in particular institutional and cultural settings. PhD writing is akin to other kinds of research writing but is shaped by the demands of the degree, just as it is shaped by the specific demands of different disciplines. Thus, what is created is a *particular* genre, which has patterns and conventions that can be learned and interrogated. But these genres are discipline-specific texts – the creation of which demands the formation of discipline-specific scholarly identities.

As researchers, we are also writers

Writers play with language to create imaginative, elegant and compelling texts. So can we – if we work at it. We can use metaphor, allegory, trope and other poetic tools to produce the story of our research in ways that engage the reader (Game and Metcalfe, 1996). All research, regardless of whether it is quantitative and experimental, ethnographic, case study or arts-based, uses writing and creates a text. Some research communities have particular scholastic conventions such as the use of the third person to narrate the story, and some research activities seem to lend themselves to a flat lexicon that gives an impression of facticity. But these are writing choices.

In sum, we are arguing for a view of doctoral writing as research. We are arguing for a combination of aesthetic judgments, technical virtuosity, epistemologies and a particular research sensibility, which goes beyond thinking of writing as 'writing up' but as the research act itself. And we are talking about writing practices, not just skills. Advice and tips will not suffice as the genre we offer doctoral researchers. Research writing involves a sophisticated set of social practices with sets of conventions and textual characteristics which we explore in subsequent chapters.

What then is the pedagogy we need to develop to teach these practices? And how will we differentiate the different kinds of writing that are involved in what we call research writing? These questions form the basis of the chapters to come. In the next chapter we introduce the remainder of our conceptual toolbox – text work and identity work, and an adaptation of Fairclough's (1989; 1992) model to view research writing as discursive practice.

Chapter 2

Writing the doctorate, writing the scholar

Kathryn is a doctoral researcher about to give her fourth conference paper. She is a part-time student in education. A teacher by profession, she has twenty years experience, five of which have been spent as the successful principal of a primary school. Despite her acknowledged expertise in her 'day job', and despite having attended more conferences than she cares to remember, she feels nervous and almost panic-stricken at the prospect of speaking in public to an academic audience. She is four years into the PhD, has spoken at graduate student conferences and has just completed her fieldwork. Yet she cannot avoid the feeling of being naked and vulnerable to the negative opinions of 'real scholars'. She dreads being either patronized or attacked, and suggests to her supervisor Janet, minutes before the presentation begins, that she hopes no one comes. But they do. A sizeable audience noisily sits down, attracted by Kathryn's topic.

Despite her qualms, Kathryn's presentation goes smoothly. The data projector fires up easily, she talks through and around the slides with little sign of the nerves she continues to feel, and finishes just as the chair signals time is up. The questions begin. The first one is easy and Kathryn responds succinctly and clearly. But then, a man gets to his feet. It is clear he is about to make a statement, rather than ask a question. Janet prepares to intervene, but as Kathryn begins to speak in response to the man's five minute exposition, she relaxes again. Kathryn skilfully defuses the negativity, responds assertively, and continues answering audience questions for a few more minutes.

At the end of the session Janet congratulates her.

JANET: Well done. You did a great job. How do you feel about speaking at conferences now?

KATHRYN: It's terrifying. It is utterly terrifying to think that you might be found lacking in some way – or boring … and the fear of being exposed. But once the focus is on you, and you have to perform or be humiliated totally, what does it do? It kind of clarifies the actual talking of the paper, rather than the writing of it. The talking of it and the defending of it. If you have to defend it, if people ask you questions, it gives you a kind of authority about your work which perhaps you can only guess at or doubt when you are siting alone at your computer.

JANET: You handled the difficult question really well.

KATHRYN: All the interaction I've had before at conferences was like 'oh that's interesting' or 'it's about time someone is looking at this'. But this man was saying, 'Well your reading of the field doesn't match with my reading of the field.' Initially it made me think ooooohhh [sucking in breath] how am I going to deal with this? But then I felt quite confident that in response to him my reading was indeed defensible and that his was a misreading or a partial reading of the field. Although I didn't think of this at the time, his was a political position wasn't it, because he was a government employee who needed to say the right things in his lit review. Once I had sort of defended my reading, I felt in some way Aha! I can do this now. I actually do know something here and it's important that I know that I know. So it made me feel no longer frightened about that happening in a way that might destabilize my sense of myself as a researcher. I thought I haven't been found lacking here. It was actually OK and quite helpful for me to be publicly questioned and asked to account for my argument.

This is a semi-fictionalized account. The actual words spoken are those of a 'real' doctoral researcher and the experience we attribute to the fictional Kathryn did happen. We open the chapter with this account because it raises some interesting questions. Why did an experienced and highly competent person, accustomed to writing and speaking in public, feel so afraid of speaking as a doctoral student to an academic audience? Why does it seem as if there are two Kathryns? Why is it that the difficult question seems to have produced a more confident Kathryn?

In this chapter we use this event, in particular, and giving conference papers in general, to introduce two theoretical resources we call upon in the remainder of the book. The first we call text work/identity work and we address supervision pedagogies through this lens. The second is a model of writing as discursive social practice, in which the supervisor mediates cultural, institutional and disciplinary rules, conventions and mores in order to support the doctoral researcher to produce an acceptable text.

Text work/identity work

As academics, we are represented by our writings and we are judged by them. In countries where audit regimes are dominant, scholarly productivity and apparent standing in the field are measured on the basis of citations, publishers, and actual writings. But scholars also pass judgment on each other, as peers, on the basis of the books, articles and papers published. Nowhere is the connection between identity and text as clear as it is when scholars get together to debate the relative merits of particular texts. There is continual slippage between the person and the text. The text is an extension of the scholar, a putting of 'self' out there which is either successful – or not.

This, however, is not the only sense that we want to make of the text/identity imbrication.

Identity is defined by the Macquarie Dictionary (Delbridge *et al.* 1991: 895) as the state of being oneself and not another. Within the humanities and social sciences this would be a contentious definition, since it suggests that each person is unique and self-contained. But our understanding of identity is that it is a social category: in other words, it brings together questions of class, gender, race and ethnicity, dis/ability, age, location and religion. We do not focus here on these social structures, but we do suggest that the identity with which we are concerned – a scholarly identity – is also a social category. It is embedded in a tangle of cultural-historical practices that are both institutional and disciplinary. The following discussion about identity then should be read, not as being about unique individuals, but rather about the ways in which the social category of scholar is produced and reproduced.

There is a large number of books written about identity from various theoretical and disciplinary positions. We do not intend to enter into these major debates here, but to indicate how we are working with particular understandings of identity. We spell out six propositions and discuss these in relation to the story we have presented about Kathryn and Janet.

Identity is a narrative we tell about ourselves. We suture together a set of experiences into a rationale which brings history, events and others together in a way that makes sense to us (e.g. Bird, 2002; Bruner, 1986; Connelly and Clandinin, 1999). People often alter their identity narrative depending on the conversation/ situation they are in.[1] So, for example, how Kathryn describes herself would differ depending on whether she was talking to her local school inspector or to her doctoral supervisor. Kathryn told a story of herself as a competent principal, but as an amateur when it came to doctoral inquiry. Indeed, she refers to her 'sense of myself as a researcher' and how easily it might have been undone, thus communicating the fragility and malleability of this part of her identity narrative.

An identity narrative is informed by the ways in which we are seen and described. In naming doctoral candidates as students, novices and apprentices, we position them as learners, particularly in relation to their supervisor(s) who, by contrast, are expected to 'know' about all matters doctoral. Many doctoral researchers, particularly those who are expert in their chosen profession, feel resentful about feeling 'unknowing'. Kathryn did feel lesser than those in her anticipated conference audience and she expected them to behave in ways that signified her 'junior' status in the academy. How we expect others to see us is also integral to our identity. This is the source of the vulnerability and anxiety Kathryn experienced. She was afraid that her audience might see through her assumed 'act' of knowing scholar and expose the 'learner' identity she ascribes to herself.

Identity is plural, not singular – identities. People have multiple identities formed in response to specific contexts, experiences and trajectories. However, multiple identities are not necessarily consistent. Kathryn the unconfident student is not identical to Kathryn the competent school administrator: different ways of being are required of each. These identities do, however, overlap because having multiple identities is not the same as having multiple personalities! In the story of the challenging incident at the conference, Kathryn seems to mobilize ways of being/doing from her other life in order to support her emerging scholarly identity. In this instance, it was her capacity to refuse the bait of confrontation and deal civilly and reasonably with an aggressive response that mattered.

Identity is not fixed. It is always in formation. Hall (1996) calls this identification. So, the doctoral researcher is not a fixed and static entity but rather is always being formed. Supervisors often expect doctoral students to move seamlessly from student to fully-fledged scholar. However, this shift involves a change in identity, self-narrative and behaviour. For a significant period of doctoral candidature, becoming an authorized scholar appears to be a remote, unfamiliar and uncomfortable possibility. And the shift is not sudden or abrupt, but rather occurs in a series of moves. Kathryn's interview shows precisely this movement – from an uncertain scholar, to one who is now able to articulate herself as a student with some authority to speak.

Identities are continually being made and remade in and as action. Identities are performed. We take this idea from Butler's (1990) work on gender as a performance. Narrative is one form of identity performance. Writing is another kind of performance. As Kathryn wrote her conference paper, she wrote herself as a researcher not as a school principal. The writing worked to continue her identification as scholar. But it had limitations. She could not imagine, while sitting at the computer, how to speak as a scholar. This had to be materially done. The conference presentation was thus another site for Kathryn to perform her identity as a researcher. In the conference she had to embody a scholar: one who knows their field and its literature, speaks with assurance, argues logically about their point of view, and listens with respect to alternative points of view. What she felt at the outset might have been an act, but afterwards seemed like the 'real thing'. In acting the scholar, she became more of one.

Identities and their performances are discursively formed. Identities are embedded in available discourses and may be thought of as a suturing together of various discursive events, modes and assemblages. In Kathryn's response to Janet after the conference, she articulated a narrative of herself as a more confident scholar. Her use of the dominant discourse of scholarly work is signified by her use of words such as 'readings and misreadings, the field, lit review, account for my argument'. She also noted the critical difference between a government point of view and her own. Such disinterested criticality is integral to social science discourse and the fully-fledged social scientist.

Our propositions about text and identity have a number of implications for supervision pedagogies, which we now consider.

Supervision pedagogies as text work/identity work

When Janet talked with Kathryn, asked her to produce a few thousand words, supported her to present a conference paper, or did any of the other things that count as supervision, what was happening was both text work and identity work. This text and identity work happened, as we have suggested, through dialogue, writing and experience. We now consider this as pedagogy, drawing on recent work by Ellsworth (2005).

Pedagogy,[2] used in the northern European tradition, encompasses the everyday formal and informal practices of education. This includes the use and development of theory about and in the work of educating, as well as the formulation of policy and the education of those who are the pedagogues. Pedagogy is a relational concept since it refers to what happens between the authorized pedagogues and students. In our story Janet was the pedagogue. And as we have noted, the supervision pedagogies used by Janet were a social practice which occurred within a specific context saturated with histories, hierarchies, customs, teleologies and narratives.

We have suggested that Kathryn's scholarly identity shifted through performing (writing, speaking and defending) the conference paper. Ellsworth (2005) in a text on the popular pedagogies of museums, art installations and websites, addresses this very shift, which she calls a 'moment'. She asks:

> What is it, then, to sense one's self in the midst of learning as experience, in the moment of learning, in the presence of a coming knowing, in this interleaving of cognition and sensation/movement?
>
> (Ellsworth, 2005: 135)

We do not see Kathryn in the moment, but we hear her reflections on it. She knows it has happened.

Ellsworth proposes that learning is a smudge between a self that knows to a self that knows more. This is the identity shift of performance (experience, textual work). The learning self is thus a moving self, in a dynamic relation with knowledge. In saying this, Ellsworth also challenges us to think not simply about knowledge as something made, but about knowledge-in-the-making.

> The experience of the learning self is simultaneously the experience of what I shall have become by what I am in the process of learning and the experience of what I shall have learned by the process of what I am becoming.
>
> (Ellsworth, 2005: 149)

Drawing on the work on British psychologist Winnicott (1989), she describes the pedagogies which allow such moments of 'smudge' to occur as transitional spaces. Pedagogy is a question of design, Ellsworth suggests. The pedagogue deliberately designs experiences, tasks, events, conversations which create the opportunity for the student to 'smudge' self, to move both identity and knowledge simultaneously.

We note here the resonance with Dewey (1897; 1916; 1934; 1938), who wrote passionately against the idea of pedagogy as inculcation, as transmission, as a closed process. Dewey suggested that a pedagogy should be focused, not on didactic instruction, but on the structuring of experiences and the fostering of conversations that are challenging, problematic, engaging, and horizon stretching. According to Dewey, the teacher's (pedagogue's) task is to create possibilities and opportunities for students to become/learn/act.

Ellsworth is adamant that the end points of pedagogy should remain open, rather than closed, in order to allow students freedom to choose what to become. Such a pedagogy of design, she suggests, 'set[s] teachers and students in relation to the future as open and ... teaching and learning as always in the making, never guaranteed and never achieved' (2005: 36). The implication for teachers then is 'work and play ... to keep the flow of difference, movement, sensation – and their destinations – open and undetermined' (2005: 175).

We find Ellsworth's ideas helpful in thinking about supervision pedagogies. Inspired by her notion of 'moving subjects' on a continuous journey towards knowings that are inevitably always incomplete and unfinished (see in particular 2005: Chapter 6), we offer the metaphor of supervision pedagogies as text work/identity work. The metaphor construes supervision as a space in which both doctoral researchers and supervisors are learning selves in transition. This is a social and relational space in which performance (experience, dialogue, writing) allows the dynamic 'smudge' of learning, the movement from one knowing-being to another. In text work and identity work, writing is performance. A conversation with the supervisor around the text provides another moment/experience which opens possibilities for becoming/knowing. Writing, in this metaphor, becomes the exercise of choices about what is written/known, and the text becomes the medium through which both knowing and knower are made together.

We turn now to a further explication of Kathryn's conference experience using our second theoretical resource, a model of scholarly writing as discursive social practice. We continue to work with notions of performance and rehearsal to emphasize the fragility and openness of identity formation.

We begin by outlining the framework we use to conceptualize doctoral texts, the student and supervisor, the institution and broader policy context.

Writing as discursive social practice

The framework we've developed for understanding doctoral writing as a social practice borrows from the fields of critical discourse analysis and new literacy studies. In particular, we find Norman Fairclough's (1992) three-dimensional model of discourse useful for conceptualizing the tensions and demands faced by doctoral writers and their supervisors. While Fairclough's model is most frequently used as a research tool for critically analysing spoken and written texts (Janks, 2002) (that is, texts that have already been written), it has also been used productively to explore the academic writing practices of 'non-traditional' students in higher education (Clark and Ivanic, 1997; Lillis, 2001). Like Clark, Ivanic and Lillis, we believe a social practice perspective must be brought into any discussion of academic writing pedagogies, but we focus on the doctoral (rather than the undergraduate) end of the writing continuum.

Fairclough[3] uses the term discourse to refer to the way people *use* spoken and written language. Referring to language use as discourse signals that using language is an action and that it is social rather than individual action. Further, language as social action cannot be divorced from any other aspects of social life and social relations. It is both produced and reproduced in social contexts. Fairclough's three-dimensional conception of discourse is represented diagrammatically in Figure 2.1. It is, according to Fairclough,

> an attempt to bring together three analytical traditions … the tradition of close textual and linguistic analysis within linguistics, the macrosociological tradition of analysing social practice in relation to social structures and the interpretivist or microsociological tradition of seeing social practice as something which people actively produce and make sense of on the basis of shared commonsense procedures.
>
> (Fairclough, 1992: 72)

In other words his conception brings together structure, agency and texts at several levels, the historical and political, the institutional, the disciplinary and the individual.

We find that this model (see Figure 2.1) provides a powerful visual heuristic for representing both the effects of broader social contexts on writing and the way writing itself is a form of social interaction, embedded in institutions and social structures. Within this framework, any instance of language use is seen to have three dimensions:

1   At the most concrete level it is a spoken or written language text (layer 1) – this is Kathryn's physical conference paper.
2   It is also an instance of discourse practice involving the production and interpretation of text (layer 2) – the conference text was produced and presented according to particular conventions and in conversation with Janet; and it was delivered to and interpreted by a particular conference audience, including the 'challenging man'.
3   At the most abstract level it is a piece of social practice (layer 3) – the conference paper and Kathryn's actions in writing and presenting it were shaped by a particular kind of academic public with particular ways of being and doing scholarship that were developed over time, within the discipline of education. In addition, everyone present was working within a particular higher education policy regime in which conference presentations were 'counted' for audit purposes.

The three boxes in Figure 2.1 are embedded to emphasize the interdependence of these dimensions of discourse. Janks (2002: 27) suggests it is easier to grasp

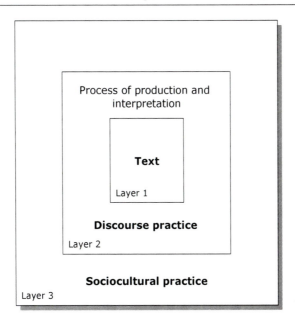

Figure 2.1 Fairclough's three dimensions of discourse (Source: Fairclough, 1992: 73; Janks, 2002: 27; Clark and Ivanic, 1997: 11)

this interdependence by thinking of the boxes three-dimensionally, as nested one inside the other rather than as concentric circles.

This interdependence is crucial when we consider how to use the framework to think about doctoral writing practices. At the centre is the text (layer 1). This may be a dissertation chapter, an abstract or a conference paper. Whatever its exact form, we are talking about the actual words the doctoral candidate puts on the page and the various linguistic features of the language used. The text, however, never occurs in isolation. It is always situated within teaching and learning relationships with supervisors and others which influence the text and how it is written. In layer 2, then, the discourse practice dimension, we are concerned with the more immediate social contexts in which writing occurs. We are concerned with the ways texts are interpreted and made – or produced and consumed. The text is inextricable from these processes that create it. Layers 1 and 2, in turn, are further embedded in the social practice dimension (layer 3). This is the broader social and cultural context in which the dissertation is produced. This includes specific academic and disciplinary practices as well as the broader relations of power and domination which shape university cultures and practices.

When we use this model to think about doctoral writing as a form of social practice, we see that the production of a thesis (text) is shaped 'not only by the local circumstances in which students are writing, but by the social, cultural and political climate within which the thesis is produced' (Clark and Ivanic, 1997: 11).

This is one of the reasons we take issue with much of the advice offered about thesis writing: it is divorced from wider institutional and socio-historical relations that pertain to any field of practice. Simple primers promising instant theses thus grossly oversimplify what is at risk in this doctoral text production.

For any supervisor working with doctoral writing, the text (layer 1) is of course a central concern. It is the tangible artefact that sits on the table between the candidate and supervisor. It is the object of concern for most university websites and for supervisors who lament that their students can't write. But the framework makes it clear that it is never a simple matter of just fixing the text or regarding the text in isolation from the conditions in which it is produced. Text work/identity work is complex. We suggest that Fairclough's heuristic illustrates graphically why supervision pedagogies need to include modelling, interrogating and explicit strategies for writing the text. These strategies will include attention to specific linguistic choices, their juxtaposition, sequencing, layout, generic and discourse conventions, expectations, and modes of address.

But what the diagram also makes abundantly clear is that the supervisor mediates the relationship between text (layer 1) and social practice (layer 3), through the processes of text production and interpretation (layer 2).

The supervisor is a key player in these discourse practices. She is a key reader and respondent to the emerging doctoral text, and in a sense a representative of the scholarly community to which the doctoral candidate seeks admission. We can think of her as an embodiment of the discourses and practices of the field. She, of course, has a personal relationship with the candidate, as illustrated by Janet and Kathryn. But within Fairclough's model of discourse, this supervisory relationship also mediates the social practices of the broader field. As an insider to the scholarly community, the supervisor both knows the field and is the first reader of the emerging doctoral text that seeks to make a contribution to knowledge in that field.

Layer 2 then, the context of situation and institutional context, are made more immediate through the supervisor's mediating processes of interpretation and production. Power within fields and disciplines is translated through the supervisory relationship and requirements of the institution. In doctoral supervision, the mediation of institutional regimes by the supervisor now includes: a press for completion evidenced in ongoing production of timelines and targets; the necessity to create an audit trail through the production of multiple copies of records of supervision meetings; and ensuring the student meets various institutional requirements, such as the production of annual reports, texts for colloquium or proposal committees, participation in graduate seminars, and attendance at training courses.

The wider societal context and context of culture (layer 3) in which doctoral researchers operate are less visible to them than the previous two layers. Most supervisors, however, have a grip on key issues in this layer. Here are the politics of particular institutions and disciplines – the unspoken rules of the game. These include the hierarchies, key players and debates which shape decisions about how to position one's scholarly work. Recent books which make explicit the social practices of doctoral education (for example Leonard, 2001), particularly those in and produced by layer 3, are extremely useful to students at early stages of candidature. Traces of layer 3 surface in the dissertation text. For example, decisions about which scholars to align with or critique relate back to political contexts of the field. University policies about what counts as an acceptable artefact for examination are often subject to internecine faculty politics. The end result of these machinations will surface in the text. But there is a dialectic at work here as well. Not only are there traces of these macro-discourses in the dissertation text, but the text in turn contributes to and shapes the field. It does productive work as it makes its contribution to the field.

We propose that our two theoretical frameworks – text work/identity work and writing as discursive social practice – are useful tools for theorizing a pedagogy that promotes informed conversations about doctoral writing. To illustrate how we use these frameworks together, we turn our attention back to the academic conference to reconceptualize it as a space for taking forward doctoral writing-in-progress and for the formation of a scholarly identity (see Ivanic, 1998).

The academic conference as performance, event and practice

The strategic use of conference papers throughout the evolution and development of the dissertation is an important pedagogical intervention in terms of the identity work and the text work that can be accomplished. At one level this is hardly a new idea. Most professional conferences have student membership and are keen to recruit early career academics to their number. Many supervisors encourage students to attend and present their doctoral work-in-progress and their universities provide funding to facilitate student participation.

Using the heuristic of Fairclough's three boxes, however, also helps us see that the particular form and conventions of a conference are shaped by broader academic and disciplinary discourses in the field, and that these in turn impact on the scholarly identities of those who attend and participate. For those who are well established, it may be about display, confirmation, shoring up already developed reputations and networks. For those who are 'new', the conference can be more risky. There are dangers in performing one's scholarly identity in public before it is fully formed. But there are also opportunities to build networks, to see and meet those scholars one admires – any of whom might become potential examiners or employers – and to become/feel part of a scholarly community.

We now revisit the three boxes outlined in Figure 2.1, bringing text work/identity work into the discussion. Our goal here is to show how our concepts of texts, identities and pedagogies come together to inform a writing-centred doctoral supervision practice.

Writing the conference text

Writing the text (layer 1) is the central concern of most doctoral researchers 'new' to the game. There is much to learn and many decisions to make. Different disciplines have different conventions regarding the writing of conference papers. Some require the submission of a fully written paper for refereeing prior to the event. In countries where performance is measured by peer review processes, this is becoming increasingly the norm across disciplines. But some disciplines require only the submission of an abstract for refereeing, and it is up to presenters to further develop the paper into a print-based or electronic journal article following the conference. As part of the textual labour of conferences, then, doctoral researchers need to learn how to prepare abstracts and become familiar with the genre conventions of their discipline/conference. It is not safe to assume they already know how to do so. Supervisors, of course, are significant here, and they can use the abstract (as we argue in Chapter 6) as a rich pedagogic space for fostering both text work and identity work.

Doctoral researchers have many choices about how to write a conference paper and they also need dialogue with supervisors to determine which form is appropriate to the conference and their discipline. At a recent workshop on writing conference papers, we were bombarded with specific text-related questions from early career researchers. Should presenters make PowerPoint slides with notes to move the presentation along? How many slides are ideal? Should they also produce a fully written script to be read aloud? Should this script be different to the paper already submitted for the conference proceedings? And is it important to write a reduced version that fits the time limits imposed on their conference performance? Regardless of the possible variety of textual forms, we believe there are two crucial considerations for supervisors in layer 1: (a) how to use the conference paper as an opportunity to advance the thesis work; and (b) a recognition that the conference text – the tangible thing that is 'delivered' – is both shaped by the social practices of the field and in turn shapes the student who writes.

Certainly these were considerations for Janet in the months leading up to the conference at which Kathryn presented. Janet made a number of suggestions about how Kathryn might use the conference paper to advance her thesis. There were a few choices. Kathryn had completed a review of literatures for her colloquium panel, but it needed revisiting and updating in light of the new ways she had redesigned her fieldwork. She had also recently completed transcribing a number of student–teacher classroom interactions and she needed to begin her analysis. The conference paper would allow her to experiment with a small amount of data and make pivotal decisions about how to frame the analysis in her dissertation. As it turned out she did both, but at two different conferences. Kathryn's reflections clearly show her appreciation of the benefits of restructuring her thesis work for the specific conference audience.

KATHRYN: I was thinking about how writing a conference paper demands that you
    take it apart and put it back together in a new way, which I think gives you

a bit of distance on it. This allows you to tell a coherent story about your research which is a bit snappier than you do in a dissertation. It's the concept 'paper' which enables you to make links perhaps. You can foreground different things and it allows you to play with ideas and put things together in ways that I might not have been thinking about in the overall dissertation, but which may have a coherence for an audience. It's that ability to play with structure and to select to foreground something and de-emphasize something else that's a useful conceptual tool.

Like Janet, we suggest to our students that they use writing a conference paper as an opportunity to sharpen ideas and hone the thesis argument. In this way the text produced in layer 1 serves multiple purposes. It allows doctoral researchers to rehearse understandings that will become integral to the dissertation. And it is an opportunity to experiment, to try things out that can be abandoned if they don't work out as planned. It thus contributes positively to the production of the final text.

But of course there is more to a conference presentation than work on the text. There is also work on the self.

Discourse practice: performing the conference paper

Because so much time and energy goes into the performance of writing the text (layer 1), students often overlook the crucial labour in performing/presenting their work (layer 2) – for a public audience prior to submission and examination as a thesis. Some doctoral researchers read their paper over a few times, even out loud with a timer. But they overlook that what they are performing is not just the intellectual content of the work, but also their scholarly identity. It is not only the paper that gets 'read' and interpreted at the conference, but the scholar as well.

Most advice books will tell students to make sure their presentation is polished, but we find it a useful pedagogical strategy to extend the metaphor to help doctoral researchers think about what makes a good performance: the need for sufficient rehearsal, attention to staging, costume, timing, and an engaging start and conclusion. There is nothing more tedious than attending a boring, turgid conference session. Presenters who drone on in a tedious monotone and read dense, impenetrable text that has not been written like 'speech' are a nightmare (see Chapter 7 for our discussion of the differences between spoken and written language). Worse still is having presenters run out of time, encroach on the time and space of the next presenter and conclude by waving the paper in their hand, saying 'You can read about it later'. Not much incentive there.

The notion of performance, by contrast, foregrounds the importance of planning these events. It also implies opportunities for rehearsal and we have found it important to provide these for students individually, as well as collectively. Many universities run small, local departmental or faculty seminars that create 'safe spaces' for graduate students to rehearse prior to the 'big conference'. These trial runs allow doctoral researchers to get feedback and amend their presentations accordingly. When these opportunities are not part of institutional life, we have found it important to create informal gatherings for this purpose, thereby building an expectation that performance requires rehearsal and that a discourse community of emerging scholars can assist one another with this work. Students can also be assisted in supervision sessions to articulate key arguments or identify the three to five major points they will make in their PowerPoint slides. This allows them to cut through the excess of information, in which they are often drowning, and to identify what kind of data makes the point best 'in person', as opposed to 'in writing'.

Social practices: networking the field

When students understand the conference as discursive event and engage seriously with the social practice dimension of the conference (layer 3), it becomes clear that there is more to be done beyond writing the paper, performing it and listening to other people's papers. Boden *et al.* (2004) provide an extensive discussion of the politics of academic networking and the kind of work early career researchers might engage in to foster their work and make their scholarly identities known. They argue that conferences offer invaluable opportunities for meeting people, having conversations and arguments with them and finding intellectual/research buddies. Conferences are a tangible way to get in touch with current debates/ideas in the field; to access 'what people are thinking now rather than what was in their past published paper' (2004: 43) and to gain different perspectives about how things are done/researched elsewhere. Conferences also provide opportunities to gain visibility by asking questions and joining in discussion on other people's papers, as well as to meet publishers and journal editors.

We agree that such activities are central to negotiating the politics of one's field. But we also recognize that emerging PhD scholars who may be performing their identity publicly for the first time find these suggestions overwhelming. Again we see the supervisor as a buffer (layer 2) in this regard, creating safe spaces, smoothing the way for connections.

The politics of conference attendance can be ameliorated by supervisors. Some supervisors co-present with students to facilitate the acceptance of their papers onto large conference programmes and guarantee an audience (the supervisor is known, hence others will attend). Joint presentations also provide a kind of intellectual scaffolding and a more direct modelling of how to perform a paper and engage with an audience interactively.

We have also found it helpful to guide doctoral researchers in differentiating the kinds of questions they may be asked at conferences so they can prepare accordingly. We suggest there are at least three difficult types of interrogators they may encounter: (1) people who want to talk about the paper the student did not write; (2) people who want to make themselves look smart and assert their identity by chopping away at the presenter's; and (3) people who have not got the point. We propose to our doctoral researchers that it helps to listen to which 'type' of question it is, and then act accordingly. They can deal with comments about an alternative paper, for example, by simply thanking the questioner for their contribution. By contrast the belligerent put-down or aggressive contradiction needs a very calm and succinct rebuttal. This is precisely what Kathryn did with surprising effects on her sense of scholarly authority. If that cannot be managed, then it is again a polite thanks for the point. But the third type of question requires a serious re-explanation of the points made. Indeed, it may be the case that someone who does not get the point is making a very positive contribution to the further development of the thesis argument in pointing to things that were obscure or conflated.

In sum then, in combining the two ideas of text work/identity work with Fairclough's three layers of discourse, and in emphasizing the idea of performance, we have come to see the academic conference as a rich site for doctoral writing pedagogies. We suggest that these frameworks allow an embodied sense of how discursive practices of disciplinary fields shape and are shaped by doctoral researchers. They build a stronger sense of the vulnerability, the emotional angst, and the elation at stake in scholarly identity formation, whether it occurs at the site of the conference paper, or as we see in subsequent chapters, in writing reviews of literature, in shaping the argument of the thesis and in writing chapters by which the scholar is known and judged.

Chapter 3

Persuading an octopus into a glass

Working with literatures

Working with the literatures is not, as some doctoral researchers in desperate and cynical moments suggest, about showing their examiners that a lot of books and articles have been read, summarized and bracketed. We believe that there are definite purposes in doctoral study for working with literatures.

We propose that the key tasks accomplished in literature work are to:

1 sketch out the nature of the field or fields relevant to the inquiry, possibly indicating something of their historical development and
2 identify major debates and define contentious terms, in order to
3 establish which studies, ideas and/or methods are most pertinent to the study and
4 locate gaps in the field, in order to
5 create the warrant for the study in question, and
6 identify the contribution the study will make.

In stating the functions of literature work, we do not want to suggest that there is universal agreement about the dimensions of any field and its themes, debates and terms. There is no one correct way for the literatures to be interpreted. As Golden-Biddle and Locke (1997: 29)[4] put it '... there is sufficient fluidity and ambiguity in any topical literature to allow it to be authentically interpreted and shaped in a number of different directions'. It is the doctoral researcher's task to canvass and interpret the field and to construct her version of its terrain. However, there are often particular disagreements and developments about the boundaries of fields of knowledge, and it is possible to locate unresolved or contentious topics. Supervisors, of course, make these issues clear in the preliminary readings they suggest to students. And there are now increasing numbers of 'Introductions to ...', 'Readers in ...' and 'Handbooks of ...' which do flag the key scholars, themes, issues and debates.

In a recent review of dissertation literature reviews, Boote and Beile (2005) deplore both the poor quality of student reviews and the lack of serious pedagogical attention given to this act of scholarship in doctoral education. A thorough, substantive literature review is, they argue, 'a precondition for doing substantive, thorough, sophisticated research' (Boote and Beile, 2005: 3).

Our work with doctoral researchers in Australia and the UK suggests they understand its pivotal importance, but are plagued by an excess of anxiety and expectation about literature work. There are many reasons for this angst. There are writing myths which complicate and make writing about the literatures a task to be endured, rather than enjoyed. And there is a lack of recognition of the intensity of identity work involved at this site of text production. We would go so far as to say that literature reviews are *the* quintessential site of identity work, where the novice researcher enters what we call occupied territory – with all the immanent danger and quiet dread that this metaphor implies – including possible ambushes, barbed wire fences, and unknown academics who patrol the boundaries of already occupied territories.

Doctoral researchers have an emergent relation to the territory (the fields which inform their research) and its occupiers (the more senior, experienced scholars of the academy). Yet they are expected to find the courage to assess the work of the occupiers – some of whom, in time, may well examine and judge their own theses. The novice researcher is not only an alien in foreign fields, but is unaware of the rules of engagement, and the histories of debates, feuds, alliances and accommodations that precede her entry to the field. This is not work for the faint/feint-hearted! There are so many decisions to make. Where to start? Which fields? Which landmines to avoid? How to be 'critical', who to be critical of, and how to escape being tangled in the barbed wire? How to negotiate the complexities of power relations in a strange land? Who to include and exclude in the negotiations? Who to engage with, who to ignore and with what effects?

While the metaphor of occupied territory may be dramatic, perhaps even overstated, it stands in opposition to a taken-for-granted view of literature work as a relatively straightforward, if time-consuming, task. It is also a metaphor which we believe gets closer to the affective experience and intensity of identity work many students experience when 'reviewing' the literatures.

This chapter focuses on the processes of naming and framing the literature 'review'. We want to both unsettle a naturalized view of literature work and also challenge advice that is too rational, too wise after the fact. But we begin by looking at examples of students' literature work that exemplify the difficulties they face and the issues that we as supervisors must address.

Literature reviews – what's the problem?

What follows are brief excerpts from literature review drafts of two doctoral researchers. It is difficult to select brief segments from such a long document, as 'problems' often range over paragraphs and pages. So our guiding principle has been to select 'pithy bits' that represent typical problems we and our colleagues encounter in relation to text and identity work.

Vera is a doctoral researcher writing about deconstruction and its relationship to both structuralism (using theorists such as Saussure, Lévi-Strauss and Lacan) and poststructuralism (Barthes and Foucault). This excerpt occurs midway through her review as she struggles with Lacan and Barthes.

> According to Belsey (2002: 57), Jacques Lacan reinterpreted Freud in the light of Lévi-Strauss and Saussure – 'to delineate a subject was itself the location of a difference'. Belsey goes on to explain that, for Lacan, the human being is 'an organism in culture'. According to Lacan, speech was central to psycho-analytic practice. He argued that during the first two months of life a child's emergent sense of self was formed in relation to subjects, capable of signifying. Lacan calls this the 'Otherness of language'. 'The big other', states Belsey, 'is there before we are, exists outside us and does not belong to us'. The early writing of Barthes, says Norris (1982: 8), was aimed at a full-scale science of the text, modelled on the linguistics of Saussure and the structural anthropology of Lévi-Strauss. In *Elements of Semiology* (1967), Barthes takes the view of structuralism as a kind of 'mastercode' capable of providing higher-level understanding. Culler (1976: 58) states that Barthes, in *Elements of Semiology*, speculated upon the ways in which 'langue and parole', 'signifier and signified', 'syntagmatic and paradigmatic' might apply to various non-linguistic phenomena. Culler goes on to say that, for a semiologist studying the food system of a culture, 'parole' is all the events of eating, whereas 'langue' is the system of rules that underlies all these events. These would define, for example, what is edible, which dishes would be combined to create a meal and the conventions governing the syntactic ordering of items.

We might characterize Vera's text as 'crowded' by the literature (Becker, 1986: 146). She is traversing complex theoretical terrain, but seems to be 'drowning' in the detail. She stands as an outsider, piling up layers of 'who said what about what' as a strategy for highlighting key theoretical ideas. 'According to Belsey (2002: 57), Jaques Lacan reinterpreted Freud in the light of Levi-Strauss and Saussure …. The early writing of Barthes, says Norris …. Culler states that Barthes …' Vera does not appear in this text at all. She has not added any evaluative comments and her somewhat confused summary is dominant in this and the writing that precedes and follows the extract. The reader has no idea how these ideas inform her study nor whether any ideas are any more important than any others.

The phenomenon of the 'invisible scholar' can also be seen in the next example. Geraldine is a doctoral researcher writing about the school effectiveness literature and while she seems more on top of the ideas in the field she is entering, her relationship to it remains hidden.

> Mortimore (1998) also contributes to the school effectiveness research agenda. He explains that school effectiveness researchers aim to ascertain

whether differential resources, processes and organizational differences affect student performance and if so, how. He is also of the view that school effectiveness researchers seek reliable and appropriate ways to measure school quality. Hopkins (2001) suggests that one of the earliest studies that was done compared the effectiveness of some secondary schools on a range of student outcome measures. Reynolds and Cuttance (1992) also point out that the effective schools research entitled 'Fifteen Thousand Hours' characterised school efficiency factors as varied in the degree of academic emphasis, teacher's action in lessons, the availability of resources, rewards, good conditions for pupils and the extent to which children were able to take responsibility. It was emphasized that effective school researchers claim that there are significant differences between schools on a number of different student outcomes after full account has been taken of students' previous learning history and family background. Hargreaves and Hopkins (1991) also endorse the view by stating that there is evidence to support the argument that the characteristics of individual schools can make a difference to pupils' progress since certain internal conditions are common in schools that achieve higher levels of outcomes for their students.

We characterize Geraldine's text as 'he said, she said'. Every sentence begins by naming the researcher, followed by a fairly neutral verb: 'Mortimer also contributes … Hopkins suggests … Reynolds and Cuttance also point out … Hargreaves and Hopkins also endorse …'. Syntactically, the lack of connection between sentences makes this more like a list, a summary of ideas. The writer piles up one study after another, but there is no evaluative stance. When, a few paragraphs later, Geraldine tries to insert some critique, she again relies on what others have said.

Scheerens *et al.* (2001) claim that many critics appear to misread the scope and limitations of what school effectiveness is all about. Therefore, they point out that school effectiveness research is about instrumental rationality, that is, how to do things right and not so much about substantive rationality of how to do the right things. The purpose of school effectiveness research raises some concerns. While it is very important to know how to do things right, it is of greater importance to know how to do the right thing because one bad decision can ruin an organization and it would take an even greater effort to set things back on the right track.

Clearly there is a debate in the field about school effectiveness as an instrumental rationality, but Geraldine does not stake a claim here. She stands aside and allows other researchers (Scheerens *et al.*) to introduce the idea of critique, but her position in all this remains oblique. The distinction between 'how to do things right' and 'do the right thing', a common phrase within the field, allows the writer to take no position, while trying to give the impression she has been critical.

In both Geraldine and Vera's texts, the literature is neither used to locate their studies, nor to advance an argument about the state of the field in order to make the case for their own work. This is characteristic of diffident scholars who lack authority and who are literally overwhelmed by the work of others.

It is our argument throughout this chapter and the next that there are two sides to reviewing literatures: knowing the genres, conventions and textual practices; and assuming what we call a 'hands on hips' subject position. When the doctoral researcher writes about literatures, she is constructing a representation of the scholar and her scholarly practice. The struggle with writing occurs because of the difficulty of negotiating text work and identity work simultaneously. The challenge is to learn to speak/write with authority, standing back with 'hands on hips' in order to critically survey and categorize texts and the field itself.

To better understand why doctoral researchers find this work so difficult, we asked them to describe how they felt about literature work.

Metaphors that students live and work by

We have run several workshops for graduate students in Australia, South Africa, Norway, Canada and the UK on writing literature reviews and we find students inevitably anxious about the task of positioning and justifying their own research in relation to The Literature. We begin our workshops by putting identity issues on the table as a starting point for the text work that will follow. One strategy we have used is to ask: When you think about doing a literature review, what is it like for you? What image or metaphor[5] comes to mind? These metaphors are written on small cards, collected and discussed amidst the whole group. We approach the task with humour and some irreverence, as we are keen to make visible the feelings of inadequacy shared by many students and identify these as a genre problem, rather than as simply an inadequacy of individual writers.

To give some structure to the discussion, we ask questions of the metaphors:

- How is the literature represented?
- What is the researcher doing?
- How powerfully is the researcher represented?

We use the term representation to emphasize that metaphors are a particular way of using language, not 'the truth' but a way of seeing and understanding and therefore acting.[6] That there are many ways of seeing is evident from the multiplicity of metaphors used across the group. These metaphors have power. They influence how doctoral researchers approach the task of literature work and how they think of themselves as writers. They are therefore worth eliciting and interrogating in order that supervisor and student can together confront and change them.

For the purpose of our discussion here, we have pooled metaphors from three workshops to highlight commonalities. These include a myriad of ways in which the doctoral researcher is represented as lost, drowning and confused while the literature is pre-eminent, strong and needing, somehow, to be conquered.

Water images are particularly popular, where the literature itself is figured as dangerous territory and unmanageable:

- a chaotic whirlpool
- an ocean full of sharks
- a stormy ocean

and the researcher as unprepared or impeded from taking action:

- trying to swim with concrete blocks on my feet
- setting off across the ocean in a canoe
- floating on the ocean without an anchor
- diving into a pond of water weeds and trying to find my way out
- tossed between currents in the sea, all pulling in different directions
- trudging through a mangrove swamp.

The puzzle/maze metaphor also features widely as a representation of the literature, nuanced by images of light and dark. Here the researcher is lost, stumbling, unable to find their way:

- walking into a tunnel
- walking through a maze blindfolded
- walking in the dark
- going through a maze in search of hidden treasure
- searching the night sky without a telescope for connections between illuminated stars.

Students also use bodily pain and discomfort imagery to represent the process of literature work, with popular clichés dominant, including:

- pulling teeth
- sweating blood
- being hit by a truck
- sinking in quicksand
- getting caught in knots of other people's writing.

While such images dominate the groups we've worked with, highlighting a lack of agency and being overwhelmed, a small number of students have offered more benign images of searching the literature, as:

- gold mining: extracting the golden threads that provide the value
- collecting seashells

- digging in the ground for precious metal
- building a brick wall, laying down one brick at a time until this magnificent wall has been created.
- looking into a kaleidoscope, a mosaic which keeps shifting.

These images highlight the value of the search and the satisfaction of the process, but possibly romanticize the labour involved. The rewards (gold threads, precious metals, magnificent walls, lovely mosaics) have an Enlightenment ring which suggests that for these students, some kind of 'truth' resides somewhere in the texts with which they were working.

For us, however, the richest metaphors are those that attribute the difficulties in writing to the nature of reviewing literatures. Two of the metaphors we find most delightful use animal imagery:

- eating a live elephant
- persuading (selected arms of) an octopus into a glass.

These metaphors differ qualitatively from the others in that they highlight the almost absurd difficulty of the task, with humour. Feelings of inadequacy or lack of preparedness are absent. Rather, the obstacle is huge and unruly (the live elephant, those unmanageable octopus arms), and the researcher is active. She is 'eating' and 'persuading' – doing what she needs to do in the face of what seems an impossible task.

Such metaphor work is powerful for tapping into student anxieties. It has the potential to create a pedagogical conversation through which supervisors can orient doctoral researchers to the importance of identity work in the project of becoming a scholar and, more specifically, doing the literature work. Our aim as supervisors is to shift disabling metaphors so that students can begin to imagine other subject positions where they might be in charge of this journey, however hard it is. Beginning a conversation about literature work with a discussion of metaphor is a way to start a different kind of conversation with doctoral researchers, one which addresses their intellect and emotions, and which takes up the tangled nature of text work/identity work.

We think at least part of the problem, however, lies in the term itself – the literature review.

Literature review – what's in a name?

Just as we were concerned in Chapter 1 to question the phrase 'writing up', because of its negative and mythologizing effects on the process of thesis writing, here we reflect on and reject the notion of *the literature review.*

A few things stand out about the phrase. First it is singular, preceded by the article *the* or *a*, suggesting that it is a single object of importance which occurs in one place in the thesis, conventionally the second chapter. Whether we are talking about *the* (as in one and only) or *a* (somewhat less definitive but still singular) literature review, it is linguistically marked as a unified piece of writing, rather than being used throughout the dissertation.

Even more worrying is any implication that the writing of the review occurs only once at the beginning of the doctoral research, with only minor editing and tidying after the fieldwork has concluded. There is no doubt that at the outset of doctoral candidature, an intensive immersion in literatures is essential. But most commentators (e.g. Dunleavy, 2003; Hart, 1998, 2001) stress that literature work is an evolving and ongoing task that must be updated and revised throughout the process of writing the thesis. We rephrase this advice to suggest that reading and writing are integral to all phases of doctoral study.

The term literature itself is also curious, as it seems to elevate research reports, books, articles and monographs to the status of canon – *the literature*, with all its evocation of high culture and importance. We don't ask doctoral researchers to do a review of *research*, but of *literature*, and usually of literature as singular, literature *not* literatures.

Finally, the verb *review*, which has been transformed to a noun, implies a collection, a showing and summarizing of what others have done. The doctoral researcher is to create a review by 'doing' one (Hart, 1998) or 'writing' one (Murray, 2002). When the term review is used as a verb, as in *to review* the literature, the researcher is positioned linguistically as onlooker. Our emphasis, by contrast, is on positioning students as agents who *use* and *evaluate* the research of others, in order to make a place for their own work.

As we progress our discussion in this chapter and the next, we return to some of the issues raised here, including what it means to *use* the literature, rather than be used by it and where/how literature work might be located in relation to the overall structure of the thesis. As our aim is not to invent new terms unnecessarily, we continue to use the term literature, but always in the *plural* and with a lower case l – literatures. This is to signal that there is neither one monolithic research *canon*, nor necessarily one place only in the thesis where it belongs. At times we will also use the abbreviation LR to further defuse and undermine the potency of the taken-for-granted terminology.

We now consider how literature reviews are discussed in the advice books in order to clear the way for more productive metaphors and strategies.

Literature reviews and the advice books

Advice books on how to write the LR are rife with intimidating expressions and exhortations to be rigorous, systematic, respectful (but critical), and comprehensive (but not all inclusive). Burton and Steane (2004) are a prime example of how not to help. Writing from the field of management, they construct what we would call an excess of expectation about the significance of the LR. Calling it alternately 'a critical part of the thesis' and 'the foundation of the research project' (2004: 124), and crediting it with doing an enormous amount of work, they say:

All parts of the thesis are strengthened by the comprehensiveness and rigour of your review of relevant theories. Understanding the literature sharpens the focus of your argument and will help to clarify your proposition or research question ... define the arena of your study, and can suggest hypotheses that you need to test, methodologies appropriate for your study and perhaps even a sample size.

(Burton and Steane, 2004: 125)

This is high stakes LR. This is a make-or-break activity. While we agree that getting a grip on literatures is important, this kind of heightened do-or-die focus hardly helps to make the LR project seem doable.

Burton and Steane also use a journey/water metaphor to represent the process of reviewing, warning of the dangers of getting lost or trying to include everything.

The task of identifying the relevant literature can be likened to a journey of discovery, like tracking a river to its source. If you are exploring the river, there will be tributaries and creeks that invite exploration, but these are side trips and diversions from the main task and from the general direction – some of them fruitful and some of them not. If you explore every creek and stream that flows into a river, you will have a much greater understanding of the whole river, but you also run the risk of becoming so distracted by the small streams that you will never reach the source. So you need to decide what are the important branches of the river that need to be explored, and to decide what branches are less important and can be ignored.

(Burton and Steane, 2004: 126–7)

This river metaphor constructs a rational landscape, a considered set of choices. The literature (singular) is represented as a river with branches and is subdivided in a fairly orderly manner. Somewhere there is a source (or sources) out there to be found. All the journeyperson need do is navigate, decide whether to move this way or that, here or there, and decide how long to stay. While the position of navigator has agency, navigating is presumably hard to do if, as our students suggest, they are wearing concrete blocks on their feet or they are caught up in the weeds and sludge of the river bottom, entangled and lost or on the verge of drowning.

Burton and Steane send their student out on a journey with no map, into uncharted waters, with little guidance about how to approach the plethora of decisions to be made. On what basis does she decide which streams are worth exploring? How does she avoid being stuck on a mud bank, or swept off course in white water? This river metaphor, and others like it, construct an overly rational version of what is possible after the fact. Once the writer knows the river and can presumably see its tributaries and branches, she can navigate them.

It is little wonder, we suggest, that advice such as this does little to help students and probably adds to their anxieties. It is crucial to move LR conversations with students in more positive and enabling directions. We think of this as re-naming and re-framing. In the remainder of the chapter, we consider two metaphors for rethinking the practice of working with literatures.

More helpful metaphors: tables and dinner parties

Not all advice books are so unhelpful. Becker (1986) in a chapter aptly entitled 'Terrorised by the literature', suggests that students need to think of scholarship as a cumulative enterprise. They are adding to something that already exists and they re-use scholarship in order to advance their own study. Rather than sending students out on a river in a *Deliverance*[7] style test of endurance, Becker uses the metaphor of a table to get at what is new, and what is old or borrowed/used. He says:

> Imagine that you are … making a table. You have designed it and cut out some of the parts. Fortunately, you don't need to make all the parts yourself. Some are standard sizes and shapes – lengths of two by four, for instance – available at any lumber yard. Some have already been designed and made by other people – drawer pulls and turned legs. All you have to do is fit them into the places you left for them, knowing that they were available. That is the best way to use the literature.
>
> (Becker, 1986: 142)

Becker suggests that the LR is a particular kind of text, an argument. (This is a genre we explore in more detail in Chapter 6.) Here we allow Becker to make the initial point:

> You want to make an argument, instead of a table. You have created some of the argument yourself, perhaps on the basis of new data or information you have collected. But you needn't invent the whole thing. Other people have worked on your problem or problems related to it and have made some of the pieces you need. You just have to fit them in where they belong. Like the woodworker, you leave space, when you make your portion of the argument, for the other parts you know you can get. You do that, that is, *if* you know that they are there to use. And that's one good reason to know the literature: so that you will know what pieces are available and not waste time doing what has already been done.
>
> (Becker, 1986: 142)

One positive feature of the table metaphor is that of familiarity. We have all used tables and know what they are, whereas not many of us will have paddled a river from top to bottom. A table is also of a manageable size because it has to fit into a room: even the grandest table can be seen in entirety and walked around. The table metaphor thus makes the LR appear doable. And, making a table is a crafting activity. It is pleasurable work with the hands, both mental and manual, aesthetic and utilitarian. This resonates with the notion of writing that is honed and polished through labour that is both aesthetic and functionally directed. Of course, there is always the occasional hammered thumb to contend with, but that is a far cry from being submerged or being stranded oarless up the proverbial creek.

In our own search for useful metaphors that might put some agency back into the process yet foreground the crucial identity work involved, we have been particularly taken by a metaphor developed by our Australian colleague John Smyth. It is of literature work as a dinner party. We have elaborated this metaphor in our workshops with students to counter the overwhelmingly *swamped*, *lost* and *drowning* images they usually offer.

We like the domestic, familiar image of the dinner party and its emphasis on conversation with a community of scholars. The party occurs in one's own home, in the familiar territory where one belongs (not the ocean or the swamp or the river). The doctoral researcher invites to the table the scholars she would like to join her for a conversation over the evening meal. The emphasis is on the company and the conversation that happens at the table. The candidate has selected the menu, bought the food, and cooked the dinner which she offers her guests. As host to this party, she makes space for the guests to talk about their work, but *in relation* to her own work. Her own thesis is never disconnected from the conversation, for after all it lies on her table. It is part of the food the guests eat, chew and digest.

And because it is her dinner party the doctoral researcher has a great deal of agency. The dinner party metaphor makes it clear that she cannot invite everyone because they will not all fit at her table. She is not just a bystander or 'reviewer' of the conversation, but a participant. While she may not always comprehend the conversation or catch all its nuances and complexity, she is present. And she can reflect on these conversations later, mulling them over as one might do at the end of a good night out. But having made the contact and the connection (between their work and her own), there is a starting point for other dinners, coffees, conversations and the option of not inviting some guests back or including others.

We find students warm to this metaphor because it is such a stark contrast to the more powerless images they offer. It does not seem out of reach. Its very domesticity makes the LR seem doable. Most importantly it creates a very different subject position for the writer. It is the doctoral writer who does the inviting, it is she who initiates the conversation with her scholar guests and it is she who *uses* what they have said, rather than just being grateful that they have come.

Of course, counter metaphors, as important as they are, are not enough in supervision pedagogy and so we move on to strategies that help students operationalize the dinner party organizer as subject position, that is, to find agency through text work. But our argument throughout is that identity work is as central as the text work and should not be underestimated. This is not just an added extra, it is part of the work of writing the thesis.

Adopting a critical stance

As we noted earlier, most advice books suggest that the LR needs to be critical. On the surface, the term *critical* positions the doctoral researcher more powerfully as judge and evaluator of the research that has preceded her. But we have found this is where many students come undone. Critical is taken to mean *critique*, to find what is *wrong*. Many students are intimidated and sometimes paralysed by the prospect of being critical of (esteemed, elevated) scholars who are senior, more powerful and acknowledged experts in their fields.

The seemingly innocuous and commonplace phrase *a critical review of the literature* carries with it a set of presuppositions that create a particular stance for the doctoral writer, what we call a difficult subject position, which makes the task of writing more onerous. Doctoral researchers often revert to writing summaries, we believe, because they are nervous about taking on the subject position of 'critic'. They are often cautioned (through advice books, supervisors, university websites) that the LR is not a summary genre, that it involves making a case for their work and finding which research literatures are like/unlike/connected to what they are doing. But such advice is often not sufficient.

The dinner party metaphor can help here. The doctoral researcher can make her dinner party a dull affair where all the guests speak one after another, but engage in little interaction, debate or challenge. Or her soirée can be one in which she serially holds the floor, ridicules all of the guests and prevents them from talking back or to each other. Of course, all students know that in reality neither of these events will be entertaining or informative. Getting the mix right is not easy.

We can capture this dilemma by considering a text where the doctoral researcher has difficulty achieving a critical stance. The text is written by Gina, a senior school administrator who is researching what is 'known' about school reform.

> Fullan (1993) proposes some paradoxes about change that would help one to understand and deal with the complexities of change. He claims that you can't mandate what matters since the more complex the change, the less you can force it. He also explains that change is a journey, not a blueprint and that we will encounter problems. However, we should see problems as our friends. Can one ever regard problems as good? This could be the most feared thing and could become an obstacle for some, knowing the stress and headaches that problems can cause. Nevertheless, the author is of the view that because they are inevitable, we can't learn without them. In this light, I share the author's view because the old adage goes 'experiences are our greatest teacher'.

Here Gina shows a grasp of the issues and debates about school change, but a difficulty in positioning herself in relation to the writer Fullan, a senior scholar in the field of educational reform. In this passage she talks of herself as 'one' and 'I' and of an anonymous 'you' and 'we' as the audience the writer is addressing. She is critical of the proposition Fullan is making, but in order to make the critique she resorts to rhetorical questions. Gina then absents herself from the text to make another critical comment which is based on her own considerable professional experience, but which she is reluctant to assert, saying 'knowing the stress and headaches that problems can cause'. She does not produce counters from other literature at this point. She reasserts herself, as the 'I', only when in agreement with the author.

It would be easy to respond to this text as a piece of 'bad writing', but a closer reading shows that the problem is not primarily about style and expression. The lack of intertextuality and some of the tongue-tied-ness derive from Gina's inability to find a comfortable 'hands on hips' stance. She is mute at her own dinner party.

For Gina to move forward, an expanded notion of critical, beyond praise and blame, is required, together with the adoption of a stance that we characterize as appreciative.

Becoming critical

To be critical is not just about praising and demolishing the work of others. To continue with our dinner party metaphor, the task is not to invite the guests in order to poison, gag or humiliate them. Nor is it simply to contradict in the style of the famous Monty Python argument sketch, where 'Yes it is', 'No it isn't' constitutes an argument. These are commonsense versions of critique and argument. The scholarly meanings of these terms are different.

Being critical involves making a number of judgments and decisions about which literatures to engage with, and which to ignore, which aspects of texts to stress and which to omit or downplay. Adopting a critical stance to a text means paying attention to: definitions; underpinning assumptions; theoretical resources mobilized; epistemology and methodology; method (who, what, where, how); and findings. These perspectives can be brought together to establish points of similarity and points of difference. It is through such focused interrogation and intertextual work that students come to identify major debates in the field.

But to be critical is also to be respectful of what others have done, to look at what they have contributed, rather than going on the attack. A key question to ask is: What does this work contribute? Rather than, what does it fail to do? This creates an evaluative frame which does not privilege 'criticism' as negative or destructive behaviour. The following example, written by doctoral researcher Sean, illustrates what an appreciative stance might look like.

The Stages Heuristic is widely acknowledged to have been the first formal policy theory established in the 'new' field of policy science (Deleon, 1999; Sabatier, 1999; McCool, 1995). Although it is no longer in active use, I mention it here as an historical antecedent to later policy theories. Originally conceptualized by Lasswell (1951), the *stages* approach was refined by Brewer

(1974) and identified six key stages: (1) policy initiation, (2) estimation, (3) selection, (4) implementation, (5) evaluation, and (6) termination. The Stages Heuristic represents a delineated, sequential policy process framework where some overlap between stages is possible, but where each stage has distinctive characteristics. While much of the policy research since the 1970s has been shaped by this framework, its critics now characterize the approach as disjointed, episodic and linear (Deleon, 1999; Sabatier, 1999).

For all practical purposes this theory has become outdated and irrelevant in that it is no longer studied by scholars. But the *stages* approach represents a point of departure for other theories and more stringent and holistic models. It also served to open policy studies to a range of academic disciplines and provided space for later ideas based on social norms and personal values (Deleon, 1999).

Here Sean demonstrates a grasp of a body of literature which was important to policy scholarship. While noting the critiques of scholars who built their work in dialogue with and against this body of work, he is able to insert his own evaluation of its importance. Without resorting to 'I agree (or disagree)', or 'Deleon says', Sean puts forward his assessment of the body of scholarship, namely that the work was important as a kicking-off place for others and as the beginning of a new field.

This is a graceful recognition of the work of other scholars. It is neither deferential nor obsequious nor harsh. But it does, nevertheless, point out that the actual theory in question has largely been superseded.

Some students arrive at a generous and generative criticality by themselves. Others benefit from a more direct pedagogical strategy. The work of Jon Wagner (1993) is particularly useful in establishing an analytic framework for criticality that moves beyond liking or disliking, agreeing or disagreeing. Wagner distinguishes between what he calls the 'blind spots' and 'blank spots' in others' research. What we 'know enough to question but not answer' are our blank spots; what we 'don't know well enough to even ask about or care about' are our blind spots, 'areas in which existing theories, methods, and perceptions actually keep us from seeing phenomena as clearly as we might' (1993: 16).

So, for example, surveys typically give a broad snapshot of a phenomenon using respondents' perceptions. What they cannot do is provide in-depth reasons about why those particular answers are the way they are. This requires a different kind of investigation. The lack of in-depth reasons are a blind spot of this type of research (and indeed, are typically why mixed methods are seen as preferable to single surveys). To identify the blind spots in others' research, students need to focus on the things a particular methodology or method does not do, that is, areas that have been overlooked for theoretical or methodological reasons.

Identifying blank spots, by contrast, involves asking what this research could have seen or done that it does not. That is, what are the shortcomings of the research? So, if a survey omitted questions or failed to take up opportunities for informative cross-tabulations, then these are arguably blank spots.

This distinction assists students to see the difference between research that is poorly executed, and research that can only provide a limited data set. Furthermore, when there is a limited data set by virtue of a blind spot, the student is then able to check the blind spots against the claims made of the findings to see if they stack up. Combining the notion of blind spots and blank spots with an appreciative stance allows doctoral researchers to focus on what the research contributes and how/where/why more might be required. The combination also provides evaluative detail beyond summarizing content and themes.

In workshops we encourage doctoral researchers to assess the individual texts of other scholars by asking such questions as:

- what is the argument?
- what kind/aspect of x is spoken about in this article?
- from what position?
- using what evidence?
- what claims are made?
- how adequate are these (blank spots and blind spots)?

Asking and answering such questions allows students to write about the specific contribution, and then to compare it with other texts that have been written, possibly as a history of the field, or as a synthesis of the current state of understanding. Working with blank and blind spots across many texts provides important understandings about the gaps and spaces in the field, one of which the doctoral researcher will occupy.

Modelling good literature work

It is helpful for supervisors to collect examples of student writing, including texts that don't work, as well as texts that do (and negotiate permission to use these). Supervisors can thus make concrete how identity issues surface in text. Doctoral researchers and their supervisors can look together at this writing as a set of strategies, asking: What does this text accomplish and what does it fail to do? Such writing becomes part of the resources of a writing-centred supervision. It makes writing-in-progress more public and less a source of embarrassment. It creates an opportunity to get specific, rather than provide only general feedback to students.

Here is an example of student writing which demonstrates what a sound LR looks like. Anne, a senior public servant, is focusing on traditional and critical perspectives on the role of bureaucracy. In this excerpt she demonstrates that she can handle with facility and generosity complex ideas and an important corpus of scholarship.

> The question of whether senior bureaucrats play an active role in policy development or if their influence is more limited, even an impediment to the

will of elected ministers, is contested. There seems to be a pervasive view that ministers set the policy agenda of government with the bureaucracy represented as a 'necessary evil' for enacting policy. Meanwhile, there is literature that positions the bureaucracy more favourably, even suggesting a more authoritative role in policy development. But, there appears to be no concurrence on the extent of involvement. While many scholars agree that bureaucrats, either actively or tacitly, do play an important role in policy development, it is safe to say that this does not represent the consensus view (Levin, 2002; Stone, 2002; Birkland, 2001; Lynn, 1996; Majone, 1989; Goodsell,1985).

The casting of politicians as policy leaders assumes that a public servant, senior or otherwise, is a 'servant' to the public, but more to the point, a servant to the minister. Some see senior public servants as instruments of political processes but with a severely limited role in policy formulation (Wilson, 1999). This theoretical orientation is consistent with new corporate management ideologies that are believed to foster a stronger separation between public administration and politics but, as I will argue, do more to motivate bureaucrats to seek a more direct role in government policy. As Cohn (1997) suggests, under such arrangements ministers rely on deputies and other senior administrators to provide direction and advice on policy, but the actual decisions are made at a political level. In framing policy development in this way, there is some recognition of the role of the permanent public service, to be sure, but it is one of implementation, stopping short of policy formulation.

We could characterize Anne's text as 'in charge of the literatures'. Anne frames her discussion from the outset as a debate, a set of ideas in competition with one another. This allows her to make ideas central, rather than other researchers, and to take the lead in guiding the reader through the different positions in the field. She uses evaluative language to sort and clarify positions: 'There seems to be a pervasive view; there is literature that positions the bureaucracy more favourably ... there appears to be no concurrence ...'. She also makes links to broader discourses, 'This theoretical orientation is consistent with new corporate management ideologies ...', and to her own argument, '... as I will argue, do more to motivate bureaucrats to seek a more direct role in government policy'.

This is a dinner party where the host is orchestrating the conversation and calling the shots in an elegant and respectful way. Such writing, together with other examples, might serve as a model for students. It stands in contrast to the work by Vera and Geraldine with which we began this chapter. It demonstrates that the doctoral researcher is neither overcome by the literatures, nor in possession of unrealistic expectations of their finality and unity. It shows a healthy degree of appreciation and criticality, and a clear sense of where the doctoral research argument is to go.

In the next chapter, we build on this set of pedagogical strategies to develop more finely-grained mapping strategies that are the foundation of scholarly authority and persuasion.

Chapter 4

Text work in the field of knowledge production

In Chapter 3 we argued that the ways in which language names and frames the literature review is significant. We deconstructed the very idea of the LR and interrogated metaphors used by students as well as advice books. And we proposed counter metaphors, making a table and holding a dinner party, as productive frameworks for the text work/identity work doctoral researchers need to accomplish when working with literatures.

We still need, however, to think about the literatures themselves. Instead of talking about The Literature or even the literatures, we propose thinking about *the field of knowledge production*. We borrow this phrase from our Australian colleague Susan Nicholls to capture the complexity of sources that may constitute 'the literature'.

A *field* may be comprised of bodies of scholarship that have natural boundaries and affinities; but it is just as likely these divisions are blurred and in process. Scholars bring together disparate areas to create different and new fields. *Knowledge production* emphasiszes the constructive capacity of this intellectual work. It is productive and ongoing: the agency of the doctoral scholar as a producer within fields and disciplines is foregrounded. We opt for the notion of *working in the field of knowledge production* because it highlights the physical, mental and emotional labour of text and identity work and is less passive than 'reviewing'. Similarly the term 'field' suggests something less fixed than 'literatures' – a canon, sacrosanct, hard to touch.

We also want to stress that what is in the field may be more than scholarly journals and books. Equating literature to the academy is deeply problematic. It suggests that only the products of academic research ought to be taken seriously: the rest is somehow inadequate, invalid, unreliable, irrelevant. This kind of binary is not in keeping with our understandings about how and where knowledge is produced, nor, indeed, where the need for research might be located.

These are times when scholars cannot keep up with change and when advanced knowledge is produced by governments, by industries, and by all manner of quangos (Beck, 1992; Burton-Jones, 2003; Delanty, 2001; Gibbons *et al.* 1994). These are times when the ways in which people think are influenced by media, by information freely available on the web, and by populist texts (Franklin, 1999; Seaton, 1998; Taylor *et al.* 1997). These are also times when professional work produces problems that only practically informed research can adequately address, and when policy makers increasingly call for evidence to back up as well as inform their actions (Edwards, 2000; Sanderson, 2002). Furthermore, students may find that the 'gap' their research aims to fill derives from a cultural, professional or policy issue, as opposed to coming simply from scholarly activity. Thus, the kinds of texts that are important for doctoral research might well include a great many from a range of sources, not simply those found in academic papers and books.

In addition to opening up what constitutes a valid text, the idea of a field of knowledge production focuses attention on some critical questions:

- Who is producing knowledge about x and who is not?
- How are these knowledges produced?
- What knowledges are included and where, and which are excluded?
- What connections exist between these different sets of knowledge?
- Who has access to these knowledges and who does not?
- What discourses are common across the field of knowledge production?
- In whose interests does this work?

These kinds of questions are not featured in advice texts, but are important for doctoral researchers to consider as part of formulating the kind of contribution they wish to make through their study. The questions also bring to the fore issues relating to Fairclough's third layer, discussed in Chapter 2. In particular they foreground, and render problematic, decisions about which scholars to align with or critique, in light of the political contexts of the field. However the prime focus in this chapter is Fairclough's first layer, that of the research text itself.

In this chapter we focus on pedagogical work in the field of knowledge production. We illustrate a number of strategies for supporting doctoral researchers, including mapping, locating, and creating a warrant. These strategies all produce a more hands-on, interactive textual position for supervisors than is usually suggested in most books available on supervision. While our illustrations are specific, we assume supervisors will remake these for their own disciplinary and institutional contexts.

Mapping the field of knowledge production

When we rethink the LR as working in the field of knowledge production, we are also creating a pedagogical space for work. Within such a space, we need tangible strategies to guide students' labour. Tips and advice will not suffice when helping our doctoral researchers move through 'occupied territory'.

Mapping is one such strategy, where we envisage the field geographically and position the candidate as a map maker. The aim is for doctoral researchers to map the field and identify key players that intersect with their project. As it is unlikely there will ever be a discrete body of work that neatly and comprehensively applies to their research, the aim is to think about literatures in a more aggregated way, identifying what is relevant and pertinent. This kind of mapping encourages a grouping of articles, chapters and books that share common characteristics – either theoretically, methodologically or substantively in terms of thesis topic.

Hart, a scholar who has devoted an entire book to 'doing literature reviews' and another to literature searches, also recommends mapping as an important part of reviewing the literatures.

> Mapping ideas is about setting out, on paper, the geography of research and thinking that has been done on a topic. At one level, it is about identifying what has been done, when it was done, what methods were used and who did what. At another level, it is about identifying links between what has been done, to show the thinking that has influenced what has been produced.
>
> (Hart, 1998: 144)

Hart suggests a number of methods for mapping ideas, arguments and concepts. These include *feature maps* (making a summary schema of arguments proposed by a study and similarities/differences with other studies on the topic); *tree constructions* (showing the way major topics develop sub-themes and related questions); and *content maps* (organizing a topic into its various hierarchical arrangements). These techniques are useful. They help doctoral researchers identify connections between ideas and arguments and identify relationships that exist between individual pieces of work.

Our approach to mapping places more emphasis on identity work and the relationships *between different bodies* of research. In selecting, rejecting, and categorizing research in the field of knowledge production, students are actively framing their research. They are entering a conversation with other scholars via texts. They are finding out where their research 'fits' in relation to those fields and sharpening their own arguments.

As preparation for making a visual map, we ask doctoral researchers to talk about their difficulties in selecting and categorizing bodies of research. We ask about inclusions and exclusions, their worries about who to put in and who to leave out. We have used this strategy in workshops with groups of doctoral researchers, and we find the physical act of making a visual representation helps them produce new connections. Shifting to another modality helps them see things more graphically and often produces new insights. Maps can identify gaps in their control of literatures, and/or consolidate their thinking to date and make it visible.

Figure 4.1 shows the map produced by Lucinda, a doctoral researcher we met in an LR workshop in Australia. Her topic is childhood behavioural disorders in educational settings. She was in the first year of full-time doctoral candidature when she drew the map, and had just completed her first draft review of literatures for her dissertation proposal confirmation.

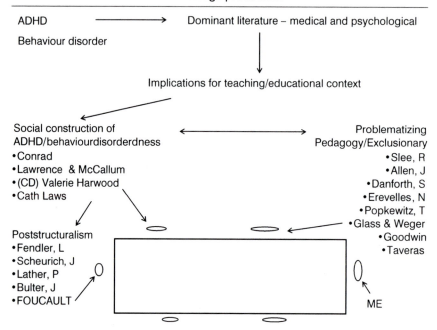

ADHD   ——————→   Dominant literature – medical and psychological

Behaviour disorder

Implications for teaching/educational context

Social construction of   ←——————→   Problematizing
ADHD/behaviourdisorderdness   Pedagogy/Exclusionary
•Conrad   •Slee, R
•Lawrence & McCallum   •Allen, J
•(CD) Valerie Harwood   •Danforth, S
•Cath Laws   •Erevelles, N
   •Popkewitz, T
   •Glass & Weger
Poststructuralism   •Goodwin
•Fendler, L   •Taveras
•Scheurich, J
•Lather, P
•Bulter, J
•FOUCAULT   ME

Figure 4.1   Lucinda's map of the field of knowledge production

In email correspondence with Lucinda following the workshop, we asked her to reflect on her map. She wrote the following, evoking the dinner party metaphor (introduced earlier in the workshop and described in Chapter 3) as part of her representation.

> The dominant literature that surrounds the psychological and medical conceptualisation of childhood misbehaviour is clinical 'disorderedness'. Personally I'd prefer not to invite them to the table, but they have to be acknowledged, so perhaps I could annex a table near the windy doorway?
>
> You will notice I put Foucault at the head of my table but I seldom mention Foucault in the lit review, apart from the point I make that my choice of Foucauldian theory guides the way I perceive and organise everything else. So to me, Foucault should be at the head of my table, opposite me at the other head because I understand that I, as researcher/writer/designer am making decisions about what and who to include. I am cognisant (perhaps because of my background in literary analysis) that I am making choices and interpretations of texts that are contingent upon my theoretical and political persuasions.
>
> Next to Foucault, I position writers that interpret Foucault's writings (like Maria Tamboukou, Mark Olssen) and on the other side, writers who have used Foucault to trouble the kinds of things I wish to problematize (Julie Allen, Valerie Harwood). On one side of me (the researcher) at the other

head of the table, I put the work that looks to ADHD behaviour disorders. As mentioned previously, there is the dominant group (who have to be acknowledged) and then there is a much smaller group that looks to the social construction argument (Conrad, Laurence & McCallum, Glass & Wegar). Basically I am weaving and spinning a web by jumping from each of these places and drawing connections as I go.

(Email correspondence 7 December 2004)

Lucinda went on to say she found it 'reassuring' to make the map at this point in her candidature for 'someone with an inferiority complex'. We were surprised by this phrase, given her able control of the theoretical and methodological relationships in her discussion of the map. Lucinda is confident in her discussion of Foucault and his place at her table. She has clarity about different theoretical positions and debates in the field of ADHD. Yet her email stresses her need to be reassured. Her troubled history of being expelled from Year 11 at age 17 continued to be a burden to her. As she says, 'I have never completely got that monkey off my back, as I feel like I have always been coming from behind'. Such commentary is testament to the enmeshed nature of text work and identity work, and to the fact that as supervisors we need to attend to both, even in our most accomplished and adept students.

Mapping strategies can be used at various points of candidature, recursively, as doctoral researchers progress and revise their understandings of the field of knowledge production. Sometimes they will not be able to do the mapping. Perhaps it is too early or they are not yet able to think about their contribution to the field. But this inability is also useful information. At times like these, supervisors can jointly construct maps with doctoral researchers, calling on the supervisor's greater knowledge of the field.

Supervisors can also do effective pedagogical work by modelling maps that inform their own research. Julie McLeod, an Australian colleague, runs an online seminar for doctoral candidates on reviewing literatures, where she asks students to identify key players and debates in the diverse fields in which they're researching. As preparation for their online contribution, she models how her own research intersects with diverse bodies of research that shape her inquiry. This is an excerpt from her verbal mapping.

The *12 to 18 Project* is a longitudinal research project, which studied girls and boys as they go through each year of their secondary schooling and into their first years of post-school life. The project is concerned with the development of young people's identity and with education, and with the interactions between these in Australia today ... My project intersects with many different fields and styles of research in terms of its substantive research focus (literature on youth studies, schooling differences and school effects, gender and class differences, identity development), its methodological focus (literature on interviewing, longitudinal studies, the role of the researcher and researcher reflexivity) and in terms of theoretical interests (literature on identity formation, accounts of modernity and social change, feminist discussions of gender) ... I can nominate several 'key players'.

One example is a recent book by Valerie Walkerdine, Helen Lucey and June Melody (2001), *Growing Up Girl: Psycho-social explorations on Gender, Class,* which addresses several issues that are also of concern for *The 12 to 18 Project.* First, *Growing Up Girl* is based upon a longitudinal, qualitative study of young women from age 4 to 21; it explores gender and class differences and identities, and theorises social change and late modernity. Second, the authors are very well known, and Walkerdine especially has a strong international reputation for her innovative research on gender and identity and social and educational change. Third, while the empirical research is based in the UK, there is some overlap in social and educational trends and there are some parallel methodological and theoretical interests. Fourth, although the specific foci and analyses developed in *Growing Up Girl* are not the same as the ones we develop, it is clear that we need to engage with the ideas and identify how our work is different from it, and delineate any criticisms we might have of the approach and analyses. Finally, given the reputations of the authors, their previous work, and the book's close relationship to our own project, not to engage with this work would be seen as a serious omission. Further, judging from the attention the book is receiving from other scholars, it is going to be a 'key player' not only for our research but for the larger field of psycho-social research on young people and class/gender identities.

(McLeod, 2005)

McLeod's mapping discussion is 'written' and hence more formal than the way supervisors might talk about their research to students. But it makes visible the kind of thinking experienced researchers engage in when locating their own work in the field of knowledge production. It highlights that doctoral researchers need not include everything in their maps. They are occupying parts of the landscape, detailing those parts that are germane to their project, while still flagging that they know the field.

Such texts from experienced researchers can be used in multiple ways with students, and we turn now to using them to model location and occupation strategies.

Modelling discipline-specific location strategies

It is easy for doctoral researchers to be overwhelmed by the bodies of knowledge produced by others and to lose sight of their 'contribution' to the field. To encourage them to make space for their own work, we have developed location strategies which model different ways of identifying gaps or trends in a field. Our approach is to collect sample LRs, written by experienced researchers in particular fields. We ask doctoral researchers to look carefully at the way other scholars write, to read like a 'writer'. But we find they need guidance to do this kind of text work and it helps if they have some sense of the generic conventions being used in different fields.

To illustrate this strategy, we consider the genre conventions used in two LR excerpts. The first comes from a research article by Patricia Dunsmire (1997), from the field of critical linguistics. The second is from a book introduction by Ken Jones (2003) on education in Britain.

Dunsmire's article, 'Naturalizing the future in factual discourse: a critical linguistic analysis of a projected event', analyses the front-page coverage from the *New York Times* and *Washington Post* newspapers during the 1990 Persian Gulf Crisis, 3–7 August. This excerpt comes from the beginning of the article, where she reviews a wide body of research in an economical way in order to situate her own approach. We number her sentences so we can refer to particular strategies used by the writer.

> [1] The study builds on and contributes to work in critical linguistics (Caldas-Coulthard and Coulthard, 1996; Chilton, 1982; Fairclough, 1989, 1992a, 1992b; Fowler, 1991; Fowler, Hodge, Kress and Trew, 1979; Seidel, 1985; Van Dijk, 1989, 1991; Wodak, 1989). [2] Although studies in critical linguistics have examined the discursive construction of past events, there has not been an extended study of the construction of a projected event. [3] As such, this study provides additional insight into the constructive processes of language by explicating the linguistic and rhetorical processes through which a projected—future—event is constructed as a discrete and autonomous state of affairs. [4] The analytic focus on a projected event enables another contribution. [5] This study analyzes how the political and social interests underlying accounts of the Iraq/Saudi Arabia projected event were rhetorically managed in *The New York Times (NYT)* and *Washington Post (WP)*. [6] Although numerous studies (Bruck, 1989; Clayman, 1990; Fairclough, 1992c; Fowler, 1991; Fowler and Kress 1979a; Glasgow University Media Group, 1976, 1980; Hall, 1978, 1982; Hodge, 1979; Tuchman, 1978; Van Dijk, 1988, 1989, 1993; Zelizer, 1989) have identified sourcing (i.e., using spokespersons representing so-called elite groups and institutions as sources for information) as a constructive social and ideological practice, little analytic attention has been paid to the implications of this finding for how texts are linguistically constructed within newspaper discourse, a discourse context guided by the professional canon of objectivity, balance and neutrality. [7] I address this issue by demonstrating how assertions about a hypothetical future event attributed to a specific group of spokespersons were transformed into unmediated and presupposed information.
>
> (Dunsmire 1997: 222–3)

Typically, we ask a number of questions to guide researchers in their analysis of articles, including:

- How does the writer align herself with certain scholars or bodies of work?
- How does she show where she belongs?
- How does she create a gap to insert her work?

We then work together on the text, either individually or in small groups, to see how it works. So in the Dunsmire excerpt, we highlight how sentence 1 locates her analysis within critical linguistics, the place where her work belongs. We look at the way she signals a gap by pointing out what other researchers have *not* done in sentences 2 and 6. And we consider the way she signals the contribution her study will make to the field in sentences 3 and 7: 'As such, this study provides additional insight'; 'I address this issue by demonstrating how'.

But this is only one kind of textual locating. We find it important to collect multiple LR examples to show doctoral writers that there are many ways to stake a claim for one's work. The conventions used depend on the purposes of the review as well as the discipline. Our second example is a pithy excerpt by Ken Jones (2003) from the introduction to his book *Education in Britain: 1944 to the Present*. We like it because it shows in a short space the kind of text work more experienced scholars use to create a warrant for their work in the broader field of scholarship.

> [1] The book differs from other accounts of the post-war period. [2] It owes a factual and interpretative debt, as any writer in this area must, to Brian Simon's *Education and the Social Order* (1991), to Richard Johnson and his colleagues at the Centre for Contemporary Cultural Studies (1981; Johnson 1989), to McPherson and Raab's *Governing Education* (1988), and to the work of Gareth Elwyn Jones on Wales (1990, 1997) and of several writers including Sean Farren and Penny McKeown, on Northern Ireland. [3] In other respects it has benefited from the consciously gendered history presented by Arnot et al (1999), and from Iain Grosvenor's treatment of race, identity and nation (1997). [4] In these writings it is possible to find descriptions and analyses of national or 'sectoral' histories of schooling whose detail this book does not intend to match. [5] What it rather does, I hope, is to present a broader perspective on educational change than is usually managed, with a more consistently maintained cultural dimension, a greater attention to political conflict, a fuller sense of the range of social actors involved in policy, practice and the educational space, within a framework which conveys something of the varying national experience of schooling in Britain. [6] If it is successful in these respects then much is owed to the educational activists with whom I have worked in the past, and to my present colleagues on the journal *Education and Social Justice*, whose pages are much referenced in my final chapter.
>
> (Jones 2003: 2)

Again, we find it useful to propose questions to ask of the text. These focus the reader on the strategies and conventions used, not just the content:

- How does the writer acknowledge the work of other scholars?
- How does he distinguish his contribution to the field?

In the Jones excerpt we find a fine example of the appreciative stance to others' scholarship we discussed in Chapter 3. This is a criticality which is respectful of what others have done. In working with this text, we highlight how sentences 2 and 3 use verbs such as 'owes' and 'benefited' to show the writer's debt to previous scholarship. But we also look at how sentence 1 distinguishes Jones' contribution right from the start, for example, through the use of the verb 'differs'. And how sentence 5 uses a number of comparative terms, 'a broader perspective … with a more consistently maintained … a greater attention to … a fuller sense of', to further mark the book's distinctiveness. Thus we see generosity, expressed in sentence 6, is not a cover for false modesty and humility and can enhance the writer's authority, rather than diminish it.

Working with these kind of LR samples creates a context for talking about the kinds of strategies doctoral writers might employ in their own writing. It is text-specific work which makes explicit how more expert writers create space for their scholarship. Modelling these geographies of working in the field of knowledge production is useful. But we can go further and more directly 'mess' with our students' writing. We are not proposing an old-fashioned 'bring out the red pen' strategy. Rather, it is a collaborative kind of text work where supervisors and doctoral researchers work together to develop a 'hands on hips' textual authority. We now elaborate two of these text work strategies which we call joint texting and syntactic borrowing.

Joint texting

The joint texting strategy is one where we work side by side with doctoral researchers at the computer to revise their draft LRs. The basis for this strategy is our belief that modelling and deconstructing text is not always enough. Remaking text and manipulating it until it speaks more assertively is more tangible. It makes the process of knowledge production 'hands on'. The supervisor takes the lead in this strategy and models revision-in-action, often with powerful effects on doctoral researcher identities.

To illustrate, we consider an interaction between doctoral researcher Mia and her supervisor Andrew. Mia is reviewing literatures for her dissertation proposal. She has summarized trends in the field of homework research as a foundation for her own qualitative study on the effects of homework on families in diverse sociocultural contexts. Like Dunsmire, Mia consolidates a large number of studies into a short space. Like Vera, whose LR we considered in Chapter 3, Mia also starts most sentences by naming previous studies and reviewers of homework. We highlight this syntactic pattern in italics and number her sentences to facilitate our analysis of the text.

Mia's LR

[1] *All reviewers of the homework literature agree* that much research into homework has been poorly designed, short term, experimental and narrowly focused on academic achievement (Cooper, 1989; Coulter, 1979; Paschal, 1984). [2] *Further, studies* have been premised on partial or commonsense definitions which either assume an understanding of homework or narrowly define homework as time spent in completion of school assignments (Hoover-Dempsey, 1995). [3] *Many studies* have been based on self-reported quantitative data alone; *such data* is inevitably limited in its potential to provide insights into the relationship between homework and achievement.

[4] *Several scholars who have reviewed the academic literature on homework* (Hoover-Dempsey, 1995; Coulter, 1979) suggest that the equivocal nature of the findings into the effects of homework, despite a century of research, reveals more about the methodological challenges of researching this complex subject than can be stated conclusively about the relationship between homework and achievement. [5] *Apart from the quantitative studies previously discussed, many studies* have used evidence *from* interviews with children, parents and teachers. [6] *There has also been little research evidence derived from classrooms* which explores teachers' framing of homework or children's understandings of their tasks. [7] *Further, the majority of studies* have concentrated on homework practices of adolescent secondary students. [8] *Scholars who have reviewed the academic literature on homework* (Hoover-Dempsey, 1995) have directed little research attention to primary school students' homework, with the exception of the role of parents in the development of child literacy. [9] *Few observational studies* have examined the webs of social interaction between children and their parents, siblings, friends and schools within which homework is constructed (Coulter, 1979: 27). [10] *A few influential studies* have looked at the family interactions around homework in diverse socio-cultural contexts (Breen et al, 1994; Freebody et al, 1995; Lareau, 1987) and will be discussed in a later section of this review.

Mia is neither drowning in the literature nor overwhelmed by it. There is 'nothing wrong' with her writing in terms of fluency, syntax or clarity. Andrew was concerned, however, that she was absent from the text. She succinctly summarizes the equivocal findings of the homework research, but her own opinions and evaluations are backgrounded or attributed to other researchers. As a result, a critical and authoritative stance is missing in her writing.

To interrupt this way of writing, Andrew began the supervision session with Mia's text displayed on the computer screen. His aim was to 'mess' with the text on screen to model how Mia might foreground her own point of view. It is important that this text work occurred in her presence, rather than as red-pen correction in her absence. In this way she was part of the process. Andrew talked out loud about what he was attempting. He was tentative and playful, trying things on the screen and rejecting them. Mia, in turn, was both witness and participant, making suggestions and seeing the text change before her eyes. The interaction was punctuated by Andrew asking Mia questions about the text.

His first move was to make visible how Mia had attributed everything (every idea, trend, opinion) to other researchers. So, for example, he looked at sentence 1 where Mia begins, 'All reviewers of the homework literature agree', and asked whether Mia agreed as well. When she said yes, he shifted her sentence structure so that the assertion came first, and the citation last.

> In sum, it appears that much research into homework has been poorly designed, short term, experimental and narrowly focused on academic achievement (Cooper, 1989; Coulter, 1979; Paschal, 1984).

This is a subtle shift, but one that lets Mia take a stand in this community of scholars and join them, rather than exclude herself. Andrew used a similar strategy in the second paragraph. He looked, for example, at sentence 4 where Mia begins: 'Several scholars who have reviewed the academic literature on homework suggest'. He shifted the pattern of attribution to the end of the sentence and allowed Mia's claim to come first.

> It seems, then, that despite a century of research, the equivocal nature of the findings says more about the methodological challenges of researching this complex subject than about any definitive relationship between homework and achievement itself (Hoover-Dempsey, 1995; Coulter, 1979).

His next move was to create a third paragraph, missing altogether from the first draft. His aim was to model how Mia might highlight the gap her own research was addressing. He looked, in particular, at sentence 10, where she refers to 'A few influential studies' without making any link to her own work. He asked: What is the link between this work and what you will do? How do you plan to use these influential studies?

On the basis of this conversation, he started adding phrases and sentences, asking: What will you say here? How do we mark your contribution? Gradually he inserted Mia's words, acting as her scribe and text worker. This conversation provided a scaffold for Mia to learn syntactic conventions for staking a claim. Mia worked *with* Andrew to make textual connections between her work and the wider scholarly community – thus locating her place more firmly in the field of knowledge production. Her revised LR constructs a more authoritative stance for Mia as doctoral researcher. We use italics to highlight the new syntactic pattern at the beginning of sentences and the change in writer stance it achieves.

Mia's revised LR

[1] *In sum, it appears that much research into homework* has been poorly designed, short term, experimental and narrowly focused on academic achievement (Cooper, 1989; Coulter, 1979; Paschal, 1984). [2] *Studies have been premised on partial or commonsense definitions* which either assume an understanding of homework or narrowly define homework as time spent in completion of school assignments (Hoover-Dempsey, 1995). [3] *The over-reliance on self-reported quantitative data alone* has led to limited insights into the relationship between homework and achievement.

[4] *It seems, then, that despite a century of research, the equivocal nature of the findings* says more about the methodological challenges of researching this complex subject than about any definitive relationship between homework and achievement itself (Hoover-Dempsey, 1995; Coulter, 1979). [5] *The qualitative research evidence to date* has relied heavily on interviews with children, parents and teachers, that is, on what people say they do. [6] *There has been little attention* given to the practice of school homework as it occurs in the family context. [7] *There has been little classroom-based research evidence* which explores teachers' framing of homework or children's understandings of their tasks. [8] *Further, little research attention* has focused on primary school students' homework, with the exception of the role of parents in the development of child literacy.

[9] *In this proposal I* attempt to address these methodological gaps by designing an observational and interview-based study which examines the webs of social interaction between children and their parents, siblings, friends and schools within which homework is constructed (Coulter, 1979: 27). [10] *I focus* on the primary secondary school nexus and work with a more complex understanding of homework as a social practice. [11] *A number of influential studies which have examined family interactions around homework in diverse socio-cultural contexts* (Breen, 1994; Freebody, 1995; Hill, 2002) provide a foundation for my study and will be discussed in Section 3.3 of this review.

In this revision, Mia now takes a 'critical' stand on the trends she identifies. She incorporates evaluative comments at the start of sentences, for example, 'The over-reliance on self-reported quantitative data alone has led to limited insights' (3). She identifies gaps: 'There has been little attention given to' (6); 'There has been little classroom-based research' (7); 'Further, little research attention has focused on' (8). And like Jones, she acknowledges her debt to previous scholarship: 'A number of influential studies ... provide a foundation for my study' (11).

The textual outcome is a more assertive, less descriptive construction of the field of knowledge production. The identity work was also profound. Mia was not only pleased with the revision, but astounded at how little it took to make her sound more authoritative. This joint texting with Andrew affected her deeply and almost seemed to be written into her body as she left the supervision seemingly taller. She spoke later of the session as a pivotal event in helping her 'get how to become critical'.

This collaborative strategy was certainly more powerful than simply explaining or correcting Mia's draft. As supervisor and student remade the text together, they also remade her understanding of what was required to get the kind of textual authority she desired but was unable to create on her own – particularly at this early stage of her candidature. There was also something pleasurable about the sociality of this joint texting. It created a different subject position for the doctoral researcher, not just as novice but as text worker, working collaboratively with the supervisor to strengthen the text so that it speaks with greater authority. We now consider one final text work strategy that also works closely with syntactic patterns.

Syntactic borrowing

Map-making strategies can encourage doctoral researchers to position their work in relation to the wider scholarly community, but they still often struggle with the 'words' to do this location work. We find it is useful to 'borrow' the words of others to help students learn new ways of speaking that may seem foreign or intimidating. Our syntactic borrowing strategy relies on Swales and Feak's (1994) notion of the 'sentence skeleton'. The aim is to make explicit the linguistic patterns in any passage of research writing by removing the content and identifying the skeleton of rhetorical moves. To illustrate, we represent the skeleton of rhetorical moves from the Dunsmire excerpt we looked at earlier.

1 The study builds on and contributes to work in _____ .
2 Although studies in _____ have examined _____
    there has not been an _____.
3 As such, this study provides additional insight into _____ .
4 The analytic focus on _____ enables another contribution.
5 This study analyses _____ .
6 Although numerous studies (   ) have identified _____
    _____ ,
    little analytic attention has been paid to _____ .
7 I address this issue by demonstrating _____
    _____ .

In this strategy we ask doctoral students to write about their own research using this sentence skeleton. The skeleton creates a linguistic frame to play with. It encourages writers to take on the subject position of an experienced, authoritative writer – at least linguistically. It allows them to write themselves into an authoritative stance they may not be able to take by themselves. Thus the syntactic framework scaffolds a kind of linguistic identity work. Doctoral writers take up 'ways of asserting' and 'staking a claim' in their field and make these their own.

Then they discuss the results with supervisors and/or in small groups with other students. This is not plagiarism as they are not copying content. Rather it is a syntactic strategy for getting *inside* the patterning language and making explicit how others write LRs in particular fields of inquiry.

Supervisors can adapt the strategy to a wide variety of scholarly articles across disciplines to make explicit the discipline-specific conventions they wish their researchers to grasp. So, for example, we can make the same kind of skeleton frame from the Jones excerpt, making a few modifications from *book* to *thesis*.

1 The thesis differs from other _____ .
2 It owes a factual and interpretative debt to _____ ,
   _____ and_____ .
3 In other respects it has benefited from the _____presented by
   _____ and from _____'s treatment of _____ ( ).
4 In these writings it is possible to find descriptions and analyses of_____
   _____ which this thesis does not intend to match.
5 What it rather does is to present a broader perspective on _____
   than is usually managed, with a more consistently maintained _____
   _____, a greater attention to _____, a fuller sense of the
   range of _____within a framework which conveys _____
   _____ .
6 If it is successful in these respects, then much is owed to _____
   _____ .

We suggested earlier that the Jones passage was powerful in modelling how to make a warrant for one's research. When we also use it as a frame for student writing, we take the modelling a step further. We are not concerned if students end up using the skeleton in their writing – or even that it perfectly fits. Rather it is an identity strategy, a way to write themselves into more authoritative ways of speaking. Given our assertion that the LR is the quintessential site of identity work, such strategies can be useful for supervisors who mediate the student struggle to become critical. Looking critically at the rhetorical strategies used by experienced writers can help doctoral researchers learn to 'read like a writer', a strategy we elaborate further in Chapter 8.

In this chapter we have been working in the discursive space of Fairclough's layer 1, the text. We have proposed a number of pedagogical text work strategies for working in the field of knowledge production: mapping strategies, location strategies, hands-on joint texting strategies and borrowing the syntactic patterns of expert writers.

In the next chapter we move back to layers 2 and 3 to consider what is at stake in developing a personal stance in dissertation writing.

Chapter 5

Reconsidering the personal

Is the use of 'I' acceptable practice in doctoral writing? This is a question we are frequently asked in workshops and we have little choice but to say that, once forbidden, the use of 'I' has now become more accepted within academic circles. We hasten to add that doctoral researchers must check the regulations at their university and discuss the question with their supervisor. Sometimes we find they have done precisely that and are asking the question to seek a contrary opinion. We emphasize that while questions of style or acceptability may be foremost in students' minds, using 'I' is not just a matter of personal choice. There are epistemological/methodological and rhetorical reasons for choosing to use the first person pronoun.

More than two decades ago, feminist scholars argued that the use of the third person in academic writing was a masculinist strategy intended to create the impression of an objective view. Instead of resorting to what Donna Haraway (1988) described as a 'god trick', in which the researcher is nowhere and everywhere via the use of the third person, it was imperative, the feminist argument went, to explicitly situate the researcher in the text. One way to make herself visible was through the use of the first person (Jones, 1992). The use of 'I' was also a deliberate political strategy designed to unsettle notions of objectivity. First person textualizing of the researcher often provoked accusations of subjectivism. But it did nevertheless create opportunities to engage in debate about the nature of knowledge and the inevitable imbrication of the researcher in the practice of research (e.g. Alcoff and Potter, 1993; Lather, 1992; St Pierre and Pillow, 2000).

Of course, different feminisms have different ways of theorizing language and situating the researcher does not necessarily mean writing as an 'I'. But scholars writing from critical race and postcolonial positions also argue for disruptive autobiographical writing that challenges the neutrality of academic genres (Bishop and Glynn, 1999; Smith, 1999). Fictional and non-fictional storytelling are used to reconstruct the past (King, 2003), critique the law (Lynn, 2004) and challenge existing race, gender and social class relations of power and privilege (Barone, 1989; Bochner and Ellis, 2002; Parker, 1998). Other research traditions have extended their object of study to include the self and there are now examples of personal inquiry throughout the social sciences (e.g. Cixous and Calle-Gruber,

1997; Cotterill and Letherby, 1993; Ellis and Flaherty, 1992; Neumann and Peterson, 1997; Reed-Danahay, 1997). Indeed, there are now journals largely devoted to the political/personal dimensions of research: *Auto/Biography* (Arnold journals, UK), *thirdspace* (www.thirdspace.ca) and *A/B* (University of Wisconsin-Whitewater), for example. These kinds of texts all use the first person within a specific genre of self-study which has its own internal debates (Burdell and Swadener, 1999; Clements, 1999; Prain, 1997).

And, *we* have named ourselves throughout this book as a deliberate writing decision. We felt that it was important in a book which addresses our academic peers to write in the first person plural, in order to establish a collegial dialogue. We have imagined ourselves building a conversation space as we write. We have framed explanatory sections of the text in the first person, to make our decision-making and rationales open and available to colleagues who are our readers. We have also described some of our own practices and these narratives are offered, not as imperatives, but in the spirit of sharing ideas.

We thus do not want to begin this chapter by suggesting that it is inappropriate to write in the first person. Nor do we want to engage in endless debate about the propriety of first person texts. But we *do* want to suggest that when it comes to research writing, confining the personal to a matter of pronouns is a mistake. The research enterprise cannot be separated from the researcher, and it is imperative to put the personal on the agenda through doctoral study. In this chapter, we argue that the question of the personal and doctoral writing is more complex than that suggested by advocating or abhorring the use of I/we.

To begin our discussion, we turn to examples of doctoral writing that highlight the difficulties of using 'I' and the issues we as supervisors must address. We then consider strategies where important 'personal' work can be accomplished through writing. We look at how 'writing along the way' can assist in building reflexivity. We then show that the personal is still present in texts that are written in the third person. We propose that supervisors can help doctoral researchers develop a distinctive personal 'stance' through conscious attention to language conventions which signify evaluation and judgment.

Using I – what's the problem?

Some fields permit more writer presence than others, as do certain methodological paradigms. But doctoral researchers often take up the first person as an individual choice, not tied to the disciplinary community they have entered. We can illustrate the problem in using 'I' with brief extracts written by doctoral researchers early in their candidature. Not surprisingly, these examples come from sections of their dissertations which focus on methodology or literature work – where the writer's relationship to a more authoritative community of scholars is uncertain or in formation.

In Samantha's writing, the 'I' is prominent as she discusses her impact as a researcher on the production of data. Her dissertation uses a practitioner research design to explore aspects of nurses' work. We place *I*, *my* and *me* in italics to highlight her pattern of pronoun use.

> Another ethical issue is the question of what constitutes research. Whilst *I* may make efforts to restrict *my* data to that which is gathered through formal means such as interviews, there is no doubt that *my* prior knowledge of the participants through *my* daily work with them will impact upon the meaning that *I* make of what they tell *me*. That *I* might be considered a peer rather than a superior could be seen to reduce the likelihood that they will tell *me* what they think *I* want to hear. However, this does not prevent *me* from interpreting what they tell *me* to fit with any hypotheses that *I* might have.

Almost every sentence here includes two or three uses of *I*, *my* or *me*. In response, Samantha's supervisor wrote: 'You might refer to some literature here too. This is not just a problem you have identified'. Her comment captures the problem: Samantha's 'I' is disconnected from a community of prior scholarship. Samantha is trying to assert her methodological dilemma, but she writes as if it's only 'my problem'. There are no traces in her writing of interactions with wider scholarly communities and discourses. If we think in terms of Fairclough's (1989; 1992) model of discourse, there is no connection to layer 3. There clearly are broad literatures which investigate similar power and representation issues in participatory research, but as her supervisor's comment signals, there is no one in Samantha's text but 'I'.

As a consequence, her writing ends up sounding somewhat naïve. It constructs a novice researcher, writing about her experience as an individual. Samantha may not yet know other ways to write herself into her research, but her use of 'I' does not create an authoritative stance when used in this way. And it raises questions for supervision. When and how often should Samantha's person be made explicit? And what are the consequences of doing so? How do we help her think about 'I' as a rhetorical strategy or representation, rather than a simple reflection of her 'real self'?

In the next example, doctoral researcher Patricia also constructs an immature way of using 'I' to create an alliance with writers whose work she supports and finds useful. These three extracts come from her dissertation on inclusive schooling and are numbered to facilitate our discussion of them.

> [1] Deal and Peterson (1994) argue very succinctly that leadership itself is a paradox as it involves working with so many participants. *I* could not agree more when *I* consider leadership in inclusive schools.
> [2] To help us explore this concept a little further, *I* particularly like the following quotation: 'Man's capacity for justice makes democracy possible, but man's inclination to injustice makes democracy necessary' (Niebuhr, 1994).

[3] Thomson and Blackmore (2005) have an interesting take on the process versus product debate. They point out that in relation to leadership allegiance, neither the process nor the product debate is particularly helpful. They cite several useful examples of leadership viewed as design, which steps away from the idea of orientation to process or product, and in stepping away, creates different solutions to leadership that can be trialled. Similarly, *I* feel, that dealing with the paradox of process and product in relation to inclusion ultimately requires leaders to step away and look at creative solutions which do not locate themselves in either of these orientations.

We might characterize the strategy at work in these texts as: 'Scholar X says this, and I agree/disagree with/like what they say'. The personal pronoun 'I' highlights the doctoral researcher's presence. It leaves little doubt about her opinion, but do we need to know? Or, do we need to know in this way? We could, for example, rewrite example 2 without 'I'.

Niebuhr's (1994) work is *particularly useful* to help us explore this concept further.

In this rewrite there is no 'I' to set the writer apart from Niebuhr's words. Instead, she uses Niebuhr to make *her* case and inserts the evaluative phrase 'particularly useful' to signal her opinion. Example 3 also represents the doctoral researcher as separate from the scholarly community: '*they* say this and *I* think that'. Patricia makes three consecutive moves: identify the debate, say what the writers argue and then agree or disagree with them. But what if we deleted 'I feel' from the fourth sentence? The rewrite might look like this.

Dealing with the paradox of process and product in relation to inclusion *is a significant move, because it requires* leaders to step away and look at creative solutions in which they are not located in either of these orientations.

The rewrite does more explicit 'hand on hips' work in evaluating Thomson and Blackmore's work. And the evaluative phrase *significant move* creates greater textual authority than 'I'. In each of these instances it is possible to *not* use 'I' and still make the writer's opinion explicit.

These examples highlight that using 'I' is not just a straightforward way to write the doctoral researcher into the text. 'I' can be easily overused or misused, without the writer realizing it. And when it is used in individual terms, rather than in terms of participating in a scholarly conversation, it can undercut the writer's desire to be authoritative. One final example suggests that the overuse of 'I' can also mark the researcher as more significant than the research. This excerpt comes from a journal abstract written by a more experienced academic writer discussing her work with students as co-researchers.

Participatory research methods are often assumed to alter the roles, relationships and responsibilities of researchers and participants in research projects
reframing research as collaborative inquiry. In *my own* research on urban
schooling, whenever possible, *I* have attempted to craft research projects
with and for the participants in the project, rather than conducting research
on them. For instance, in order to document urban adolescents' perspectives
on their schooling, *I* asked high school students to join research projects as
co-researchers. *I* learned that the core principles of participatory research
become complicated and, at times, problematic when put into practice with
adolescents. In this article, *I* describe three of the collaborative relationships
I developed with high school students in a single research project. *I* use this
work with adolescents to call for the reconsideration of conventional notions
of collaboration, participation, action and representation in participatory
research.

(Schultz, 2001: 1)

Here the 'I' foregrounds what the researcher has done ('I have attempted, I asked, I
learned, I describe, I developed, I use'), but possibly at the expense of highlighting
the broader significance of this scholarly work, none of which is referenced at this
point. The focus on self could thus even be read as excessive self-promotion which
ignores previous research. The writing constructs a world where this research is
the only or major effort at collaboration, possibly an unintended consequence of
the overused first person pronoun. This is somewhat ironic, given that the topic
here is *participatory* research, a paradigm which emphasizes the significance of
all participants, not just the researcher.

The tendency to over-inflate the self or make it too prominent can also occur in
doctoral writing, although in our experience it is less common. This example from
Charles' thesis, where he discusses key theorists framing his research, illustrates
the problem.

In his discussion of self-writing, Foucault *agrees with me* when he says:
'These practices are nevertheless not something that the individual invents by
himself. They are patterns that he finds in his culture and which are proposed,
suggested and imposed on him by his culture, his society and his social group'
(Foucault, 1998:11).

The *me* suggests that Foucault, were he alive, is not only reading the doctoral
candidate's work, but is confirming its worth. It is fairly humorous for us to
think of Foucault agreeing with Charles, but not for Charles. This is not self-
aggrandisement, but rather Charles asserting his authority: this is a far cry from
the anxious scholarly identities we saw in Chapter 3 struggling for a place at
the dinner party. However, Charles is not clear how to manage his position.
Such textual overconfidence skews power relations to the extreme and is just as

problematic for creating a credible doctoral text as diffidence. This is a dilemma we address later in the chapter as the 'Goldilocks dilemma', when we ponder how much textual authority is 'just right'.

It is clear that questions of how to 'write' the person into the dissertation text need careful consideration of textual, representational and identity practices. Janet Giltrow (1995) makes a useful distinction in this regard between the personal I and the *discursive* I of scholarly writing. While it is not uncommon, she argues, for the first person to be used in published scholarship, there are constraints which control its use. The *discursive* I describes the writer in her capacity as writer/researcher. It often occurs with verbs that refer to some discourse action such as: 'I want to suggest'; 'I intend to begin'; 'I shall focus'; 'I begin with a discussion'; 'I explore'; 'I examine'; 'I evaluate'; 'I close'; 'I draw on evidence'; I provide'; 'Let me conclude' (Giltrow, 1995: 252). That is, while writers of scholarly genres often refer to themselves, the identity signalled by the textual 'I' is limited.

We use Giltrow's distinction between the personal and discursive 'I' as organizers for the remainder of this chapter. Later in the chapter we focus on the discursive 'I' and explore a variety of language resources (other than pronouns) for creating a persona in academic texts. But first we consider how supervisors might use personal 'I' writing as a pedagogic strategy to support dissertation identity work.

Writing biographies

Many doctoral researchers delay writing. They may have successfully completed undergraduate and postgraduate work, but often find the very idea of 'doctoral writing' an enormous obstacle. When supervisors ask them to write about what they've been reading, or discuss aspects of fieldwork, or consider issues related to method, they proffer excuses. They need to read more, they don't understand what is expected, they have done something but it's only notes and it isn't fit to see yet. These delaying tactics are not necessarily the equivalent to 'the dog ate my homework', but arise (as we argued in Chapter 2) from the imbrication of texts and identities.

In such situations it is beneficial to make space during supervision to talk about writing. The earlier in a student's candidature, the better. Writing biographies is a strategy that can be used to begin the conversation. It is particularly helpful for part-time students who have had a break between study and doctoral work. Part-time students often feel hesitant about their capacity to play the academic writing 'game' and some resist. Others adopt a turgid, awkward style which they equate with the requirements for scholarship. The strategy is also helpful for successful professionals who find it difficult to switch from authoritative modes of workplace writing where they are used to producing short summaries and bullet points. Here there are clear connections with identity: such students are experienced professionals at work, and 'learners' in the doctoral context.

To create a writing biography, we first ask doctoral researchers to generate a set of adjectives that they would use to describe themselves as writers. Next, we ask them to sketch out a brief history of the kinds of writing they have done over their school and professional life, no matter how short or long this has been. We suggest they focus on types of writing and/or pieces of writing that were particularly satisfying and/or difficult. We then ask them to talk us through the biography within a limited timeframe, say fifteen minutes. To illustrate we represent the writing biography prepared by Daryl in Figure 5.1.

Daryl described himself as a confident and quick writer, but not a good one. This prompted an immediate conversation about his ideas of a good writer. Daryl's supervisor Marie took up his assumption that writing is a 'gift' afforded some but not others, in order to deconstruct the embedded anti-learning attitude and address the necessity of hard work and time.

In his writing biography, Daryl represents himself as someone with little recent history of academic work. His authority as a psychologist and the genres of writing in which he demonstrated success will not necessarily morph into those required for a doctorate in social policy. But he has enjoyed the success of writing for a professional journal. This allowed him to move out of a tight report and case note format into more chatty articles, which strongly advocate for consumer participation in service delivery decisions. These articles have not required the production of evidence, but have argued on moral and ethical grounds for particular courses of action.

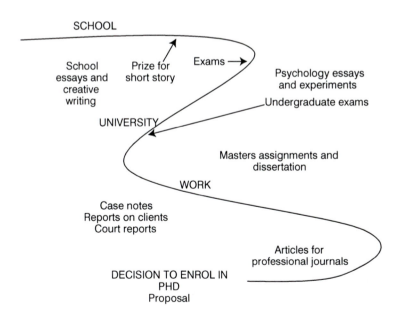

Figure 5.1   Daryl's writing biography

This information allowed Marie to begin a conversation about different types of writing and how their features differ from standard sociological texts. A journal article and a completed doctoral dissertation were used to discuss some of the particularities of writing within social policy. Having examples of writing from within the discipline is useful in that it makes concrete and tangible the points under discussion. It assists students to read not only for argument, content and method, but also to read for genre and conventions.

By opening up discussions about the different types of writing in which doctoral researchers feel proficient, those which are regularly undertaken and those which promote uncertainty, the supervisor can begin to tackle the mutual construction of text and identity. She can bring this idea into the conversation and talk about the connections between confidence and professional identity: the need to build scholarly text and identity at the same time, together.

The writing biography also affords the opportunity for supervisors to deal with academic practices more explicitly. Supervisors can address the conventions of scholarly writing and make visible why they are 'the way they are' within specific disciplinary and institutional contexts. Understanding these expectations is integral to the formation of scholars. It can, of course, happen through a diffusion process, as it did when students knelt at the feet of dons. But this is rather haphazard. At a time when students pay large sums of money and come to supervision with high expectations, and when supervisors are expected to assist students to complete in a timely fashion, it is important to move beyond the tacit to the explicit, with reassurances that these new kinds of genres can be learnt.

We move now to a pedagogical strategy which follows on from the biography. It also deals with the personal 'I' and it too is 'writing along the way'.

Fostering reflexivity

A 'reflexive scholar' is not someone who reflects on their writing at periodic intervals, in journals and/or in quiet moments. Such a person would be reflective, but not reflexive.

The dictionary definitions of reflective and reflexive make the difference between the two quite clear. According to *The Macquarie Dictionary* (Delbridge *et al.* 1991) to be reflective is to be given to meditation whereas to be reflexive is to make the subject and object of an activity the same. Thus a reflexive scholar is one who applies to their own work the same critical stance, the same interrogative questions, and the same refusal to take things for granted as they do with their research data. Developing a reflexive disposition is profoundly about the being and doing of scholarship. It is about the personal and the person of the researcher: reflexive practice uses both the personal and discursive 'I'.

Reflexivity means looking for the social in the individual account, asking how particular events, categories and assumptions might have been produced through discourse, culture, political affiliations, and/or social practice. It means learning not to take for granted the ways in which we have narrativized our identities, the 'how we got to be where and who we are' stories that we comfortably (re)produce. It also means interrogating how we might be perpetuating particular kinds of power relationships, be advancing particular ways of naming and discussing people, experiences and events. Reflexivity thus involves critical self-interrogation and discursive movement between Fairclough's layer 1 (the text) and layer 3 (social practices).

Many doctoral researchers arrive at their supervisor's door with passionate beliefs related to their proposed topic of study. For example, in our field of education, there are students who were, as undergraduates, non-traditional higher education entrants and who now want to research the barriers to participation in universities. There are students who were teachers and who want their doctoral research to change the ways in which particular disciplines are taught in schools. There are students who are passionate advocates of feminism or anti-racism and who want to do doctoral research that will make a difference.

Our job as supervisors is not to change their passions or intentions. Indeed, we support work on changing participation in higher education, on improving teaching, and in working for social justice. But it *is* our task to ensure that doctoral researchers examine *how* their concerns might contain taken-for-granted assumptions, might bias their research, or prevent them from 'seeing' what is in front of their noses. In other words, our job is to help doctoral researchers look for and probe their own blind spots. To foster the kind of reflexivity Delamont and Atkinson (1995) call 'fighting familiarity', we have developed two strategies which we call critical questions and critical incidents.

Critical questions

We ask doctoral researchers to write one to four pages about why they want to undertake a particular study. Why this topic – why now? We then ask them to generate a set of critical questions which interrogate their text. They write both their questions and answers, and then come to discuss their responses with their supervisor. After the conversation, the text is rewritten.

This strategy is particularly helpful for researchers who have a strong narrative about who they are and how they got to be where they are, thinking as they do. It encourages them to see how the structural/cultural (Fairclough's layer 3) operates within their own identity narrative. To illustrate, we present an extract from Mona's text. Mona is a doctoral researcher in the field of social work.

> I want through my narrative writing to be released from a cycle of compliance!!! And helped to see value in what I do and know. I am looking for new confidence to take risks to look critically at myself and my organization and protest about what is narrow, constraining and uncaring! I want to pose questions about organizational processes and consider what actions I might take to remake the … experience offered to clients.

In this writing, Mona positions herself as a reformer in her organization. In order to help her become more reflexive her supervisor Peter asked her to deconstruct her position by asking questions about the categories she had created and the desires she was expressing. The questions Mona wrote and answered included:

- On what am I basing my view that this organization is narrow, constraining and uncaring? Are there any counter examples within the organization?
- Is there anything I can now say looking at the kinds of practices of which I am critical and those that are different?
- How might my reformer stance be doing the work of the organization?
- How do I know that clients want the organization reformed in the ways I think are necessary?

In asking these questions Mona took two important steps. First of all, she moved beyond her own personal narrative to consider the broader context in which she worked. She opened up questions of power and authority and allowed herself to ask questions she would not ordinarily ask in everyday professional life. She allowed herself to entertain the possibility that others might think differently and that their views might be quite rational. She thus began to position herself in a way that would facilitate the conduct of interviews where she could 'hear' what others might have to say, and open herself up to other ways of thinking/ being.

Second, Mona engaged with the notion that all texts can be deconstructed and interrogated, including her own. It is important for doctoral researchers to understand that their text is a representation, a version of the truth, that it is the product of writerly choices and it is discursive. As such, representations can be refashioned, choices can be remade and discourses can be probed.

Critical incidents

A second strategy to assist in the development of reflexivity we call 'critical incidents', adapted from the work of David Tripp (1993). When Tripp talks about critical incidents, he is not discussing traumatic events. He is suggesting that events are made critical by virtue of the questions we ask of them. In Tripp's critical incident work, the student writes one or two pages about an incident in which they were involved that seems to epitomize a particular issue, theme, problem and/or attitude. Tripp argues that the written account is important because it formalizes experience and allows it to be questioned and then reshaped. He encourages the writing of successive versions which are checked against the original for misrepresentation. Reflexivity is produced through students

> trying to understand the so-called 'objective' phenomenal world they are investigating, examining the way in which their developing understanding changes them and their relation, not only to both the phenomenal world they

are observing and their knowledge of it, but also to how they are observing and understanding the phenomenal world.

(Tripp, 1993: 39)

We ask doctoral researchers to do the same kind of exercise. They write one to four pages about something that 'captures' a professional or everyday dilemma related to their research. It does not have to be traumatic, but rather a puzzling, irritating or worrying experience. They write their narrative in the first person.

These narratives are very different from the kind of writing students think of as 'academic'. Yet we find that by writing outside the boundaries that they construct as 'academic', they often produce a far more confident 'persona' in their writing. We illustrate by comparing two texts written by the same doctoral researcher, Sadie, who is a school principal. Sadie's critical incident reports an event that happened at her school, while her second text comes from dissertation literature work.

Critical incident: Sadie

Five-year-old Amy's anger fills my office. It is 9:15 on Monday morning. This morning Amy has lasted in her class for less than an hour. She arrived late and joined the other children as they began to get their books and lunch orders organised ready for the day. She is fascinated by the fish in the tank near her book tray, and squats down to get a better look at it. Joe tries to squeeze past her to get to the trays and bumps Amy's arm. Instantly, Amy retaliates with a push sending Joe crashing into another desk. Joe is hurt and begins to cry.

Amy knows the system well, she has tested it many times in the short time she has been at school.

Amy is asked to apologise, she refuses.

Amy is sent to time out, she refuses.

The teacher sends another child to the office to get me.

Discussion of literatures: Sadie

Strauss and Corbin (in Mellor, 1998: 461) explain 'Choosing a research problem through the professional or personal experience route may seem ... hazardous'. Mellor cites Moustakis' research into his own loneliness as 'heuristic research ... this involves self search, self dialogue and self discovery; the research question and the methodology flow out of inner awareness'. As Moustakis says 'I begin the heuristic journey with something that has called to me from within my life experience, something to which I have association and fleeting awareness but whose nature is largely unknown' (Mellor, 1998: 461).

These two texts differ greatly in the authority they convey. In the first extract, Amy is the focus of the story. Sadie uses powerful short sentences to describe what has happened. She is able to create economically and vividly a picture of Amy, her actions, and hint at some of the issues at stake. Sadie appears in the text, but not in a self-conscious way. She is simply one of the actors in the story.

In the second extract, Sadie attempts to discuss the difficulties of practitioner research. But she makes scholars, not the ideas they are discussing, the subject of her sentences. There is no strong narrative to carry readers along; instead a 'he says, he says, he says' formula is used. The confident Sadie as narrator, evaluating and judging actions, has all but disappeared. While she does not employ the naïve 'I' we saw earlier in the writing of Patricia and Samantha, she nonetheless separates herself from the scholars she reviews by making herself invisible.

A simple conversation about the differences between Sadie's texts may not be sufficient. The challenge for supervisors is to figure out how the knowing and assured writer of the first piece might be enabled to write about literatures with the same assurance. Or alternatively, how Sadie might *use* the literatures to rewrite her critical incident into a more theorized, less personal account. In both cases the supervisor is working to relocate the personal (Kamler, 2001). By this we mean to produce writing that is less individual and situates the personal in social/institutional practices and discourses (Fairclough's layer 3). We have tried a number of tactics to push student narratives in this direction, from layer 1 to layer 3 and back. These texts then become the basis of discussion with the supervisor.

One tactic is to ask doctoral researchers to rewrite their critical incident in the third person. Rather than writing as 'I', it is 'he', 'she' or 'they' who retell the story. This creates textual distance and allows the writer to re-see the experience as if it had happened to someone else: for examples of third person narrative work see Haug (1987) or Kamler (2001). We also ask doctoral researchers to consider the positions and perspectives of other actors in the story. This was what Sadie did, rewriting the narrative from the point of view of the child Amy.

A second tactic is to give doctoral researchers key readings that might help them move away from the purely personal. This exercise is difficult but important for those who may have difficulty hearing points of view radically different to their own. Being asked to consider the logic and emotions attached to other positions is a helpful precursor to interview studies, both for the actual interview and for the analysis of subsequent transcripts. However, students like Sadie, who are already predisposed to reflexive work, also find the exercise useful.

After she had rewritten her story from Amy's point of view, Sadie could see herself, as school principal, as a very powerful figure. She also saw how from Amy's point of view, this was not just an incident, but part of an ongoing struggle with schooling. Her supervisor then recommended she read an article by Convery (1999) which suggests that teachers often paint themselves in the best possible light in their narratives. They are inclined to tell 'comfortable stories' about themselves, their experiences and motives. After reading it, Sadie wrote further about her 'self'.

Her supervisor also asked her to consider the following questions:

- If this narrative is not simply about individuals, but also about social/institutional relations and practices, what are they?
- What is at stake in this incident? Whose interests are involved?
- What are the power relations here?
- Who might benefit from this incident and how?
- How did this situation (conflict, difficulty, way of doing things) get to be like this?
- What discourses might produce this kind of narrative?
- Is there an ideal(ized) person here in this text – what is this ideal?
- How might it have been different?

Sadie's written response illustrates a greater degree of reflexivity than in her first telling of the incident in the office.

> I have thought a lot about why I chose this particular incident. ... One of the reasons I chose it relates to Convery's point about presenting an attractive identity. I think this story, the way I have told it, shows my commitment to equity, collaboration and relationships, however, I do not touch on more political aspects of status and power in a primary school. This could open up a completely different and nowhere near as attractive story about me!
> ...
> Convery's writing hit some real nerves. I read his article after I had written the incident from my perspective and I realised that I had created myself as the type of Principal I wanted to be. I had chosen particular aspects of the incident in my telling of the story. I had left out significant aspects in order to create a personal identity. I had left out whole underlying themes. To use Convery's words 'my narratives were not just the simple recall and recital of a series of definitive personal experiences; these stories provided opportunities to display my moral individuality through the selection, organization and presentation of personal experience ...' (Convery 1999: 132). I think, in my narrative I used 'a self reassuring strategy' which explained 'rather than explored my intentions and practices' (141). My narrative construction of this situation had in a way covered some difficult and political issues by simply not including them or glossing over some aspects.

Sadie's realization through this writing is that a taken-for-granted narrative, illustrating her commitment to social justice, omitted important power relations in the school context. In moving past the surface of the critical incident, she eventually produced a much more complex narrative about the difficulties school principals face working for social justice, given their positional power in an educational system which continues to (re)produce inequality. This conceptual work was an important precursor to fieldwork with colleague school principals.

There is also an interesting shift in the way Sadie mobilizes the literature here compared to her earlier extract. Here she foregrounds the relevant ideas from Convery, and while she has used direct quotations, Convery is not the major actor – rather it is his ideas. Sadie is in conversation with Convery, but she controls the dialogue. This is a good example of what we mean when we say that doctoral researchers must *use* the literatures, rather than let the literatures use them.

In addition, what we see in this journal entry is a productive interrogation of a professional identity. Sadie brings scholarly practice to bear on her principal self, and notes that it is a comfortable fabrication. In this transaction we see a move characteristic of critical practitioner research which must be reflexive in order to challenge naturalized ways of doing, thinking and saying.

It is important to reiterate that the purpose of this writing is not to produce anything directly for the dissertation. This is 'writing along the way'. It is writing that helps produce the scholar by shaping scholarly dispositions. It helps to produce the researcher 'stance'. It is working with the personal in order to accomplish scholarly work and to build scholarly practices.

There is, however, a possible dissertation application of such work. Sometimes dissertations begin with a first person narrative. The purpose of such a narrative is to locate the researcher in the research, to make visible their passions and investments, or to trace the history of a research question and its evolution. Often, however, dissertation narratives are uncritical and not worked on or worked over. They are personal accounts dotted with the personal 'I' but they neither engage the reader nor do serious intellectual work. They do not move to the discursive 'I' in the way that Sadie has begun to.

To promote more reflexive narratives, Barbara (Kamler 2005b) asks students in an online doctoral writing seminar to read a number of published academic writers who write autobiographically. These readings are analysed and unpicked as a set of possibilities for doctoral researchers to interrogate, reject or take up in their own writing. Students experiment by writing their own introductory segment, which they submit to an online discussion for critique. Suggested questions guide their discussion of each other's texts:

- What strategies and resources are used for talking about the self?
- Is the researcher foregrounded or backgrounded? Does she/he use first or third person?
- What stories are selected from the researchers' lives and with what effect?
- Are they confessional? How do they illuminate the argument? How might they detract from the research story being told?

These kinds of critical strategies for 'writing along the way' promote a more theorized approach to the personal. They move students away from naïve accounts which make easy and unreflexive connections with the topic of their research. They focus explicitly on identity work and aim to encourage the development of confident scholars and writers.

However, the problem of the personal in the dissertation, journal articles and conference papers requires a different approach. Dunleavy (2003) argues that it is the personal stamp, the angle that students take on their research problem, that really makes their contribution to knowledge original. And we argue that doctoral researchers cannot help but be in the dissertation text. Text work and identity work are inseparable. The question is then, how will they represent themselves on the examinable page? What are their choices?

Building a credible persona

In order to be persuasive and have their argument accepted in their disciplinary communities, doctoral researchers need to build appropriate social relationships with readers. This is as important as relevance and plausibility of ideas. It involves creating a *credible persona in the text*. We use the term *persona* to signal that this is a textual move.

At the start of the chapter we saw doctoral writers using 'I' to create a persona in the text, but not always in relation to the practices of disciplinary communities and not always effectively. We suggested that this was because they were using the personal rather than the discursive 'I'. We now ask: How can supervisors help doctoral researchers project themselves into the text with credibility and authority? What practices are used by different disciplinary communities for constructing knowledge and how do these shape the persona formed?

We find Hyland's (2000; 2002) discussion of *writer stance* useful to make these matters more explicit. Hyland is a linguist who investigates the ways academic writers project themselves into their writing. He argues that academic writers are never just communicating information, ideas and knowledge. They are also conveying 'their integrity, credibility, involvement, and a relationship to their subject matter and their readers' (Hyland, 1999: 101). They use language to convey judgments, opinions and degrees of commitment to what they say. They can boost or tone down their claims and criticisms, they can express surprise or importance, and sometimes address readers directly.[8]

This interactional aspect of writing is often overlooked by doctoral writers, but it is important in determining whether their argument will be considered persuasive by others. We suggest that supervisors need to engage with Hyland's idea that writer stance is *not* peripheral to a more serious goal of communicating content. Rather, there are choices about what stance to take and these differ by discipline. Hyland outlines a number of resources for creating writer stance which we present in Figure 5.2. This classification scheme is useful in helping supervisors get a more explicit sense of the wide variety of language features doctoral researchers can use to create writer stance.

Hyland collected 56 research articles from seven leading journals in eight disciplines to see how these features were used by different discourse communities. The broad cross-section of disciplines included: microbiology, physics, marketing,

Hedges include terms like *possible, might, perhaps, believe* which explicitly qualify the writer's commitment about a proposition. They may show uncertainty and indicate the information presented is opinion, not fact. Or they may convey deference, modesty or respect for the view of more experienced colleagues.

Emphatics include terms such as *clearly, in fact, definitely, it is obvious, of course* which signal the writer's certainty and emphasize the force of a proposition. They stress shared information with an audience and group membership.

Attitude markers express the writer's affective attitude to propositions in more varied ways. They might convey surprise, obligation, agreement or importance, for example. They are most often signalled by attitude verbs (*I agree, we prefer*); by necessity modals (*should, have to, must*); by adverbs (*unfortunately, hopefully*). Attitude can also be signalled by putting particular terms 'in quotes' or using *italics* and exclamations!!! for emphasis.

Relational markers are devices that directly address readers, either to focus their attention or encourage their participation. These include the use of second person pronouns (*you can see*), questions (*Where does this lead? How might we understand this?*); commands (*consider, recall that, note that*); and asides that directly address the audience but may interrupt the ongoing discourse (this will be familiar to readers who ...).

Person markers refer to the degree of explicit author presence in the text. This includes the use of first person pronouns (*I, we*) and possessive adjectives (*our, my, mine*) to present propositional, affective and interpersonal information. The pronoun system allows writers to present their information subjectively (*we believe, my analyses involved*) or interpersonally (*we can see from this, let us consider*) or objectively (*it is possible that, the data show*).

Figure 5.2 Hyland's resources for building writer stance (The chart borrows from Hyland 2000: 111–13 and Hyland 1999: 103–4.)

applied linguistics, philosophy, sociology, mechanical engineering and electrical engineering.

He found that stance was an important feature of all the articles, confirming that 'academic writing is not the faceless discourse it is often assumed to be' (Hyland, 1999: 107). *Hedges* were most frequently used, followed by *attitude markers* and *emphatics. Person markers* and *relational markers* were less frequently used, in all disciplines. That is, experienced writers in most disciplines did not convey their stance by using the first person or directly addressing their reader. By contrast, in the student texts we've looked at, writers rely primarily on person markers – often with unintended effects.

Hyland also found significant disciplinary differences between the sciences and humanities/social sciences in the use of stance features and their expression. Not surprisingly, journals in applied linguistics, marketing, philosophy and sociology contained almost 30 per cent more stance expressions than those from science and engineering. This confirms the stereotype that the sciences tend to produce more impersonal texts. But it also reflects, according to Hyland, the different structures of knowledge domains and argument forms in these disciplines.

According to Hyland, for example, the sciences have a more formalized reporting system than the social sciences. This allows science writers to represent arguments fairly compactly and to minimize their presence in the text. So, while writers in all disciplines used *hedges* to modify their claims, Hyland found those used by science writers were generally less explicit in offering a personal judgment. Writers revealed their opinions only by commenting on what readers should attend to. The following examples are taken from Hyland's (1999) data pool, abbreviations (EE, Phy, Bio) signify the discipline of the writer.

> It is clearly necessary to use improved device structures and to employ ... (EE)

> In simulation studies, one must check any limiting case of calculations. (Phy)

> ... it is important to consider the hydration of the plant, the minimum temperature and ... (Bio)
>
> (Hyland, 1999: 116)

The social sciences, Hyland argues, require greater intervention to achieve an authorial self and mutually shared context. Writers have to work harder to engage their audience and shape their argument to the shared perspective of the discipline. As a result, social sciences/humanities writers were more likely to indicate the subjectivity of their own evaluations. This occurred, for example, through the use of verbs such as *believe, suspect* and *suppose*, which carry a sense of personal conjecture.

> I suggest that certain ways of thinking about social movements are likely to be very fruitful ... (Soc)

> I believe that these are different notions that may well involve different objects. (Phil)

> On the basis of this pilot investigation, I consider the following implications relevant to ... (AL)
>
> (Hyland, 1999: 117)

In the sciences and engineering, Hyland found writers more likely to use verbs such as *indicate, imply, suggest*, which emphasize the reliability of information over its certainty and which allow them to distance themselves from their claims.

> The results presented here suggest ... (Bio)

> The code equations imply that ... (ME)

> ... agreement between the measured and the calculated performance is quite good and indicates ... (EE)
>
> (Hyland, 1999: 117))

Perhaps Hyland's most surprising finding relates to the use of first person markers 'I' and 'we' – an obvious matter of concern for our discussion of the personal in dissertation writing. While we typically associate the use of first person pronouns with the social sciences, Hyland found that biology had similar figures to sociology, and that physicists used the first person more than linguists or sociologists.

> The choice of first person helps writers to construct a more authoritative discoursal identity and to adopt an explicitly accountable stance. The suppression of personal agency is therefore considered to be a means of concealing the social constructedness of accounts in academic writing, and scientists are generally seen as most guilty in this regard, concealing their interpretative practices behind a screen of empiricist impersonality.
>
> (Hyland, 1999: 117–18)

On closer inspection, however, Hyland again found that disciplinary differences were operating. So, first person was used in the sciences to construct the text and present writers' decisions, but rarely to take a personal stand on the object studied. In the social sciences, personal markers were more often used with verbs such as *argue* and *think*, and with *believe* and *propose* in marketing – placing writer claims in a framework of personal perception. In engineering and science, by contrast, 'I' or 'we' occurred more with verbs referring to experimental activities such as *assay, measure* and *analyse* and verbs used to structure the text, such as *note, discuss* and *refer.*

This finding extends our earlier analysis of student use of first person discursive markers. First person is complex in the ideological and interpersonal positions it offers to writers. Hyland's study suggests broad differences in the way academic research writers employ the vexatious 'I'. But it is not a matter of yes-no, on-off, science-no, humanities and social sciences-yes. Writers have to make decisions to either foreground or downplay their involvement in 'creating a text and creating knowledge' (Hyland, 1999: 119). There *are* socially authorized conventions that guide these choices, but these are not the same as strict rules of conduct. They constrain rather than determine linguistic choices.

Supervision and the personal

It is useful for supervisors and students to have a more conscious understanding of how such conventions operate. However, the process of drawing on conventions is not, as Clark and Ivanic (1997: 143) argue, 'completely free ranging'. It also depends on the writer's social history, 'experiences and affiliations to particular groups', as well as 'the pressure to conform to the prestigious conventions for the type of writing in the institutional context'. It is important to make these choices a topic of supervisory conversation and one way to do this is to use real examples of published dissertations.

When working with completed and successfully examined dissertation texts, the aim is to help the doctoral student see beyond the simplified notion that academic writing is impersonal – or that the only way to create a persona is through the use of 'I'. To illustrate, we compare the opening paragraphs of two dissertations. Both use the personal pronoun 'I' effectively to create an authoritative persona and situate the researcher's own history in relation to the research problem. The first example comes from the first page of *Learning Literacies in the Law: Constructing Legal Subjectivities* (Maclean, 2003).

> This thesis had its genesis in a project that *I* and a group of colleagues conducted in 1994 to study the academic writing of first-year university students. The problems students experience in coming to terms with the demands of university writing are well-known (Ivanic, 1998; Lea and Stierer, 2000). As literacy educators with skills in discourse analysis *we* believed *we* had something to offer to colleagues in other faculties seeking to find a way of helping their failing students.
>
> Following the conclusion of the academic writing project, *I* decided to pursue the issue further by making student legal discourse the focus of this thesis. *My choice* reflected the factors which influenced the direction of the earlier project. Choice of law as a focus for study was influenced by its linguistic character. 'Language is both the core technology and the core topic of law and legal work' (Dingwall, 2000). Law is very much concerned with language and texts, both as a tool used to accomplish action and as a medium used for representation (Phelps 1989). Reflecting these claims, the linguistic and discourse analytical methods *I* was using proved to have considerable leverage in the study.

There are a few observations to make about this writing. There are three uses of 'I' in these two paragraphs, and two of 'we', but the personal pronoun does not appear in every sentence. Each use of the *personal marker* achieves a particular purpose. The first is to signal an intellectual history – where the project comes from. The second is to make a link between Maclean's past research and the dissertation research. The third is to emphasize the researcher's methodological credibility. Each use of this discursive 'I' signals the location of the researcher within a credible field of study with a track record. The reader is left in no doubt at the outset that this dissertation comes from a researcher who knows what they are doing and where their work fits. The claim is pegged out right from the beginning.

In the second example, from a dissertation titled *Professional Learning Through Narratives of Practice* (Hogan, 2005), we also see 'I' and 'my' used skilfully to mark the territory of the writer and her research.

This research folio began with the banal observation that almost everything *I* know about teaching has been learned from stories, both from the stories of other teachers and learners and from my own experiences reconstructed as narrative. Many of *my experiential narratives* have been told or written for others, but many more have been composed only in *my mind* for the purpose of making something coherent and meaningful out of the chaos of events and impressions. Like all aspects of culture, teaching is intertextual; the long narrative of *my career* in education is formed from the stories of others *I* have observed, read or heard about. Or, to use Tim Winton's metaphor, they have provided the 'debris and nutrient and colour' in the river of *my professional life*.

The research texts included in this folio have as a common current the argument that narratives of practice are central to teachers' ongoing construction of their professional identity. Narrative is a powerful and dynamic means by which educators (like other humans) establish a sense of what it means to be a member of a particular community. Through shared stories the community's norms, expectations and enduring values are transmitted, problems and setbacks are framed in ways that enable them to be understood, and the work of the best (and worst) practitioners is preserved in legend. Narratives can function to conserve certain practices, values and ideas, yet paradoxically they can also foster change by enabling teachers to imagine alternative ways of doing their work. If we accept the argument that narratives of practice are a primary means by which educators make sense of their work, and that narrating is a fundamental social process, it follows that teaching narratives have significant constitutive power in shaping the identities and practices of the teachers who engage with them.

Here we find first *person markers* in the first paragraph only. While there is some reference to self in almost every sentence, it is done with a view to engaging the reader. References to *my narrative*, *my mind*, *my career*, *my life* create a link between the reader and the writer. The researcher authorizes herself as an educator with a rich history of stories and uses metaphor to conjure her territory in a lively way. In the second paragraph she disappears altogether as a presence and moves on to argue her case for the power of narrative, her chosen methodology.

In sum, both Maclean and Hogan make linkages and to bring the reader in: links with previous research they may have done, with their professional lives and careers, with the discourse communities (law, education and narrative inquiry) to which they are appealing. So unlike our earlier student examples, the 'I', when used purposefully, is not personal. It is the discursive 'I' which leads the reader and links the research to scholarly communities and practices. And this makes all the difference.

But how do supervisors, once their students are clear about the differences between using the personal and discursive 'I', help them sort out when the 'I' should be mobilized?

The Goldilocks dilemma

Hyland captures the 'I' challenge for scholarly writers when he says, 'Writers need to invest a convincing degree of assurance in their propositions, yet must avoid overstating their case and risk inviting the rejection of their arguments' (Hyland, 2000: 87). For doctoral writers, making choices about writer stance is even more complex. They are not writing for peers. Relationships between doctoral candidates and examiners are culturally constrained as unequal. They are not yet 'accepted' in their scholarly communities and are seeking entry through the writing of the dissertation itself.

So the question of 'what kind of stance is appropriate for doctoral writers' creates a genuine supervisory quandary, what we call *the Goldilocks dilemma*. How much persona is appropriate? *Not too cold*: passive, tentative, over-cautious or evasive. *Not too hot*: overly confident, too brash and assertive. *But just right*: confident, in charge, leading the reader through the dissertation.

Finding the right mix is complex. It is not simply determined by the use of the personal pronoun or the linguistic resources outlined by Hyland and others. But linguistic tools can be useful as a starting point to make such matters more conscious for students and an object of ongoing supervisory conversation.

We have experimented with a few strategies to help doctoral researchers come to grips with questions of textual authority and writer stance. The aim is to explore the choices in constructing the certainty of their assertions – what some linguists call modality.

Modality includes the hedges, emphatics and attitude markers described by Hyland, but classifies these somewhat differently. According to linguists Halliday and Matthiessen (2004), modality expresses two kinds of meanings: *probability*, judgments about the likelihood of something happening or being; and *usuality*, judgments about the frequency with which something happens or is. Choices of modality express how powerful writers feel in a particular domain and how knowledgeable and authoritative they feel. In short, modality encodes relations of power and affect.

We often give students a chart which sets out some of the explicit markers of modality, shown in Figure 5.3.

In workshops we experiment with two dimensions of modality: (1) the authority of doctoral researchers in relation to examiners and scholarly experts and (2) with respect to the truth or probability of their research assertions and findings. We talk about how difficult it is to strike an appropriate balance between confidence and tentativeness, to write with authority but not fall into the trap of claiming too much. Some advice books offer rules, cautioning students to use the language of tentativeness or what we'd call low modality: '*it is likely that, it seems obvious here, one tentative conclusion that might be drawn ...*' (Glatthorn, 1998: 112–13). But such rules oversimplify the decisions doctoral writers need to make. Qualifying every statement will lead to weak, unconvincing prose.

- **Modal auxiliary verbs** (*may, might, must, should, can, can't, ought*) *which* modify the verb to express degrees of possibility, probability, intention or necessity:
  She may win
  She should win
  She might win
- **Modal adverbs**, such as *perhaps, probably, possibly, obviously, questionably, definitely*:
  She will probably win
- **Conditional clauses**, i.e. by adding a whole clause:
  She will win, if she has the skill
- **Hedges**, such as *sort of, a bit*, or *something*:
  She had a bit of a win

Figure 5.3 Modality markers

Our approach is to ask students to play with the extremes of modality. First of all they rewrite a passage of text with high assertive modality. We ask them to be extremely confident and sure of their propositions, using whatever language resources they can find to assert the truthfulness of a claim and express maximum affect. Then we ask them to rewrite the same passage with low modality: to be as tentative, cautious and careful as they can imagine, in full recognition of their unequal power relationships in the academy. This can be fun when done in pairs or small groups. It creates a playful approach to the Goldilocks dilemma. But it raises a serious issue for doctoral writers – and makes it public.

There are many choices to be made in taking a stance and creating a persona in text. It helps to look more carefully at how other scholars in their field approach this puzzle. Put another way, this is a quandary located in Fairclough's layer 2 – in the social context of the reader–writer relationship, where the reader is an examiner. Playing with modality encourages a more explicit engagement with the identity consequences of dissertation text work.

We think doctoral researchers need to develop resources that enable a more authoritative, impersonal stance, so that they have a choice about which way to represent themselves and their work in their dissertation texts. If they are to be successful scholars in the academy, they must come to the 'just right' combination of certainty, humility, personal claim, dis/agreement and authoritative stance. Doctoral writers also need to come to see that it is not wrong to use the 'I' in academic writing, but it is instead a matter that is guided by disciplinary conventions as well as personal inclination and epistemological beliefs. And when this pesky personal pronoun is used, it needs to be used in moderation and with some sophistication, or the unintended consequences may undercut the reasons for its use.

The self of the researcher, and her representation in textual form is integral to the construction of a persuasive argument and it is an argument we address in the next chapter.

Chapter 6

Choreographing the dissertation

The American novelist Frederick Busch, in interview, noted that 'You discover your book as you write it' (Walker, 1999: 34). Writers of fiction often describe writing as a process that unfolds mysteriously and speak of characters who come alive, of narratives that unfold into plausible virtual worlds. In one sense writing research is also like this. As we have argued elsewhere in this book, writing and understanding are mutually constructed. Scholars write and think simultaneously and their writing develops their ideas and then pins meaning on the page. The process of writing advances insight in research writing, just as it does in fiction.

However, many fiction writers also have a rough plan. This may change as the story goes along, but they do not craft a narrative with nothing in mind. It is even more imperative to have a structure in mind when undertaking doctoral writing, whether for a conference paper, a journal article, or the dissertation itself. This chapter addresses the question of structuring a scholarly text.

We begin by discussing received wisdom about the 'correct' way to write a scholarly text and we consider the differences between recount, summary and argument. We argue that much social science writing would benefit from having a stronger focus on argument. We consider pedagogic work with what we call 'tiny texts' to help doctoral researchers focus on argument. We then go on to explore the construction of argument through the metaphor of a choreography of 'moves'. We examine some of the textual features that characterize the academic dance: signposting and headings. We conclude the chapter with a brief discussion of the overall shape and flow of the dissertation and the relative weightings given to various scholarly elements – literature, methodology, conclusions.

Recount, summary and argument

Scholars regularly craft particular kinds of writing. Here, we consider three, all of which are vital to the sound construction of academic texts. We provide definitions of each type in order to make the case that the apparent orthodox structure of academic writing has significant problems. These problems are related to the particular mix of three types of writing: recount, summary and argument.

Recount

A recount is a text which talks about what happened, and what we/I/others did. Two types of recounts occur regularly in scholarly texts: (1) a personal recount in which the writer retells events/activities in which she has been involved; (2) a factual recount which recalls the details of a particular event or sequence of events.

As we saw in Chapter 5, academic writers often mobilize personal recounts. They write about events in which they have been involved as a form of evidence or to trace an intellectual history. While some disciplines frown upon the use of personal experience, in others, such as those in which practitioners/professionals are now actively engaged, the use of personal recounts is more accepted: 'My experience of this policy is important and it informs the way I have developed the research design'. Personal recounts are also used to establish the mandate for research or for a particular methodological approach: 'I am using this approach because the following happened to me and because I don't want to do that to others, I'm going to do this instead'. However, as we also argued in Chapter 5, a reflexive and critical approach is more desirable than a simple recount, and 'relocating the personal' often shifts the writing into a different genre – an argument (we discuss argument shortly).

Many academic journal articles use a factual recount when they detail the process of constructing the research: 'We used this kind of method and sample and generated this kind of data. We wanted to do this but something got in the way and we couldn't. Therefore our research findings can only address this aspect of the issue', or, 'We consulted these particular books in the library and spoke to the following people for the following reasons'. In research papers and dissertation texts, factual recounts can be more extended and some go as far as providing an 'audit trail' of steps taken in the research – from conception to implementation through to analysis. This kind of recount certainly makes it easy for examiners to follow what doctoral researchers have done, although the risk can be that too much detail is provided.

Summary

A summary is an economical and accurate representation of events, actions, ideas, texts or speech. To produce a summary, the writer needs to make decisions about what to include and exclude, what to highlight and background and how to frame the text.

Summaries form the basis of much academic work, but they are less often a published genre. Scholarly summaries, for example, underpin engagement with literatures. Doctoral researchers may be asked by their supervisor to summarize sets of texts in order to advance their understanding and/or to begin the process of identifying their position within the field.

Janet Giltrow (1995) suggests that a good summary shows a knowledgeable reader that the writer understands something important. This knowing is not accomplished by cutting and pasting together the words of others taken out of context, but through doing new work. This new work entails identifying important ideas and evidence and providing abstract terms to capture major themes and enough detail to provide 'proof'. Such text work requires careful reading and/or highlighting of key ideas, grouping these ideas together to produce commonalities and differences, and then developing evaluative categories to describe them. The writer can then use these summary blocks to build a cogent introductory framing or a coherently structured narrative.

But doctoral researchers are generally required to do much more than simply produce economical summaries: they are expected to take a critical, evaluative stance (see Chapters 3 and 4). This positions them within the field of knowledge production and allows them to demonstrate the intertextuality of their research and its dependence on, and position in relation to, the work of others.

Argument

Writing an argument involves taking a position on a particular issue, event or question, and justifying that position. An argument attempts to persuade the reader to a particular point of view and to the veracity and worth of that point of view. In its simplest form an argument consists of:

- a statement of position (a thesis),
- a series of points arranged in logical order, supported by evidence and examples, linked together by connections that emphasize their cumulative nature, and
- a summary in which the thesis is reaffirmed and restated. There may also be recommendations at this stage (see Derewianka, 1990).

A scholarly argument generally follows this structure. It may also entertain counter points of view, in order to strengthen the case being made. Scholarly arguments can be concise, as in the form of an abstract, or in their most extended form they become a dissertation or book. Because scholarly argument does not take evidence and examples as givens, it also incorporates analysis, interpretation and evaluation. There are generally sub-arguments contained within the larger overarching case being made.

Having briefly outlined the purpose and form of the genres of recount, summary and argument, we now use these to deconstruct the formulaic thesis and suggest an alternative.

Research writing by numbers

Many doctoral students believe that scholarly writing must follow a set pattern: introduction, literature review, methodology, findings, discussion and conclusion.

While this formula might produce a text, we suggest it also hardwires in numerous difficulties.

In Figure 6.1 we present a table which categorizes the kinds of writings that are used in producing this dissertation orthodoxy. While it may over-exaggerate the effects of a thesis-by-numbers approach, it serves to illustrate the point that we want to make. The formula fosters particular kinds of writing which can lead to a boring, reader-unfriendly text.

Figure 6.1 suggests that a formulaic dissertation text is likely to be dominated by factual recounts and summaries. Arguments will form *sections* of chapters, except in the case of the mandatory discussion section/chapter. An overuse of factual recount and summary can lead to a mechanistic and tedious text. It is rather like reading someone's lengthy diary without having a purpose for the reading. It is the argument that provides a compelling read. And readers are more likely to lose the thread of the argument, we suggest, if it is embedded in sections of chapters.

Thesis segment	Narrative	Genre
Introduction	Here is my experience.	Factual recount
	Here is what I am going to do and why.	Factual recount plus argument
Literature Review	This is what other people have said about the topic.	Summary
	Here is how my research fits in.	Analysis (possibly) Argument (some)
Methodology	Here is what other people have said about methodology.	Summary
	Here is what I did.	Factual recount
Findings	Here is what I've found: themes, graphs, questionnaires, results.	Factual recount and summary. Possibly small pieces of argument.
Discussion	Here is what this means and why it is important.	Argument
Conclusion	Here is what I did, what I found and some things that might happen next.	Summary
		Argument

Figure 6.1 Dissertation genres

This does not mean that doctoral researchers who use the dissertation recipe do not know how to argue or fail to argue. It means that when pieces of argument are scattered throughout a formulaic text, the reader can easily get lost. (In Chapter 7 we look at linguistic tools that can help writers flag rather than bury their argument.) Stated another way, the problem for the reader is that she is not given an extended and overarching argument to follow. As a consequence, she must piece together the bits and pieces of argument along the way to make her own coherence. This is a lot to ask of any reader. However, if that reader is also an examiner, she may become impatient with the expectation that it is her job to do the hard work of tying sections of the dissertation together.

We believe it is important to assist doctoral researchers to make the argument the major organizer of the text. There are two further reasons, besides constructing a reader-friendly text, for suggesting that supervisors take this approach.

First, doctoral study should be concerned with a problem, justify the importance of attending to that problem, and persuade a reader that the evidence they have accumulated on the topic sheds new light on the issue. The essence of the doctoral dissertation is thus not recount or summary. It is very extended argument – indeed, that is why it is called a thesis. A dissertation that contains little argument may well struggle to achieve the stated goal of making a scholarly contribution.

Second, scholarly work at doctoral level is also meant to be about the unique contribution to knowledge production made by the student. Even if the focus of the research has been subject to countless other studies, doctoral researchers must place their particular stamp on their work. While critical summary may rely on framing and locating the work of others, factual recounts do little more than say what happened, not why, nor why this was important. It is argument that provides the opportunity for doctoral researchers to make their mark, to state their case, to stake a claim.

In the remainder of this chapter we discuss pedagogical approaches that help doctoral researchers focus on argument. We begin with the notion of 'tiny texts'.

Tiny texts

Crafting a thesis argument is not easy. And it doesn't happen all at once. Doctoral researchers need to 'write along the way' (as we also argued in Chapter 5) to learn how to write persuasively about their research. One excellent strategy to assist them is writing abstracts for academic conferences and journals. Writing abstracts creates a pedagogical moment for supervisors to focus on the making of an argument. Abstracts highlight issues of authority and thus identity and authorial voice. All in just a few sentences! We call abstracts 'tiny texts' because they compress the rhetorical act of arguing into a small textual space using a small number of words. But they are 'large' in the pedagogical work they can accomplish.

In order to gain entry to journals or conferences, doctoral researchers need to learn how to write a compelling abstract. Abstract writers not only seduce others to buy their wares and/or bid for inclusion in scholarly events, they position themselves, via the abstract, to be seen as legitimate knowers within particular scholarly communities. But for the most part, abstracts are a taken-for-granted academic practice which researchers are just expected to know how to produce.

When we investigated abstracts in a wide array of journals (Kamler and Thomson, 2004), we found a motley and often bland array of conventions and genres. Guidelines given to prospective journal writers were most often inexplicit, focusing on word length and spacing, rather than offering any substantive advice. We undertook our own analysis of abstracts in order to identify textual features and characteristics to provide our doctoral students with more guidance in writing.

Based on this work, we have found that far from being a tiresome necessity of academic life, the abstract is a rich site for text work/identity work (see also Kilbourn, 2001 on the benefits of close work with first paragraphs). It creates pedagogic space for doctoral researchers to practise writing a persuasive argument and become more familiar with institutional and scholarly discourses, conventions and genres.

To illustrate how supervisors might work with tiny texts, we consider two examples. The first occurred in the context of the supervisory relationship, the second in an abstract workshop which involved more explicit genre guidance and less hands-on labour.

Elizabeth gets abstracted

Elizabeth wrote an academic journal article based on her dissertation on young children's interactions with Information and Communication Technologies. She did not attempt to write the abstract until after she completed the article and she found it very difficult to write. Elizabeth's first draft abstract consisted of only one sentence.

> In this article I argue that careful analysis of very young children's use of ICT and other technologies suggests that both the dominance of print in emergent literacy education, and school expectations of the literacy achievements of children prior to formal schooling, may require review.

The text is short and consists of 45 words. Elizabeth does not situate her research on young children and ICT in relation to any social or educational issue, or previous research. She does not mention that she is reporting research. Strangely, the term *research* is omitted entirely. She uses the personal pronoun 'I' with the verb 'argue', but the abstract does not make an argument. Her use of the modal verb 'may require' creates a cautious stance, but it is not clear what it is that may require reviewing.

Elizabeth's supervisor marked this draft with suggestions which they discussed. They also did some joint writing on the computer, not unlike the joint texting strategy we described in Chapter 4 between Mia and her supervisor Andrew. Their explicit goal was to explore how Elizabeth might construct a more authoritative stance in the abstract. The supervisor sat at the keyboard, trying options, asking Elizabeth to amplify her reasoning. Elizabeth then produced a second draft which still had traces of her struggle to produce an argument.

In this paper I explore how three young boys in the period of pre-school transition use ICT and other technologies. I suggest that neither the dominance of print in emergent literacy education, nor school expectations of the literacy achievements of children prior to formal schooling, attend to the versatility with literacy technologies demonstrated by these very young children and that this failure could inhibit their continuing literacy development both in ICTs and print.

This second draft is longer (73 words) and now consists of two sentences. Elizabeth uses the personal pronoun 'I' in both sentences, but the verb argue is now left out and 'explore' and 'suggest' are used instead. However, some sense of argument begins to emerge. There is still no reference made to Elizabeth's research, but the 'three young boys' are now more visible as research participants. The use of 'neither/nor' also creates a slightly more critical stance, and an implicit contrast between what children can do outside school and what schools offer them. There is, however, still no sense of how this research relates to a wider field of practice, although this emerges in Elizabeth's third draft.

Recent investigations of early and emergent literacy seriously underestimate young children's capacity to use ICTs and other technologies in becoming literate, and print continues to be privileged as *the* dominant literacy for young children. In this article I examine how three young boys used ICT in the period of pre-school transition and highlight the complexity of their multimodal reading and writing practices. I argue that unless schools attend to young children's versatility with literacy technologies, this failure could inhibit their continuing literacy development both in ICTs and print.

This rewrite is clearly a more successful bid for journal inclusion because it adopts a more authoritative stance. The ideas are more elaborated, signalled by an increase in the number of sentences (3) and words (from 45 to 73 to 94). Importantly, the three sentences correspond to three rhetorical moves. The first sentence locates the paper in relation to a body of research on early and emergent literacy and takes a critical stance through the evaluative phrases 'seriously underestimate' and 'continues to be privileged'. The second sentence identifies the same data as draft two, the 'three young boys', but now a purpose for looking at the boys is stressed – 'highlight the complexity'. The third sentence concludes by making an explicit argument, and uses evaluative terms 'unless', 'failure', 'could inhibit' to assert the writer's point of view.

To experienced academic writers, this struggle to become authoritative in such a 'tiny text' may seem unusual. Initially, we too were surprised at how difficult many of our doctoral students found writing abstracts, but we now know this is not uncommon.

The difficulty emerges, we argue, primarily because of the identity work involved. Publishing out of their PhDs presents a new set of identity challenges as doctoral researchers negotiate a place for themselves in the wider academic community. An abstract requires both clarity and an authoritative stance towards the argument developed, and doctoral students may not yet have achieved either. Their thesis argument may still be in formation or they may not know the genre conventions for writing abstracts. The opportunity to write drafts with supervisors makes these issues visible so they can be worked on.

The opportunity to engage in joint texting with a supervisor is far more useful than applying a set of rules, or simply following what other abstracts have done. But we have also developed workshops as a 'mass pedagogy' to guide students through the text work required to produce successful abstracts, as our work with Robert illustrates.

Robert abstracts

Robert was one of fifty doctoral researchers who attended a workshop on writing abstracts. We had asked participants to bring a draft abstract with them. In the workshop they established writing pairs whom we asked to share information about their dissertation research as a context for the abstract work. With some audience participation, we then developed a set of genre questions to ask of the abstracts (see Figure 6.2). First we used these questions as a heuristic to critically read a series of published abstracts which we projected onto a screen. We then asked each pair to use the heuristic to consider what needed to be included/ changed in their own abstracts.

- What's the research problem being addressed?
- How do I locate the significance of my work?
- What conversation am I in? Where am I standing in relation to research on this problem?
- What do I offer as an alternative to existing research?
- What is my argument?

Figure 6.2   Genre questions to ask of abstracts

We paused the pair conversations to consider questions of identity and authority. This, of course, generated an enormous amount of conversation by anxious scholarly identities hungry for guidance and worried about how to represent themselves as researchers. We then asked the pairs to collaboratively rewrite the abstracts they had brought with them. During this time we overheard many conversations about authority and identity, as well as other writerly and scholarly matters. Conversations swung from the choice of particular kinds of adjectives and adverbs, to discussions of the nature of the claims being made, to questions of policy and related research. Dialogue is central to this kind of pedagogical text and identity work. It is the talk and movement from one draft to another that produces the movement to being 'author-ized' as a knower, rather than a learner, occurs (Ellsworth, 2005).

The changes Robert made to his abstract illustrate the powerful effects of this kind of explicit text work, even in a short period of time, and without the intense supervisory input Elizabeth received. Robert's original abstract looked like this.

Education research using the ideas of Vygotsky's sociocultural theory as a theoretical framework is increasing. This presentation discusses the foundations and key concepts of sociocultural theory with regard to activity theory. Sociocultural theory originated with the work of Vygotsky and his interest in the relationship between human activity and thought. The central tenet of sociocultural theory is that human consciousness emerges through the assimilation of experience from goal-driven activities mediated by tools and artefacts. Activity theory evolved in an attempt to organise an empirical method to investigate a 'genetic analysis' of human behaviour within a sociocultural framework by looking at 'activities', 'actions' and 'operations'. Specifically, the presentation describes the application of these ideas with respect to my own research in language education that examines the practices and behaviours of foreign language teachers.

Robert foregrounds Vygotsky's sociocultural theory, its importance and tenets. The writing is descriptive. It shows off what Robert knows about Vygotsky and the evolution of activity theory. But it is not until the very last sentence that Robert mentions his own research, and then, entirely without argument. Instead he promises to 'apply' the ideas of others, hardly a compelling bid for inclusion in a conference programme. His invisibility and over-deferential stance begin to shift in his revised abstract.

Research using Vygotsky's sociocultural theory has increased markedly over the past two decades following the translation of his works into English, emerging as a distinct, though nascent, tradition in its own right. The first half of the paper concentrates on two ideas central to sociocultural theory: mediated action and genetic analysis. The second half then moves to a discussion on how these ideas might shape a methodological framework for empirical research around the classroom practices of foreign language teachers. In the spirit of this conference, *New Perspectives in Educational Research*, the paper argues that sociocultural theory has the power to shed new light on how we might conceptualise future research agendas in teacher education.

The revision is more succinct (114 words compared to 131 in the first draft). Vygotsky's work still goes first, but it is now used to validate and locate Robert's own research. He uses a two-part rhetorical strategy ('first half 'second half' of the paper') to explicate how he will *use* Vygotsky's theory, rather than be *used* by it. The final sentence articulates an argument about the theory's usefulness for the field of teacher education as well as foreign language teaching. This is a more compelling conference bid written in a fairly short period of time. Again it illustrates the possibilities for encouraging doctoral researchers to write arguments.

Our final activity in the workshop, and in subsequent work with our own students, is to focus on what we call the 'So What' question. We ask, 'Given that there is a plethora of published research available, why read this text and not something else?' This question fosters the notion that abstract writing is an invitation to a public conversation about things that matter. In asking doctoral researchers to consider the importance of their work, we challenge them to take up an authoritative position within the academy; to write, if not with confidence, at least with certainty that what they have to contribute is important.

However, even if students master the tiny text and can construct a convincing argument in a few sentences, moving to a much, much bigger text requires a different approach. We now consider the dissertation, the big book, because constructing and sustaining an argument over 80,000 to 100,000 words is a daunting and difficult task.

Chunks, moves and choreography

Conventional advice says that doctoral researchers should start the process of writing the dissertation with a chapter outline which provides a map of what the thesis will be about. There is no doubt that a thesis usually ends up with chapters and students do need advice about negotiating the larger structure of the thesis. But the question is whether or not it is useful to start with chapters. We say no.

Doctoral researchers often refer to the writing they do throughout their candidature as chapters: 'I'm doing the literature review/methodology chapter now'. Obviously, there is some satisfaction and even a sense of relief in thinking that pieces of the dissertation can be written off early. The remaining labour is then automatically reduced and seems more manageable and less threatening.

But premature elaboration of chapters often coincides with the problematic thesis-by-numbers approach we discussed earlier in this chapter. The difficulty with early chapter production is that there is no context into which the chapters might fit. No overarching story. No continuous and sustained argument. The most likely result is that these early chapters will either sit somewhat incoherently in the overall text, or they will require extensive rewriting in order to produce 'flow'.

This is not to suggest that early writing work is not useful. We urge our students to write all the time about every aspect of the doctoral research process. We suggest that they produce *chunks* of writing, and more *provisional* groupings around key ideas, data, methodologies. These chunks might be 'writings along the way', or they may end up being incorporated with minor finessing into eventual chapters. We ask students to write about the problem they are researching, about the field of knowledge production, about their methodology – often several times. These chunks are important for sorting out ideas and working on the writerly stance (see Chapter 5) they will take in their final text.

Chunks have substance. They are not a few pages in length. They are substantive pieces of text that probe, test out, argue and interpret specific aspects of the research. We have written chunks in order to construct some of the chapters in this book. We find that getting out the ideas, so that we know what we have to say, is a helpful precursor to putting those ideas into sequence and framing them through a key idea.

When our students finally come to the end of their fieldwork, and begin to worry about how to construct the actual dissertation text, we ask them to write chunks about their data, to develop their analysis and theoretical ideas. They then know the dimensions of what they have to say. Then, and only then, after most of the analysis is completed, do we turn to the metaphor of choreography.

The metaphor of choreography conveys more than a set of moves strung together. Even if a choreographer uses a restricted repertoire, there are many ways that the moves can be put together. This is how it is with data: there is likely to be more than one argument in a set of research findings and analyses. Some sequences of moves, however, are more pleasing than others. Some seem to 'just work' because they flow on from one another. And this is how it is with argument. There may not be a set pattern of moves to a dissertation argument, but some moves work better than others: some segue neatly while others construct too abrupt a shift.

We suggest guiding doctoral researchers to look at dissertations as choreography, as a set of carefully designed moves that comprise the overarching argument. So, rather than construct chapters or set out contents pages, we think a better strategy is to map the moves of the argument; to see how it is set up, staged, and substantiated to allow convincing claims to be made.

Supervisors can use already published dissertations, especially ones they consider 'good models' from their disciplines, to talk through the macro-choreographic structure with their students. This can be a non-technical discussion, couched in terms that are familiar. The aim is to make explicit and sensible how the argument is staged *across* chapters. The supervisor takes the lead, demonstrating that structure is not just an arbitrary set of conventions or the formula we critiqued earlier: introduction – lit review – methodology – findings – discussion – conclusions.

In Figure 6.3 we illustrate how such a discussion might occur around a dissertation that examined the current situation in disadvantaged schools in Australia. Here Pat uses her own unpublished thesis (Thomson, 1999) to set out the textual moves for a doctoral student. Her thesis is on the table between them as she articulates the moves, explaining how they connect with the division into chapters.

By engaging in this conversation, Pat is doing a kind of modelling. Working through the structural skeletons of theses as choreography allows supervisors to make explicit the propositions and moves involved in constructing a big text. Such moves are not transparent in the complex chapter organization of a large document and students do need help to tease them out.

Conversational Moves	Chapters
So here's the problem I'm working on – what's happening in disadvantaged schools. This is why it's important and here is what I'm going to do in this dissertation.	Chapter 1 Framing the research Flagging the argument to be made
There are various ways policy makers, teachers, academics understand the problem, theorise it, tackle it. Unfortunately most seem to have stopped talking about it – and there is nothing doing in policy. Or they tackle it in this way, which limits what they can do.	Policy analysis and some work with literatures
So I'm going to do this research in a particular way (narrative) because I worked in the field for 27 years and the vast majority of the research already done annoys me. I dislike the way people's life experiences are chopped into tiny quotes between long slabs of researcher voice. I'm going to do something that represents the experiences I had and those of my colleagues.	Chapter 2 Critique of existing body of research from methodological point of view and mandate for particular approach
To really understand what's going on in disadvantaged schools I have to delve into the history of education policy and deal with broader political questions. I have to re-problematize the question of equity and go outside education to talk about what is happening to people and why. I have used methods and theories from a range of other disciplines.	Chapter 3 Contextual analysis More literature work Framing of findings
Here is the situation. Disadvantaged schools struggle to make a difference because: • They have to do more with less. • They have much more to do than wealthier schools. • Governments do some good things but mostly are not very helpful to disadvantaged schools which must largely go it alone. • No one takes what disadvantaged schools are saying very seriously.	Chapters 4–8 Major themes that emerge from data analysis Connections made with literatures
Because this is what re-problematization has allowed me to 'see', I now have something to say to policy makers about what they ought to do. Even though each disadvantaged school is unique, there are some common issues: • Disadvantaged schools have less money and they should have more. • Working with tough kids takes a lot of time and special skills which schools find hard to get – staffing policies need to be changed, more professional development offered. • There are other aspects of public policy (health, housing, transport, jobs) that would help disadvantaged schools.	Chapter 9 Meta-analysis
Well that's interesting, what can be learnt from this project? • Education researchers can benefit from using approaches from other fields. • Most of this was said by Connell et al. twenty years ago – and it is not acceptable that it is still the same. • There are more things to research.	Chapter 10 Specific contribution of the research identified Conclusions and recommendations Staking a claim for more research in the field

Figure 6.3 Dissertation choreographic moves

To illustrate further the benefits of thinking about argumentative moves, here is an example of doctoral researcher Tracy beginning to map out her dissertation in chunky moves. Her research has focused on the Widening Participation agenda in England, a policy and programme which aims to get more working-class students and under-represented groups into higher education. Tracy is conducting a longitudinal qualitative study following twenty school students in their final year at school through to university.

Moves in the dissertation, Version One

1 Own narrative (motivation behind study)
2 Methods
3 Individual's narratives – choices made
4 Widening Participation – situate the sample
5 'Structuring' elements: class and education, class and choice, Bourdieu
6 Students' responses to moves 4 and 5
7 Findings and analysis
8 Summary
9 Implications

This first attempt shows that it has not been easy for Tracy to move from describing what she is going to do – methods, findings and analysis – into the actual argument. She has not been able to resolve whether this is the right order of moves. While she understands that chunks are not the same as chapters, she doesn't seem to know what should go into each chunk. She has a sense of movement, but it is as if she is describing the choreography she might do, rather than actually doing it. We outlined a similar problem in our pedagogic work on tiny texts. By taking a passive stance in relation to the research, Tracy writes herself with lack of authority and an uncertain scholarly identity.

Tracy's supervisor then talked through a dissertation, just as we demonstrated in Figure 6.3. She suggested that Tracy write herself into the moves she had outlined. She proposed that Tracy rewrite the first two moves using the personal pronouns 'I', 'me' and 'my', and the third move using 'the students'.

Tracy then produced a second version of chunks.

Moves in the dissertation, Version Two

1 This study is framed by *my* own educational journey and the way in which the decisions and 'choices' *I* made were influenced by the structuring principles of educational processes.
2 *I* chose to study a group of 'working-class' *students* who attended a summer school for disadvantaged students intending to go to university.
3 The 'working-class' *students* involved in this study are not like me. They are atypical in their attitudes towards education, seen in particular through their choices of university and their educational trajectories.

4   This raises some interesting questions given the historical nature of the uneasy and problematic relationship between the working class and education.

5   In order to explore these issues *I* used a range of methods to trace the *students'* individual journeys through education from an early age.

6   The *students'* individual narratives show how they have been influenced by their history of academic success and have been supported by their parents and teachers to aspire to 'top' universities. They had decided to go to university long before their final year.

7   Unlike the literature, these *students* do not seem to feel 'out of place' in these elite institutions.

8   Bourdieu helps explain how some working-class *students* are 'structured to fit' and become upwardly mobile.

9   The experience of these *students* is clearly atypical and raises some important questions about the ways in which *students* are selected in their final year of schooling to attend intervention programmes.

Here Tracy takes up a more confident position. By putting herself and her research subjects into the frame, she was able to be specific about what each move would actually involve. However, Tracy was not happy with these sentences or with their order. She knew there was a problem in introducing the students and their stories before she had explained how she chose them. She subsequently wrote more expanded versions of each of her moves. Tracy then did something that surprised her supervisor. She put each chunky move onto a single strip of paper. She was then able to shuffle the pieces into various sequences to see which ordering was the most persuasive. She then wrote more extended chunks for each of these moves.

Telling the moves as a narrative, as Pat did in Figure 6.3, makes the dissertation seem accessible and doable. But we may do our students a disservice if we emphasize that the choreography constitutes a story about their research, rather than a set of moves. That is because story is the wrong genre. If the argument stays in the same language and narrative form as Pat's verbalized moves, it will not pass. (We discuss the difference between spoken and written language in Chapter 7.) An argument needs to be couched in the language of research writing and within the conventions of the discipline communities who will examine it. It needs to be recognizable as research and as research that is acceptable within a particular domain. Tracy has begun to write precisely in this way in her rewriting.

The major value of a verbalization of moves is to take the focus off chapters as *the* chunking mechanism of the dissertation. Finished dissertation prose always looks very neat, as if things always fitted into these textual divisions. However, chapters are constructions that take time and effort. The argumentative moves will be enhanced by a cogent chapter organization. But pedagogically speaking, keeping the student's eye on the moves of the argument across chapters keeps their agency up front and their contribution foregrounded – in their mind's eye as well as in the text.

We conclude by focusing briefly on two further aspects of textual construction that are important in dissertations.

Finessing the argumentative text

Once the basic argument is understood and able to be articulated in tiny texts and in chunks/rough chapters, there are two important types of text work still to be done to ensure a reader-friendly text. The first is to ensure textual balance; the second is to ensure adequate signposting and an economical and pointed use of headings to guide the reader through the argument being made.

Checking the balance

An issue of critical importance in constructing an argumentative text is the relative weighting given to each move. By this we mean how many words are allocated to each section and what proportion of the total they comprise.

We share with many of our colleagues the experience of examining dissertations which seem to take forever to get to the actual research. So much time is spent establishing the case for the research, trawling through what others have written on the subject in exhaustive detail or discussing the minutiae of epistemology and methodology, that by the time the reader gets to the actual research, over half the text has been produced. These kinds of texts are often under-theorized, have truncated elaborations of research findings and are followed by naïve recommendations which are detailed in only a few pages. We have also read dissertations which limit discussion of methodology to a brief description of research tools before going on to a tedious and lengthy wade through the findings produced by each tool in excruciating detail. Neither of these kinds of dissertations is appropriately weighted.

We find the notions of *frontloading* and *backloading* useful metaphors to describe texts which are either top or bottom heavy. In a frontloaded text, the writer spends a substantive amount of space working on literatures and methodology and presents a shortened section on the actual research. The backloaded text has lengthy descriptions of under-theorized findings.

Patrick Dunleavy (2003) argues that students often cannot judge the appropriate relative weightings given to the beginnings and endings of dissertations. He suggests that frontloading is a common and counterproductive strategy.

> Do not ... leave all the good bits squeezed into the last third or quarter of the text, as many people do. A recurring problem in most humanities and social sciences disciplines is that students spend so much time and effort on writing lead-in materials that they create a long, dull, low-value sequence of chapters before readers come across anything original.
>
> (Dunleavy, 2003: 51)

Dunleavy argues, and we agree, that since the purpose of doctoral research is to make a contribution to scholarship, the proper weighting of a dissertation ought to be to that point. This means that detailing the question, the field and the methodology are important. Equally important is the elaboration of the precise contribution of the research – these are not raw, unprocessed findings – and the discussion of its importance. But those who think about 'writing up' the thesis (see our critique of 'writing up' in Chapter 1) often end up with unprocessed findings, rather than the worked-on and worked-over data, refined into an elegant exegesis of the contribution. They are likely to confine their discussion to a mandatory chapter, rather than work to build a case throughout. Telegraphing the middle and final stages of the argument produces an unbalanced text which will frustrate examiners, if not actually bore them to tears, as Dunleavy suggests.

Signposting and headings

It is the doctoral researcher's job to guide the reader through their dissertation text and to make their argument accessible. This work is not external to the process of producing and understanding the argument, but an integral part of the argument itself.

We know it is not easy for students to view their thesis from the perspective of a reader/examiner, especially when they have never written a book-length text before. But we find it useful to refer back to Fairclough's model of discourse to help them consider how their text will be received and interpreted. This is the work of layer 2, the discourse practice dimension, which is concerned with the ways texts are interpreted and made – or produced and consumed. The dissertation is inextricable from these processes and shaped by the demands of those who will read and examine it.

Signpostings and headings are two important tools that can help the reader see how the thesis is organized and staged as an argument. Most of the advice books make the key point that readers should be guided through the dissertation text with an opening which explains what each chapter/section/subsection will do. Not many point to the significance of the closer. We find it useful for students to think of readers coming to the end of a chapter. At this point, they need to ask themselves: What do I want the reader to most remember from this chapter/ section? Where does this logically lead next? The answer produces the closer. A closer comes at the end of the chapter/section/subsection: it summarizes the key points made and anticipates where to next.

However, there is more to guiding the reader through the argument than having explanatory sentences and economical closers. The sensible use of headings, and second and third order subheadings is also important.

We adhere to the view that the headings and subheadings must carry part of the argument. Indeed, we suggest that it ought to be possible for a reader to simply read the headings to get some sense of the flow and major points of the argument. Each section and subsection will contain a number of paragraphs. Like nested

Russian dolls, each set of paragraphs will have openers and closers which convey the major message, and each paragraph, in turn, will also have key opening and closing sentences.

To illustrate, here is an example of signposting at the paragraph level, from doctoral researcher Alan's thesis. The sentences are numbered to emphasize the guidance he is giving the reader.

> [1] Universities in Australia have gone through a phase of rapid change and expansion. [2] As demonstrated earlier the number of institutions has increased, as a result of the creation of new institutions, and through amalgamations, and the number of students attending those universities has ballooned. This so-called 'massification' (Marginson, 1997) has also been accompanied by aggressive forays into the commercial arenas through the recruitment of international students for trade rather than aid (as had been the case in the past with programs like the Columbo Plan), both in Australia and through campuses and partnerships in other countries. [3] These are among the key influences that have made the issue of quality of education such an important topic in the debate about universities.
>
> [4] I now discuss these as contexts within which the representations of quality and online education by universities are constructed.

Alan constructs this paragraph so that it helps the reader remember the argument that is being made. Sentence 1 signals the point to be made in the paragraph. Sentence 2 reminds the reader that evidence about this expansion has already been provided and signposts that this paragraph is a move from one piece of argument to the next. Sentence 3 is a summary of points made in the paragraph while sentence 4 signposts that the next section will provide further details about each of these.

Dunleavy (2003) gives a more elaborated example of how work with headings, subheadings and paragraph sentences is accomplished, and it is worth referring to his discussion in Chapter 4 ('Organizing a chapter or paper: the microstructure'). In Chapter 7 of this book we also discuss the importance of putting major ideas first at the sentence and paragraph level, to ensure that an argument is not buried and readers know where they are in a text.

We think that it is also worth looking at actual published texts with students to see how the headings, subheadings, and paragraph opening and closing sentences work. We have on occasion given students an article they haven't read, asked them to highlight the relevant headings and sentences, read only the highlighted text, and then say what they think the article is about. We suggest that they check this partial reading against a full reading of the text. With students whose first language is not English this is a particularly helpful deconstructive exercise, as it helps them understand the choreography, as we have called it, of academic writing. They then have tangible models to help them think about how to reproduce these kinds of moves in their own texts.

Chapter 1 from Linda McDowell's book *Capital Culture: Gender at Work in the City*

Chapter title	Thinking through work: gender, power and space
First heading	*Introduction: organisation, space and culture*
First sentence	In this chapter, I want to counterpose a number of sets of literatures to draw out some questions about the changing organisation and distribution of waged work, especially in its feminisation, that will be explored in different ways in the chapters that make up this book.
Second subheading	*Men's jobs, women's jobs: employment change in the 1980s and 1990s*
Third subheading	*Explaining organisational and workplace change*
First sentence	In the next part of the chapter, I want to shift from an empirical to a theoretical focus and examine the sets of theoretical literatures about work, organisational change and culture and gender divisions of labour that influenced this study of gender patterns of recruitment, promotion and social interaction in the world of investment or merchant banking.
Fourth heading	*Gender segregation at work*
First sentence	Before moving from the organisation to the body, however, I want to review briefly the history of approaches to the analysis of gender division of labour and occupational segregation by sex through to how the persistence of such a marked division in the labour market has been explained.
Fifth heading	*Gendered organisations: sexing and resexing jobs*
Sixth heading	*Normalising the self*
Seventh heading	*Bodies at work*
Eighth heading	*The places and spaces of work*
First sentence	Despite the incisiveness of these various sets of literature about gender, work, power and organizations, they all seem to have a remarkable blindness about the significance of location.
Ninth heading	*Conclusions*
First sentence	In this chapter, I have set the scene in both a theoretical and empirical sense, demonstrating women's entry into the labour force and the ways in which it has been explained.
Second sentence opening phrase	I have argued that …
Third sentence opening phrases	The city, and The City to which I turn in Chapter 2 …

Figure 6.4 Moves and signposts

In Figure 6.4 we have reproduced, via headings, subheadings and key sentences, a snapshot of the first chapter from Linda McDowell's (1997) book *Capital Culture: Gender at Work in the City*. Our aim is to illustrate how these signposts orient the reader to the moves in an argument as well as flag what is to come and what has gone previously. This chapter is also a fine illustration of mapping the field of knowledge production (see Chapter 4) in order to create a mandate for the particular work. Figure 6.4 sometimes includes the first sentence that follows a heading, and sometimes only the heading – so that the logic of McDowell's argument can be easily followed. We have used a hierarchy of bold, italics and plain text to show the order of signposting being given.

We suspect that most readers will have a general idea of what this chapter will argue once they have read its choreography. A full reading will provide the important details of the argument, but the basic case to be made in the chapter can be seen quite simply from the moves outlined in Figure 6.4.

It is also important to note how economical McDowell has been in constructing the moves and signposts in her chapter. It is critical that the provision of signposts and headings does not become mechanistic; excessive signposting is as tedious as no signposting is confusing. This is another example of the Goldilocks dilemma we outlined earlier (see Chapter 5): not too much, not too little – but just right.

Signposting is an activity which constructs argument. When students understand that their thesis is an argument, a particular kind of genre that relies, as we have suggested in this chapter, on a set of moves which proceed logically one after another, to a conclusion, they can experiment with ways of *doing* argument. They can produce tiny texts, talk aloud the moves of their argument and deconstruct published dissertations to see how they work. With their supervisor's help, they can learn how to guide readers to keep track of their argument by making the use of headings, subheadings, and summarizing openers and closers part of their repertoire as dissertation writers. These are central to producing reader-friendly texts.

We turn now to a closer, linguistic kind of text work that supervisors can use to guide doctoral writers to produce interesting and persuasive arguments.

Chapter 7

The grammar of authority

In previous chapters we've suggested a number of strategies to help doctoral researchers write with authority, often before they feel authoritative. We've looked at ways of using metaphors, staging moves of an argument and creating a scholarly persona in the text. In this chapter we shift our focus to a closer kind of text work by introducing a linguistic toolkit for supervisors. We argue that grammar is a useful tool for helping researchers make their writing more coherent, engaging and clear. But to do this work we need a meta-language, a language about language. We need a set of tools for doing archaeological work – for digging into student text, to see how it works and how it may be remade to work more effectively.

Supervisors know when doctoral writing is unsatisfactory. It is more difficult to pinpoint the difficulty or propose a strategy for making the problem(s) visible. Written comments such as 'this passage needs more focus' or 'no structure' or 'try to be sharper in your argument' are imprecise. They provide little information about what action students might take to improve their writing. It is in the spirit of helping supervisors provide more specific guidance for revision that we discuss linguistic tools of nominalization and Theme. We have called the chapter a 'grammar of authority' to signal our goal of using grammar to help doctoral researchers produce more focused, authoritative writing.

Of course, grammar is a term that signals a universe of anxiety, controversy and misconception. Complaints about student writing are often couched in terms of 'poor grammar' or a failure to control the conventions of standard English dialect. And issues of appropriateness are often confused with issues of correctness. So we want to clarify at the start what we mean by grammar and how our approach differs from more traditional grammars which focus on etiquette and rules.

A functional approach to grammar

Grammars are never neutral in the ways they define associations of form and meaning. They always presuppose a view about how to represent and shape experience based on a set of ways of categorizing the world. Threadgold (1997) argues that there is nothing scientific or absolute about a grammar; it is just another set of categories which we use to impose structure and meaning on language. Grammar is not 'in people's heads', it is not a psychological reality and people do not actually produce language by following rules. Grammar is an attempt to describe, after the fact, some of the regularities that can be observed in the language which people produce. But the way grammars do this is always inexact and a matter of compromise, loaded with the preconceptions of the linguists who construct the grammar.

Our approach is based on the systemic functional grammar developed by the social semiotic linguist Michael Halliday (1985). A systemic approach to language differs from the traditional, prescriptive grammars many of us learned at school and those populist 'new' grammars on the bestseller lists. It asks functional questions about how people use language. It interprets the linguistic system functionally in terms of how language is organized to make meanings (Eggins, 2004). A functional grammar does *not* emphasize correct usage or formal rules. Rather, it is influenced by a view of language as social practice (which we outlined in Chapter 2), where grammar is seen as a set of tools for accomplishing social actions.

From this perspective, we think of doctoral writers as learning to acquire a repertoire of linguistic practices. These practices are based on complex sets of disciplinary discourses, values and identities (Lea and Street, 1998) and they take time to learn. A functional grammar can help supervisors make some of these practices more explicit and therefore more accessible.

But this does not mean that we treat grammar as a set of rules for fixing doctoral writing. Unfortunately, this is the kind of grammar advice many of the 'how to' manuals offer doctoral writers, as in this prescription for writing the 'mature scholarly sentence'.

> 1. Combine shorter sentences ... 2. Put the main idea in the main clause ... 3. Reduce the numbers of ands ... 4. Achieve an effect of clarity and directness by expressing the main action of the sentence in the verb and the main doer of the action (the agent) in the subject ... 5. Avoid inserting long modifiers between the subject and the verb ... 6. Avoid using subordinate clauses that modify other subordinate clauses ... 7. Place modifiers so that they clearly modify what you intend them to modify ... 8. Avoid excessive use of the passive voice ... 9. Be consistent in matters of verb tense ... .
> (Glatthorn, 1998: 117–19)

This list of rules of traditional grammar usage may be useful to some students, but it offers no guidance about context. It treats writing as a mechanical skill and grammar as a set of techniques for achieving formal requirements of correctness. This is *not* the approach we take to grammar. We advocate that the final copy of the dissertation must be professionally presented and free of grammatical and spelling errors. But this does not mean we reduce writing to matters of surface features and grammatically correct sentences.

Yet we have been struck by the inordinate attention given to issues of correctness and presentation on university websites, even though a doctoral dissertation is presumably the highest level of scholarship in the academy. This may be a symptom of the increasing diversity of doctoral candidates (Pearson, 1999) and the rich array of language and cultural formations on which candidates draw (see Paltridge, 2004 for an extended review of approaches to academic writing with second language students). As universities in the US, UK, Australia and New Zealand require students to write in standard English, there is growing anxiety about how to help students achieve this goal. And 'grammar' is often presented as a solution to a far more complex problem, as Paltridge (2003) argues:

> Dissertation writing is a difficult process for native and non-native speaker students alike. Students may have the language proficiency required for their course of study, but not yet the necessary textual knowledge, genre knowledge and social knowledge (Bhatia, 1999) required of them in their particular setting.
>
> (Paltridge, 2003: 92)

A disproportionate attention to surface features (such as spelling, subject-verb agreement, verb tense consistency) and stylistic matters (such as margin width, spacing, title page, word length) may also occur because these are the most visible and therefore accessible parts of language to address. That is, correct spelling and correct grammar are taken as code for good writing because people lack other linguistic tools for helping students.

In this chapter we try to make some of these tools visible. We examine two aspects of language that we believe are particularly useful in doctoral supervision: nominalization and Theme. For each, we balance technical explanation with examples of writing. We illustrate both the linguistic resource and how it works in scholarly writing.

In such a discussion it is always difficult to decide how technical to be. Our compromise is to provide less information than would satisfy a linguist, but more than might be of immediate use to supervisors. This is because we want to build a flexible resource that can be used for a wide array of purposes depending on the needs of students. Our metaphor is the toolkit, not a set of rules. We begin by looking at nominalization.

The differences between speech and writing

It is well known that academic writing is often dense, packed with abstractions, and sometimes difficult to read. The term used to describe this tendency is nominalization. To understand nominalization – how and why it is used – we first explore the differences between speech and writing.

A key linguistic difference between speech and writing is that writing tends to be more nominalized than speaking. By 'nominalized' we mean that much of the content of writing occurs as 'things' or nouns. In speaking, by contrast, the tendency is for much of the content to be coded as action and occur as verbs. We can illustrate with the following example.

Imagine we are late for class because we've had an accident on the way to work. We run into the tutorial room, breathless, worried about being late. We are somewhat flustered about keeping students waiting for over fifteen minutes and say to them:

[A] Look, I'm sorry for being late, but it was unbelievable, I can't believe this happened. I was on the bridge and the sun was glaring into my eyes so I could hardly see and the traffic was really worse than usual and I had a horrible headache already because I stayed up too late watching a video with my son for his exam and then I crashed. The car in front of me stopped suddenly and I went right into him and the car behind me crashed into the back of my car and it was a mess, it was just a disaster.

But what would students think if we rushed into class and instead, said:

[B] I apologise for my unavoidable tardiness. There are three possible reasons for this regrettable event, which was caused by a three car accident on the bridge: first, the glare of the morning sun; second, the unusual intensity of morning traffic; and third, my possible inattention due to a headache from fulfilling parental obligations last night.

Students would probably accuse us of being uptight or 'talking like a book'. And rightly so, because the language used in example B is highly inappropriate in this context. It is grammatical, the syntax is correct, it is not faulty language, but it sounds 'wrong' because it is patterned more like writing than speech.

Looking more closely, we can see the language in example B is organized quite differently than in A. Rather than relate a sequence of actions in which the speaker is a key player, it states a number of reasons why the accident occurred. All the words that convey the speaker's emotion and feeling are removed ('unbelievable', 'mess', 'disaster') and replaced with a pithy phrase ('regrettable event'). And much of the content is packaged as nouns (things, such as 'unavoidable tardiness') rather than verbs (actions, such as 'being late').

Figure 7.1 shows how verb forms in example A have been changed into noun forms (more nominalized) in example B to make it sound more like writing.

The point we want to make is that these differences are neither accidental nor haphazard. They are a consequence of the functional differences between spoken and written language. Typically, we use speech in interactive situations to achieve some social action. In example A, we attempt to justify our lateness and calm student annoyance, so the language is informal and unrehearsed. When we write, by contrast, we are more isolated and don't have the visual or aural dimension of face-to-face contact. We typically use language to reflect or analyse (as in example B), so it is less spontaneous. We draft, revise and edit

Example A	Example B
I'm sorry for *being* late	my unavoidable tardiness
the sun *was glaring* into my eyes	the glare of the morning sun
the traffic *was* really worse than usual	the unusual intensity of morning traffic
I *had* a horrible headache already	my possible inattention due to a
because I *stayed up* too late	headache from fulfilling parental
watching a video with my son for his exam	obligations last night

Figure 7.1   From verb forms to noun forms

our writing for an absent audience who will engage with our words when we are no longer present.

These different dimensions of the situation have a strong effect on the language we use. Speech is typically organized as a dialogue, where the participants take turns speaking and build up meaning together. Written language is typically produced as a monologue, where one person (the writer) holds forth on a topic. It's probably more accurate, however, to think of these differences as a continuum. When we are writing emails, for example, we are physically alone, but our writing is more dialogic. It is more like speech in being interactive. When we are giving a conference keynote address, we are speaking in the presence of many people. But our speaking is more like writing, in being an uninterrupted monologue of ideas and information.

Spoken language is also typically more context-dependent, because speakers are in the same place at the same time. We can say to students in our class 'pass *that* to me' or 'put *it* over here', because students can interpret 'that' and 'it' from the shared context. Writing, however, needs to stand alone and be more context independent. If students write 'I disagree with *that*' or '*It* makes that point convincingly', they must make explicit what 'it' and 'that' refer to in the text itself.

Because spoken language tends to accompany action, its structure is also more dynamic than writing. In example A, clauses are joined with a series of 'ands' and one sentence leads to another and another in a kind of complex piling up of ideas. Written language is usually a more considered reflection. So the syntax is often more tightly structured as in example B, where three succinct reasons ('first', 'second', 'third') are given for why the accident happened.

Anyone who has ever recorded speech will know that it contains false starts, repetitions, incomplete clauses, interruptions, slang and non-standard grammatical constructions. This is due to the dynamic 'thinking on your feet' mode of producing speech. In written language, we can remove all our false starts and meanderings from the text so that it *seems* more focused and directed.

These differences have repercussions for how we structure speech and writing. For the most part, we do this unconsciously. We are unaware of the differences. But when it comes to teaching doctoral writing it is useful to make this process more conscious. For example, when students' writing sounds immature, we can often trace the problem back to the fact that they are writing patterns of speech. Or when academic writing gets too dense and impenetrable, we can show students how to unpack over-nominalized prose so it is more accessible. Before we look at these applications, however, we probe further how the process of nominalization works linguistically.

Nominalization

Nominalization is the process by which verbs in a text are changed to nouns (things) and information is packed more densely into nominal (noun) group structures. We have suggested that writing tends to be more nominalized than speaking because much of the content occurs as 'things' or nouns, whereas in speaking, much of the content occurs as 'process' or verbs. We can illustrate with these examples of spoken and written language:

> *Spoken*   If you revise each chapter carefully before you submit the thesis, then you're likely to get a good result.

> *Written*   Careful revision of each chapter prior to thesis submission will increase the likelihood of a good result.

These two texts have the same content and the same set of actions, but they are organized differently. The spoken text consists of one sentence made up of three clauses (the clause is marked with a slash /; it roughly comprises a stretch of language with a verb, in italics).

> If you *revise* each chapter carefully/
> before you *submit* the thesis/
> then you'*re likely to get* a good result.

The three clauses are linked with the conjunctions 'if', 'before' and 'then'. Each clause describes a concrete action ('revise', 'submit', 'get') through the use of verbs, which are performed by a human actor ('you').

In the written text, however, the message has been condensed to fit into only one clause (with only one verb, 'will increase'). This has been achieved by turning the actions of 'revise', 'submit' and 'get' into nouns: *revise* has become *revision*; *submit* has become *submission*; *likely to get* has become *likelihood*.

As a consequence of reducing three verbs to one, there is now only one clause and more information can be packed into the nominal groups (the noun and its accompanying words) on either side of the verb.

> *Careful revision of each chapter prior to thesis submission* will increase *the likelihood of a successful examination.*

We could take this process further and continue to elaborate the nominal groups (which are very elastic) to make them even more dense.

> *Careful revision of each chapter with supervisory assistance prior to thesis submission* will increase *the likelihood of a crafted text and a successful examination.*

It is the process of nominalization, then, that makes written and spoken language so different. Spoken language is concerned with human actors, carrying out action processes, in dynamically linked sequences of clauses. Written language is concerned with abstract ideas and reasons, linked by relational processes in condensed sentences with denser nominal group structures (Eggins, 2004: 94).

Returning to our earlier example, we can see that example B sounded 'wrong' because it was too nominalized – moving away from the dynamic sequencing that goes with speaking. Its more 'written' rhetorical organization can be made visible by dividing both texts into clauses and putting the verbs in italics.

> *Example A*
> Look, I'*m* sorry for being so late,
> but it *was* unbelievable,
> I can't *believe* this happened.
> I *was* on the bridge
> and the sun *was glaring* into my eyes
> so I could hardly *see*
> and the traffic *was* really worse than usual
> and I *had* a horrible headache already
> because I *stayed* up too late *watching* a video with my son
> and then I *crashed*.
> The car in front of me *stopped* suddenly
> and I *went* right into him
> and the car behind me *crashed* into the back of my car
> and it *was* a mess,
> it *was* just a disaster.
>
> *Example B*
> I *apologise* for my unavoidable tardiness.
> There *are* three possible reasons for this regrettable event,
> which *was caused* by a three car accident on the bridge: first, the glare of the morning sun; second, the unusual intensity of morning traffic; and third my possible inattention due to a headache from fulfilling parental obligations last night.

The number of clauses in example B has been drastically reduced from 15 to 3 by turning verbs into nouns. The human actors have been dramatically removed and much more information is now packed into each nominal group (e.g. 'the unusual intensity of morning traffic', 'my possible inattention due to a headache').

This capacity to pack more information into nominal groups increases the possible content of a text and points to a key reason for using nominalization. We use it to condense meanings. We use it to make information more concise. We use it to feature abstract ideas and concepts rather than people and actions (Hammond, 1990). Not surprisingly, academic and research writing is characterized by frequent use of nominalization and abstraction-packed prose.

Janet Giltrow (1995) presents a number of rich examples to illustrate how and why the grammar of research genres uses heavy nominalization. This passage comes from a scholarly business journal:

> What appears increasingly clear is that educational attainment is not synonymous with skill requirements in the workplace, and that a single years-of-schooling measure cannot serve as an adequate proxy for the variety of working capacities required by an industrialised society.
>
> (Burgess, 1994: 31)

Nominalizations such as 'educational attainment' or 'skill requirements in the workplace' remove the agents and the verbs – the 'who did what to whom'. Giltrow suggests that these expressions eliminate the employers who hired and taught and the workers and students who learned or failed to learn. But they also provide high levels of abstraction that hold sections of the discussion together. Once introduced, these abstractions can be reinstated and used across the article to compress information and make it portable.

> Scholarly writers need a concentrated expression they can reinstate to bind together parts of their discussion and to control extensive stretches of lower-level information. These expressions are like elevated platforms from which the extent of the argument can be captured at a glance. There is not much standing-room on these platforms, so, when the arguments are complex, the expression can be complex.
>
> (Giltrow, 1995: 238)

Nonetheless, these viewing platforms or nominalizations, Giltrow suggests, are crucial because 'they compact a vast array of events and conditions, and hold them steady for scrutiny' (Giltrow 1995: 242). And they have rhetorical force as well as conceptual force. 'They engage readers' interests as Big Issues, matters of concern, and persuade them to pay attention' (p. 242). That is, they offer a way to connect the individual researcher's contribution to larger issues in a field of practice.

It would therefore be an extreme oversimplification to suggest that doctoral researchers should avoid nominalization, although they often get this kind of advice from websites and how-to manuals, for example:

Vague and wordy: orientations and explanations are important methods used by teachers in teaching writing
Better: teachers teach writing by orienting and explaining
Words like orientations and explanations are called nominalizations. Nominalizations are nouns made from verbs: orientation from orient, explanations from explain. In general, avoid excessive nominalization.

(Glatthorn, 1998: 117)

An excess of nominalization is to be avoided, certainly, as it can make writing stodgy and impenetrable. But nominalization itself is not a good or bad thing; it has important purposes in dissertation writing. Put another way, the absence of nominalization will make doctoral writing sound childish and immature, as it reduces the capacity to build up hierarchies of assumed knowledge in a text. Beverley Derewianka (1995) illustrates this dilemma by presenting excerpts from two argumentative texts. Text a is typical of the writing of children, with no nominalizations. Text b contains the same content, but is highly nominalized.

text a
We need our forests because plants can turn carbon dioxide into oxygen and if we didn't have oxygen we would die. People are worried that if the rainforest in Brazil is cut down the earth will not have enough oxygen to keep humans and animals alive.

text b
Our reliance on forest vegetation for its life sustaining capacity to generate oxygen through photosynthesis has led to concern that the destruction of the Brazilian rainforest will result in depleted supplies of oxygen.

(Derewianka, 1995: 31)

While text a spells out each concept and argument ('We need our forests'), text b takes for granted the fact that we need forests ('Our reliance on forest vegetation'). This creates a stepping-off point for building a sequence of cause and effect arguments and condensing meanings. Getting the balance right is one of the challenges writers face in using nominalization.

A considered use of nominalisation can give the impression that the writer is confidently aware of what could be assumed knowledge and what needs to be spelled out. If, however, nominalisation is overused, the reader will wonder whether in fact the writer really understands the concepts underlying the nominalisations or whether he or she is merely trying to impress. So a fine course needs to be steered between taking nothing for granted and taking too much for granted.

(Derewianka, 1995: 31)

Nominalizations, however, are not simply neutral terms. While they allow writers to condense a whole configuration of meanings, they can also have ideological effects, as the conversion of verbs into nouns has the effect of removing agency from a statement. The following nominalizations, gleaned by Giltrow (1995: 239–40) from a variety of journal articles, highlight the human action that has been removed.

> Immediate economic deprivation (being poor)
> Long-term potential for income inadequacy (worry about not having enough money later)
> Voluntary employee turnover (people quitting their jobs)
> Job satisfaction (how happy people are with their work).

We can illustrate how nominalization can be used to exclude or remove responsibility from participants in a text with a further example.

> The detonation of an atomic bomb in Hiroshima resulted in widespread mortality.

There are two nominalizations ('detonation', 'mortality') and their effect is to remove actions and actors. There are no identifiable people who either drop the bomb ('detonation') or who die ('widespread mortality'). These events just happen and who is doing what to whom remains implicit. We can make agents more explicit by unpacking the nominalization and re-inserting verb forms.

> When American planes *detonated* the atomic bomb in Hiroshima, thousands of Japanese civilians *died*.

In this less nominalized form, the ideological reasons for omitting agency and hence responsibility are made visible. We find packing and unpacking nominalizations an effective way to make doctoral writers conscious of the impact of nominalization in their writing. To illustrate, we first consider how increasing nominalization can lead to a more authoritative sounding text; and then, how unpacking nominalizations can make dense and sometimes impenetrable text more accessible.

Nominalization activity 1: making it more concise

Students who are unhappy with the maturity of their writing often consult the thesaurus and fill their texts with more complex vocabulary – bigger words. A more useful strategy is to turn 'speech-like' text into nominalized prose. This is because less developed writing is often under-nominalized. It is characterized by the patterns of 'speech' which contribute to a less forceful way of asserting opinion.

Barbara's work with Joshua illustrates how this pattern might be shifted. Joshua was writing about professional standards in management. The first step was to select a brief segment from his text, identify the verbs and break the text into clauses, assigning one verb to each clause.

> That *is* not *to say* that if you *are* highly qualified, then you *will be paid* a lot as there *has to be* demand for that profession.
> (1)   That *is* not *to say*
> (2)   that if you *are* highly qualified
> (3)   then you *will be paid* a lot
> (4)   as there *has to be* demand for that profession.

Having identified four clauses, Barbara looked at each clause to see if it was possible to change the verb into a noun form (e.g 'will be paid' into 'payment'). She discussed this strategy with Joshua and he produced the first revision.

> (1)   That *is* not *to say*
> (2–3) that a highly qualified person *will be highly paid*
> (4)   as there *has to be* demand for that profession.

Here he has reduced four verbs to three (hence the number of clauses) and created a new nominal group, 'a highly qualified person', to replace the more colloquial 'you'. As Joshua was unable to take the process further himself, Barbara modelled an even more nominalized version, which reduced the number of clauses to two and produced three nominalizations: 'high qualifications', 'high remuneration', 'appropriate demand'.

> (1)   That *is* not *to say*
> (2–4) that high qualifications *yield* high remuneration without the appropriate demand.

Joshua was pleased with this rewrite as it seemed to him 'more scholarly' and 'more impressive' than his original text. The exercise modelled a way of changing verb forms to nouns that could be built upon in subsequent writing.

A second example comes from Sheridan's writing on alternative models of teacher education. In this excerpt, she describes an integrated, team teaching approach in the university setting. Her supervisor highlighted the verb forms in the first draft.

> At the university, the courses *were staffed* by approximately nine faculty members who *came* from disparate discipline backgrounds (drama, dance, social studies, literacy and music). While this might at first *appear* as a logistic workload nightmare, in fact staff involved in the units *have noted* it *was* better sharing lesson preparation with other colleagues; that they

were continually *learning* more about themselves and their own teaching by teaching with colleagues and that they *felt* continually *supported* and in times of high stress *knew* fellow colleagues would step in to help. While many colleagues *embraced* the notion of sharing teaching, others *found* it difficult and *have worried* about the loss of their own discipline-specific content. This is indeed a cultural shift in the ways in which university educators *work* and there is a constant need *to keep* ongoing dialogue amongst staff *to establish* clear boundaries and expectations. (146 words, 17 verb groups)

The aim, then, was to reduce the number of verbs, and hence clauses, in order to produce a less verb-centred, more nominalized text. In this instance, the supervisor produced the rewrite and then spent time with Sheridan analysing the effects. Of particular interest was the way the text grew tighter and more definitive as the number the verb groups decreased from 17 to 9.

At the university, courses *are staffed* by approximately nine faculty members who *come* from disparate discipline backgrounds (drama, dance, social studies, literacy and music). While potentially a logistic workload nightmare, faculty actually *noted* two significant benefits of shared lesson preparation with colleagues; increased reflexivity about themselves and their teaching and on-tap collegial support in times of high stress. Not everyone, however, *embraced* the notion of shared teaching, and some *worried* about the loss of their own discipline-specific content. This *is* not surprising as the model *requires* a cultural shift in the ways university educators *work* and ongoing interdisciplinary dialogue *to establish* clear boundaries and expectations. (105 words, 9 verb groups)

The most extensive changes occur in the second sentence where three nominalizations are used to condense a great deal of information in a punchier and more concise way. Seven verb groups are reduced to one, and 65 words to 34 with dramatic effect.

While this might at first *appear* as a logistic workload nightmare, in fact staff involved in the units *have noted* it *was* better sharing lesson preparation with other colleagues; that they *were* continually *learning* more about themselves and their own teaching by teaching with colleagues and that they *felt* continually *supported* and in times of high stress *knew* fellow colleagues *would step in* to help.	While potentially a logistic workload nightmare, faculty actually *noted* two significant benefits of shared lesson preparation with colleagues; increased reflexivity about themselves and their teaching and on-tap collegial support in times of high stress.

The work achieved by the three nominalizations is made tangible by placing the two versions side by side. 'Two significant benefits of shared lesson preparation' replaces 'it was better sharing' to project a more definitive stance. 'Increased reflexivity' works a bit differently by inserting a complex conceptual tool to replace the simple verb form 'were learning'. And 'on-tap collegial support' uses a metaphor to enliven the prose at the same time as it replaces three verb groups: 'felt supported', 'knew' and 'would step in'.

This modelling is powerful for doctoral researchers. They can see and hear their writer's identity shift as the text shifts away from speech-like syntax. This kind of text work can help them learn to control the nominalization process, while achieving longer-term identity work. Supervisors can also reverse the strategy by making highly nominalized prose less dense.

Nominalization activity 2: making it more accessible

Nominalization, as we have argued, is not a good in itself. When used in excess, it can create inaccessible prose where meaning is obscured and/or ideological meanings are hidden. In this second activity, we use Calvin's work to illustrate how to help students unpack nominalized text and let it breathe a bit more.

Rather than condense meanings into fewer clauses with fewer verbs, the aim is to reverse the pattern. We try to insert verbs and actors, create more clauses and unpack the dense meanings around the noun so it is clearer who is doing what, when and why. This excerpt comes from a research methodology chapter where Calvin describes the method he devised to analyse websites designed by adolescent learners. These are referred to as multimodal and multimedia documents. Here Calvin discusses analytic questions developed by a well-known theorist of visual and multimodal literacies, Jay Lemke (2003). Verbs are put in bold type and nominalizations in italics.

> The above questions (Lemke 2003) **were designed to focus** my attention on *a variety of meaning types and functions during the analysis of multimodal semiotic artefacts*. The initial questions **applied** to nearly all media; some of the more advanced ones only in specialised cases. Not all meaning types **were** equally salient in all multimedia genres students designed. Most of these questions **were** relevant for my analytical purposes and research because they **were** specific and **described** some of the ways students' literacy practices **shifted and/or remained** unchanged through hypermedia design. They also **offered** *insights into the relationship between shifting or unchanged literacy practices in relation to understandings of adolescence, literacy and pedagogy*. But the questions above **were** also not entirely adequate for my research purposes. *Two additional tools for discourse analyses on multimodal documents* **were designed**: a Multimodal Semiotic Discourse Analysis (MSDA) and Hypermedia Traversal Analysis (HTA).

Calvin's supervisor focused on some of the nominalizations he uses: 'a variety of meaning types and functions during the analysis of multimodal semiotic artefacts'; 'insights into the relationship between shifting or unchanged literacy practices in relation to understandings of adolescence, literacy and pedagogy'. These are long and difficult phrases which raise many questions. What exactly is Calvin doing as an analyst? How is he using Lemke's work?

Calvin's supervisor asked him to talk about what these nominalizations meant – to unpack them. She asked him to describe how exactly he had used the questions for his own purposes. Their conversation was framed as part of the researcher's commitment to make method explicit and accessible for others to replicate and interrogate. Calvin left the supervisory session resolved to unpack the text and make his analytic labour more explicit. He rewrote at least five pages, but this revised extract gives a sense of the shift that occurred.

> At first, Lemke's (2003) questions **seemed** relevant for my analytical purposes and research because they **were** specific and **described** some of the visual aspects of students' design. However, they **did not help** me **to describe** the different kinds of meanings made in the multimodal documents themselves. I **needed** a specific metalanguage to adequately analyse the documents and then **decide** if shifts in students' literacy practices actually **occurred**. This **led** me to design two additional tools for discourse analyses on multimodal documents: a Multimodal Semiotic Discourse Analysis (MSDA) and Hypermedia Traversal Analysis (HTA).

While we might expect the process of unpacking nominalizations to result in a longer text, Calvin's revision is noticeably shorter and more concise. It is also more accessible. Importantly, he has not simply tried to rewrite each sentence or unpack each nominalization. Repetitive and confusing references to Lemke's questions have been cut out. And the focus has shifted to how Calvin used and remade the questions and why. This shift is made possible by inserting verbs ('help', 'describe', 'needed', 'led') and actors ('I', 'me') where there were none previously.

> they **did not help** me **to describe**
> I **needed** a specific metalanguage to adequately analyse
> This **led** me to design

The result is a much clearer statement of method – where the doctoral analyst is inserted and his actions and agency made visible. Theme analysis can further show why this less nominalized text works more effectively. And it is to this linguistic tool we turn now.

Theme

One of the difficult tasks in writing the dissertation is to say precisely what it is about: that is, to say what the 'thesis' (in the sense of the argument) is.

We suggested in Chapter 6 that doctoral researchers must guide the reader through the argument. They must keep the reader in mind, and provide signposting and headings, leading the way. Chapter headings and subheadings are an important way of doing this. They provide an overview of the argument. But the words or phrases that come at the beginning of each sentence are also important. They announce what is important and direct the reader's attention to the central ideas and relationships within the larger argument.

When doctoral writers are not sure exactly what they are saying and what they are not, or when they don't feel they have the authority to publicly commit to a particular point of view, the Thematic structure of their paragraphs may be really difficult for a reader to navigate. Central meanings can get buried and paragraphs can seem to be about everything or nothing.

Theme analysis is a tool that can help supervisors identify what meanings students make prominent and which they bury or ignore. It helps to pinpoint the problem when texts seem incoherent or unfocused. It allows close text work at the sentence level to help doctoral writers understand how information develops and flows. It is important to note before we go any further that the use of the capital letter *T* (*Theme* vs *theme*) here signals that we are using Theme quite differently from its everyday usage, where it means *topic* or *main idea*, as in 'the theme of my dissertation is industrial workplace relations'.

When we use Theme linguistically, we are talking about the starting point of the sentence or clause. It is what the clause is going to be about (Halliday and Matthiessen, 2004: 64). (It will be remembered from our earlier discussion of nominalization, that a clause is a stretch of language with a verb. A sentence will often have more than one verb and hence more than one clause.)

Martin and Rose (2003) discuss Theme by using the metaphor of a wave to capture the way in which information flows in a text. The sentence or clause is seen as a wave of information, in which there are peaks or crests, followed by troughs of lesser prominence. As they put it, 'the peak of prominence at the beginning of the clause is referred to as its Theme' (Martin and Rose, 2003: 177).

While these peaks (Thematic waves with a crest) occur at the sentence level, they also occur at the paragraph level. This is what many of us learned as the topic sentence. These are higher level Themes or hyperThemes which create a frame of reference to orient the reader to what is to come. They are predictive and 'establish expectations about how the text will unfold' (p. 181).

Moving beyond the clause and paragraph level to larger chunks of discourse are the tidal waves or macroThemes. These are headings and signpostings, which we identified and discussed in the example of Linda McDowell's chapter in Figure 6.4. Some of the phrases McDowell uses, such as 'In the next part of the chapter, I want to shift ...' or 'Before moving from the organisation to the body, however, I want to review …' provide invaluable guidance to the reader. These macroThemes foreground key information and put it first, as a starting point.

Here we turn our attention to Theme and how it operates at the sentence level.

Theme analysis

When we write, we make choices about the way words are ordered in the clause (even though this may not be a conscious choice). Linguistically, Theme comprises those words and phrases we put at the beginning of the clause, as in the following example.

> *Careful revision of each thesis chapter* increases the likelihood of a good result.

Here, 'Careful revision of each thesis chapter' is Theme. To identify Theme, we have highlighted those words that come before the verb 'increases'. The remainder of the message – all the other words in the clause including the verb – is called the Rheme (Halliday, 1985). Rheme generally contains unfamiliar or new information, 'since we typically depart from the familiar to head towards the unfamiliar' (Eggins, 2004: 300).

As writers and speakers of English, we have a choice about how we order Theme and Rheme. We can change Theme, in our example, by changing what we put first in the clause.

> *The likelihood of a good result* increases with careful revision of each thesis chapter.

Here, 'The likelihood of a good result' is Theme. The verb 'increases' and the remainder of the clause is Rheme. When we compare these two examples, we can see that their wording is similar. What has changed is Theme. And by changing Theme, we have created a different emphasis in meaning. In the first example, we emphasize textual work ('careful revision'), while in the second it is the purpose of textual work ('a good result') that is important.

So, when we want to do Theme analysis, we are looking for what comes first in the clause. This can help supervisors pinpoint why some doctoral writing seems to miss the point or wander about, or read less authoritatively than it might. When Barbara reads student drafts that seem disconnected or somehow incoherent, one of her first strategies is to look at how sentences begin. What does the writer put first? What meanings do they foreground? She takes her pencil and circles those words or phrases that come at the start of the clause – before the verb – in order to see if there is any pattern across sentences.

It is also possible to do a more formal analysis by dividing clauses into Theme and Rheme columns in order to make the pattern of Theme more visible. We can illustrate by using an extract from Mia's literature work, which we previously examined in Chapter 4. To do the analysis, we divide the clause at the verb, and put those words that come before the verb in Theme (this is a somewhat rough and simplified rule of thumb for our purposes here). The remainder of the clause we put in the Rheme column (see Table 7.1).

In our earlier discussion, we described Mia's review as overly descriptive and excluding her own point of view. Theme analysis shows us why. Almost every Theme in this text includes terms like 'scholars', 'many studies', 'majority of studies', 'observational studies', 'influential studies'. By taking Mia's text apart and separating out Theme, it is easier to see this pattern. While no doubt unintentional, Mia's use of Theme creates a pattern which foregrounds the authority of other scholars, rather than her own!

Her supervisor Andrew was able to use Theme analysis to pinpoint this problem. By dividing Mia's text into clauses, and then into Theme and Rheme, he could illustrate in a tangible way how Mia Thematized other scholars' work in

Table 7.1 Theme analysis: Mia's first draft

Theme	Rheme
Several scholars who have reviewed the the academic literature on homework (Hoover-Dempsey 1995; Coulter 1979)	suggest that the equivocal nature of the findings into effects of homework ...
Apart from the quantitative studies previously discussed, many studies	have used evidence from interviews with children, parents and teachers.
There has also been little research evidence derived from classrooms	which explores teachers' framing of homework or children's understandings of their tasks.
Further, the majority of studies	have concentrated on homework practices of adolescent secondary students.
Scholars who have reviewed the academic literature on homework (Hoover-Dempsey 1995)	have directed little research attention to primary school students' homework, with the exception of the role of parents in the development of child literacy.
Few observational studies	have examined the webs of social interaction between children and their parents, siblings, friends and schools within which homework is constructed (Coulter, 1979: 27).
A few influential studies	have looked at the family interactions around homework in diverse socio-cultural contexts (Breen *et al.* 1994; Freebody *et al.* 1995; Lareau, 1987) and will be discussed in a later section of this review.

every clause. Mia found this surprising. She had not realized the consistency of this pattern in her writing. With Andrew's help, she experimented with changing Theme and consequently made significant changes to what she put first in the clause. Mia's revised text shows a very different pattern of Theme (see Table 7.2).

Table 7.2 Theme analysis: Mia's second draft

Theme	Rheme
It seems, then, that despite a century of research, the equivocal nature of the findings	says more about the methodological challenges of researching this complex subject than about any definitive relationship between homework and achievement itself (Hoover-Dempsey, 1995; Coulter, 1979).
The qualitative research evidence to date	has relied heavily on interviews with children, parents and teachers, that is, on what people say they do.
There has been little attention	given to the practice of school homework as it occurs in the family context.
There has been little classroom-based research evidence	which explores teachers' framing of homework or children's understandings of their tasks.
Further, little research attention	has focused on primary school students' homework, with the exception of the role of parents in the development of child literacy.

The changes to Theme are striking. The repetition of phrases like 'little attention', 'little classroom-based research evidence' and 'little research attention' highlight gaps in the research. That is, they Thematize what is *not* being attended to by other scholars. More evaluative terms are also included in Theme ('despite', 'little', 'to date'). The result is a more authoritative, less descriptive stance to the research Mia reviews. The text now foregrounds a different set of meanings which build an argumentative or critical stance in the review – previously missing. By shifting Theme, Mia has been able to begin to stake out her territory and to make a claim for her work.

A second example comes from doctoral writer Carolina and illustrates a different kind of Theme analysis supervisors can initiate. This time the supervisor and student were separated geographically, so the Theme work was done long distance by making 'track changes' on Carolina's draft. The supervisor used her knowledge of Theme to show how changing what came first in the clause could make Carolina's writing more focused. This extract comes from the first chapter of Carolina's dissertation where she aims to define key concepts used in her study.

1.4.2 Continuing Professional Development

~~According to Fullan (1988: 326)~~ ~~c~~Continuing professional development of teachers is the sum total of formal and informal learning experiences throughout teachers' careers from pre-service teacher education to retirement (Fullan (1988: 326). ~~Guskey and Huberman (1995: 257) view continuing professional development as~~ It is continuous learning and as such not an add-on. ~~They maintain that c~~Continuing professional development encompasses the essence of teaching and learning to teach better. (Guskey and Huberman 1995: 257)

Continuing professional development, as explained by Bolan (~~date quoted by~~ ~~in~~ Stoll and Fink 1995: 155) is an on-going process which builds upon initial teacher education and training, begins with education into teaching, includes in-service training, staff development and management development, and ends with preparation for retirement. ~~They maintain that w~~Within such a framework, education, training and support activities are offered for the purpose of helping educators and principals add to their professional knowledge, improve their professional skills, and clarify their professional values.

Like Mia, Carolina puts the names of other scholars first (Fullan, Guskey and Huberman, 'They') in the familiar 'he says, she says' format. What her supervisor does is to cross out and remove these researchers from Theme position. This text work demonstrates how Carolina can shift the focus back to her own key concepts ('continuing professional development' and 'continuous learning'). The track changes make the alternative pattern of Theme tangible.

With explanation and discussion, supervisors can guide students to look for patterns in Theme in their dissertations and try alternatives. In this way, Theme analysis becomes a useful pedagogical tool for understanding the method of text development and for producing more authoritative, focused writing.

The impact of Theme on genre and cohesion

Theme also has a strong influence on the genre of a text and its overall coherence. We can illustrate this through the simple example of a recount genre. In Chapter 6 we suggested that recount needed to be subservient to argument, not vice versa. Theme analysis can help supervisors work with students to move away from excessive or inappropriate use of recount and description.

The example of a recount genre is given in Table 7.3 where the writer discusses a trip to Bali.

The items in Theme include the people (*we*) and the time when events occur (*last weekend, Saturday morning, Saturday night*). The pattern is typical of the recount genre because its purpose is to reconstruct a sequence of experiences and events over time. People and time are therefore put first to foreground these

Table 7.3 Analysis of a recount genre

Theme	Rheme
Last weekend we	went to Bali.
We	visited Denpasar
and we	stayed in a luxurious hotel.
On Saturday morning, we	went snorkelling, swimming and surfing.
On Saturday night, we	saw Balinese puppets and dancing.

Table 7.4 Changing the pattern of Theme

Theme	Rheme
A trip to Bali	is everyone's dream.
Denpasar	is waiting for you.
World class luxury hotels	are at your fingertips in this tropical paradise.
Snorkelling and swimming	will delight your senses.
See Balinese puppets and dancing	to enjoy the rich culture of the island.

meanings. But if we wanted to write a different genre, such as a travel brochure where the purpose is to sell Bali, we would need to change the pattern of Theme, as we have done in Table 7.4.

This brochure genre includes similar meanings to the recount, but drastically changes what comes first in the clause. Places, activities and events ('Bali', 'Denpasar', 'luxury hotels', 'snorkelling', 'swimming', 'Balinese puppets and dancing') now appear in Theme. By shifting the pattern of Theme, we have changed the text from one genre (recount) to another (brochure).

The same process can occur with doctoral writing. A doctoral dissertation is made of multiple genres (as we discussed in Chapter 6). But, as we have said, argument is the dominant genre. A dissertation has a thesis which is carefully argued and substantiated. It is an enormous challenge for doctoral writers to sustain an argumentative stance over a vast expanse of text divided into chapters and subsections. And they often revert to other genres, not because these are appropriate, but because it feels safer to do so. We saw this operating with Mia's literature work.

Mia's first draft was written as description, rather than argument. By consistently placing other scholars in Theme, she wrote descriptively and without authority. By shifting Theme, she began to foreground her own opinion. Theme work with her supervisor helped her shift the genre from description to argument. It helped her take up an evaluative stance towards her field of knowledge production. The point we wish to emphasize, is that as Theme shifted, so too did the genre. This is why her revised text (which becomes more like an argument) speaks with greater authority and creates a space for Mia's contribution.

As well as influencing genre, Theme also has a profound influence on the coherence of a text. As Eggins argues:

> The most striking contribution of Thematic choices is to the internal cohesion of the text: skilful use of Thematic selection results in a text which appears to 'hang together and make sense'.
>
> (Eggins, 2004: 321)

Eggins discusses three kinds of Theme strategies that writers use to achieve coherence: repetition, zigzag patterning and a multiple Rheme patterning (see Eggins, 2004: 324–5). We won't explore these methods in detail here but we do want to draw attention to the value of a focus on repetition and zigzag patterning in doctoral writing.

Repetition

Mia's revised text illustrates how repetition can be used effectively to create cohesion. The repetition of 'research evidence', 'little' and 'attention' in Theme provides unity and a clear focus to her argument:

> The qualitative research evidence to date
> There has been little attention
> There has been little classroom-based research evidence
> Further, little research attention

Repetition is a common strategy used in doctoral writing. A text with little or no repetition will seem disconnected. However, a text in which Theme never varies, will not only be boring to read or listen to, but indicates a text that is going nowhere.

> If Theme is our point of departure, constancy of Theme would mean we are always leaving from the same spot, and that the 'new' information introduced in the Rhemes would not be being followed up.
>
> (Eggins, 2004: 324)

This idea helps us understand why Calvin's text, which we looked at in our earlier discussion of nominalization, did not work as effectively as it might. Calvin used a repetition strategy in his first draft, as the Theme analysis in Table 7.5 shows. However, his use of repetition is not as effective as Mia's.

Here we see the term 'questions' repeated frequently in Theme position. This repetition creates some coherence, but it does not take the discussion of method forward. Calvin also uses a variety of adjectives to describe these 'questions' ('above', 'initial', 'some of the more advanced', 'most of these', 'above') and these descriptors actually confuse the reader. What's the difference, for example,

Table 7.5 Theme analysis: Calvin's first draft

Theme	Rheme
The above questions (Lemke 2003)	were designed to focus my attention on a variety of meaning types and functions during the analysis of multimodal semiotic artefacts.
The initial questions	applied to nearly all media;
some of the more advanced ones	[applied] only in specialised cases.
Not all meaning types	were equally salient in all multimedia genres students designed.
Most of these questions	were relevant for my analytical purposes and research
because they	were specific and described some of the ways students' literacy practices shifted and/or remained unchanged through hypermedia design.
They also	offered insights into the relationship between shifting or unchanged literacy practices in relation to understandings of adolescence, literacy and pedagogy.
But the questions above	were also not entirely adequate for my research purposes.

between the 'initial questions' and the 'more advanced ones'? Which questions were 'relevant' and which were 'not entirely adequate'? And more importantly, how was Calvin as researcher *using* these questions?

After the joint analysis with his supervisor, Calvin tried to put himself back into the text by unpacking nominalizations. But in the process of this rewriting, he also changed the pattern of Theme (see Table 7.6). As he clarified how he used Lemke's questions, he also changed what came first in the clause. And, shifting Theme also shifted the genre from description to explanation.

Calvin now foregrounds his judgment of Lemke's work and then goes on to show how this shaped his own work as a researcher. Rather than discussing the more abstract notion of research questions, Calvin is now talking about researchers and has assumed an agential position through the explanation genre.

The changes to Theme are subtle, but create an important shift in emphasis. Lemke's questions appear in Theme position in the first three clauses, but an evaluative stance is introduced through the conjunctions 'because' and 'however'. These help to change the genre from description to explanation. In the fourth and fifth clauses, Theme shifts to the researcher ('I', 'me'), so Calvin's reasoning for creating new analytic tools is now foregrounded. This new pattern in Theme works less descriptively and more cohesively to show why the analysis has been conducted in a particular way. It also suggests how supervisors can use

Table 7.6 Theme analysis: Calvin's second draft

Theme	Rheme
At first, Lemke's (2003) questions	seemed relevant for my analytical purposes and research.
because they	were specific and described some of the visual aspects of students' design.
However, they	did not help me to describe the different kinds of meanings made in the multimodal documents themselves.
I	needed a specific metalanguage to adequately analyse the documents and then decide if shifts in students' literacy practices actually occurred.
This led me	to design two additional tools for discourse analyses on multimodal documents: a Multimodal Semiotic Discourse Analysis (MSDA) and Hypermedia Traversal Analysis (HTA).

Theme work with doctoral researchers to make their writing sharper and more authoritative.

It is not always easy for doctoral writers to exploit Theme/Rheme structure as an organizational tool or to use it to build their arguments from clause to clause (Schleppegrell, 2004: 104). A better understanding of what Eggins (2004) calls a zigzag patterning is useful in this regard.

Zigzag patterning

The zigzag pattern achieves cohesion in a text by building on newly introduced information. This gives a text the sense of cumulative development which may be absent in the repeated Theme pattern (Eggins, 2004: 325).

In linguistic terms, this means that an element which is introduced in Rheme, becomes the Theme of the following clause. An excerpt from doctoral researcher Jennifer's writing illustrates this strategy for structuring information. Jennifer's dissertation examines migrant women's experiences with the law in Australia. In Table 7.7 she explores the viewpoint of a legal professional, who is commenting on the workplace discrimination case of one migrant woman, Serena. The Rheme and corresponding Theme have been placed in italics and connected with an arrow.

In this zigzag patterning, the information Jennifer introduces in Rheme, is taken up and expanded in Theme in the following clause. We find at least two clear examples of this tactic. First she draws on the Rheme 'examples of power play used against the more vulnerable party' and uses it as the point of departure in Theme of the next clause, 'such bullying behaviour'. That is, she further develops the notion of power play by naming it as bullying. This happens again in the

Table 7.7 Zigzag patterning in Theme

Theme	Rheme
Even with the assistance of an experienced lawyer, migrant women	may find themselves unequally positioned in the legal process.
The harassing behaviour of the barrister in Serena's case and the delaying tactics of the CSIRO	were *definite examples of power play used against the more vulnerable party.*
Such bullying behaviour	has no place inside the courtroom and should be reported to the Law Institute.
While the use of 'vigorous' cross-examination experienced by Serena at the Equal Opportunities Commission	is an *important feature of the adversarial system,*
nevertheless, *aggressive, adversarial court* tactics	may be more appropriate to proceedings in the criminal courtroom than in civil cases such as Serena's.

fourth clause, where she introduces the 'adversarial system' in Rheme and then picks it up again in the following Theme, 'aggressive, adversarial court tactics'. The effect is to create a text that moves forward and is cohesive.

One further feature of Jennifer's Theme is worth noting, in particular the way she uses nominalizations in Theme position:

> the assistance of an experienced lawyer
> The harassing behaviour of the barrister
> the delaying tactics of the CSIRO
> the use of 'vigorous' cross-examination
> aggressive, adversarial court tactics

These nominalizations compress information. So for example, instead of writing 'the experienced lawyer provided assistance', the verb 'provided' has been deleted. This changes a simple noun, 'experienced lawyer', into a more complex entity or nominalization: 'the assistance of an experienced lawyer'.

The move from presenting a new idea in Rheme to re-presenting similar information in a succeeding Theme, often involves nominalization (Schleppegrell, 2004). Jennifer uses nominalizations to build argument, by increasingly repackaging and re-presenting information in a nominalized form. Her use of nominalized, condensed structures in Theme works together with conjunctions, such as 'nevertheless', to mark the structure of the argument genre and build an authoritative stance.

In academic texts, the author is challenged to progressively build an argument, summarizing and recapitulating prior discourse as each clause expands the discussion. For this purpose, the academic texts use nominalizations that condense given information as the point of departure so that further comment can be made. Information from the rheme of one clause occurs again as the theme in the following clause, contributing to the density of academic texts and to the kind of organization which is often described as more complex.

(Schleppegrell, 2004: 71)

Theme analysis can thus be an extremely useful addition to the supervisor's pedagogical toolkit. It can help supervisors make the flow of information in doctoral writing more visible. We have seen that Theme patterns are strongly influenced by genre. They are also influenced by whether the language is written or spoken. In face-to-face conversation, our point of departure or Theme is most often ourselves or those connected with us. In academic or scholarly writing, abstractions and generalizations about people, situations and causes are more likely to be Theme, rather than our own experience (Eggins, 2004: 323).

If the personal pronoun 'I' is placed too often in Theme position, it alerts supervisors that student writing is following the pattern of speech. The text can give the impression that it is all personal assertion and too little argument, as we saw in our discussion of writer stance in Chapter 5. As we have seen, it is possible to remove the 'I' altogether from Theme (as in 'I believe capital punishment is inhumane') and still assert the writer's opinion (as in, 'Capital punishment is inhumane').

While conversations can have rapid shifts in Theme because of their dynamic and unplanned nature, sudden shifts work less successfully in writing. They disrupt coherence and confuse the reader. As the text becomes hard to follow, the reader may suddenly have a million questions: Why did the focus shift so suddenly? What's the point?

There are great benefits in supervisors using Theme analysis as a tool for engaging students in discussions of text organization and coherence. There is no formula for what comes first in a clause, but there are tangible effects on the genre of a text, its coherence and its method of development. Getting doctoral researchers to experiment with Theme makes them more conscious of available choices. The capacity to make choices places them in a more authoritative position as writers.

Chapter 8

Crafting a writerly text

Is it important to make the dissertation *interesting* – as well as scholarly? *Interesting* is a vague notion, but for us it involves helping doctoral writers move away from 'stodgy prose', which we characterize as soporific slabs of writing, formulaic, over signposted, bristling with brackets, crabbed and turgid, generally just a very dull read.

Most enervating dissertations pass. Their authors have conducted a thorough study and can demonstrate a clear contribution to the field. But we see no reason why dissertations should be written as graceless and intractable tomes. We see no reason to assume that lively and stimulating scholarly writing is somehow 'dumbed down': we differentiate between the platitudes about parsimonious 'plain English' and the case for distinctive and invigorating composition. There is also no reason why the scholarly requirement to interrogate complex ideas and to use precise terminology should equate with eye-watering ennui.

But we are aware that *interesting* is a potentially dangerous aim. Attempting to write a social science dissertation as a commercially published book is difficult. The two are different genres, and the aim of the dissertation must be to do enough of what is required to get the magic doctoral 'pass'. This means the final text will rarely be attractive to big publishers who generally avoid any texts resembling a thesis.

Interesting can also mean pushing at the edges of the thesis genre. Students have arrived at our doors clutching texts constructed with columns, extended footnotes, poetic forms and multiple media. With great enthusiasm, they declare their intention to be transgressive and disrupt the dissertation format. While we understand their desire to produce something akin to a novel, an art form, or a hypertext, we find their enthusiasm is rarely matched by a focus on substantive issues of content – the purpose of their research. Sometimes, we confess, we have also held suspicions that at least some of these enthusiasts lack the artistic capabilities to implement their ideas.

There *are* logical reasons for students wanting to do something different. If they have ambitions to be in the academy, they have to establish themselves via their dissertation and associated work as 'clever'. In the academic promotion economy everyone wants some kind of distinction (Bourdieu, 1984, 1988). There is such fierce competition for academic positions that standing out in the crowd means not only demonstrating a wide range of generic skills, but showing considerable flair, creativity and imagination.

We do not intend to discuss the rationale for alternative and artistic texts in this chapter (see Denzin, 1997, 2003). Nor will we give extended examples of such texts, although we do focus on alternative dissertation forms in the conclusion to the chapter. We do, however, want to devote space to the production of writerly prose and some of the dilemmas that arise when doctoral researchers choose to move beyond writing 'the big book' dissertation.

We begin with a discussion of engaging writing, move on to examine some finer points of textual polishing, data representation and the aesthetics of the page and then conclude by considering the question of the transgressive.

Writerly prose

It was Roland Barthes (1970) who argued that there are two basic kinds of texts, readerly and writerly. He suggested that *readerly* texts cast the reader as a consumer of writing that is already fixed and finished, static and straightforward. A readerly text appears to be 'transparent', seeking 'to conceal all traces of itself as a factory within which a particular social reality is produced' (Barthes, 1970: 244). The reader has no role other than to ingest what meanings have already been determined by the author. Barthes wrote that being bored by a text occurs because 'one cannot produce the text, play it, release it, make it go' (Barthes, 1986: 63).

In stark contrast, *writerly* texts require the reader to become a producer of meaning. A writerly text is open, available for infinite play, invitational and unstable. Writerly texts 'exhume … cultural voices or codes', 'discover multiplicity instead of consistency' and 'signify flux instead of stable meanings' (Barthes, 1970: 246). The reader's role is to provide their own meaning of the text through conversation with the author's words, in other words, to rewrite the text for themselves. Barthes argued that the writerly text is superior since it allowed readers – as writers – to become co-producers of meaning.

Poststructuralist scholars have both lauded and challenged the apparent binary that Barthes constructed. For example, Derrida (1976; 1978) reasoned that writerly texts are an impossibility: all readers create meaning as they respond to the text in order to 'translate' it into their context and discourse. He famously encouraged writer-readers to *vive la différance*, proposing that the meanings of language cannot be pinned down and fixed like butterflies on a board. Words and texts, he suggested, are subject to infinite interpretation.

Following Derrida's proposition, we can say that all texts are inevitably writerly. Margaret Atwood, the Canadian writer, drawing on Barthes, explains it this way:

> The printed text of a book is thus like a musical score, which is not itself music, but becomes music when played by musicians, or 'interpreted' by them, as we say. The act of reading a text is like playing music and listening to it at the same time, and the reader becomes his own interpreter.
>
> (Atwood, 2003: 44)

Following Derrida and Atwood, we take writerly and readerly, not as an either-or option, but as a combination integral to the vast majority of texts (the reading of Barthes that we favour). We recognize that some texts, such as hypertext, are structured to be writerly. They overtly set out to provide multiple pathways through which readers can find their own narratives and pleasures. But the dissertation genre we are discussing is a combination of both. What is at stake, we propose, in the dissertation and in other scholarly writing, is the question of emphasis and balance between the two.[9]

Dissertations are structured to be more readerly, in Barthes's terms. They attempt to steer the reader through a linear set of moves towards a narrative closure. They start with a proposition, a problem, a case, then go on to address or 'solve' it. They seek to avoid ambiguity. They give explicit guidance to the reader about what to expect and what to remember. In a well-constructed dissertation, a reader is led logically through a series of moves (see Chapter 6) to the conclusion. Indeed, we have argued in this book for supervision to foreground this kind of structural readerly-ness.

But in working to clarify arguments, students can sometimes lose sight of the need for deliberate writerly-ness. The lifeless, rigid prose written to pre-set textual defaults and bemoaned by our colleagues, is aptly dubbed readerly, rather than writerly, since it is profoundly unfriendly. Such tedious texts contain few invitations for readers to play with meanings, to imagine, to interpret. They are simply not writerly enough to be a good read.

But the antidote to soporific doctoral writing is neither an excess of florid fancies, nor the abandonment of a readerly structure. It *is* the acquisition of a more writerly stance.

Developing a writerly stance

Our premise is that doctoral writing can be writerly, even when texts do not consist of obvious multiple entrances, pathways and exits. What is required, we suggest, is that doctoral writers: (1) focus on audience, that is, their supervisors, examiners and potential others online and in the library, (2) hone their own writerly appreciation, and (3) experiment with writing.

Thinking about audience

Doctoral researchers can assume that their audience consists of experts who do not need a detailed account of basic characteristics of their field. What they do need is an economical mapping of the field of knowledge production and the production of a concise warrant for the research (see Chapters 3 and 4). We now want to argue that additional assumptions need to be made about their audience.

They have limited time. Doctoral students do not like to hear that their supervisors are busy people. But it is true. As often as not, supervisors read doctoral writing in fits and starts, on screens in between email, in trains going to meetings, in an hour here and there between appointments. In contemporary academic life it is a luxury to get clear time to devote to reading. It takes a long time to read and respond to a chapter, let alone 100,000 words in draft.

Doctoral researchers are even more reluctant to hear that examiners are in a similar situation. While it is common for doctoral examiners to devote large slabs of time to the task of textual interrogation, it takes upwards of a week to read complex pieces of research. What's more, supervisors and examiners have read on this topic before. What they are looking for in a doctoral text are the features that distinguish a particular piece of work from others. They are looking not simply for coverage and rigour, but also for apt phrases, innovative ideas, and elegant prose.

We suggest that students might imagine their work being examined by Foucault who wrote about his loathing for dead prose.

> I can't help but dream about a kind of criticism that would try not to judge but to bring an oeuvre, a book, a sentence, an idea to life: it would light fires, watch the grass grow, listen to the wind, and catch the sea foam in the breeze and scatter it. It would multiply not judgments but signs of existence; it would summon them, drag them from their sleep. Perhaps it would invent them sometimes – all the better. All the better. Criticism that hands down sentences sends me to sleep; I'd like a criticism of scintillating leaps of the imagination. It would not be sovereign or dressed in red. It would bear the lightning of possible storms.
>
> (Foucault, 1994: 323)

It is obviously beneficial if examiners are kept interested and stimulated as well as informed by their reading. The need to argue carefully and logically does not require writers, as Foucault suggests, to simply 'hand down' soporific sentences. If writing to 'bear the lightning of possible storms' is somewhat daunting, students *can* be encouraged to write more engagingly by thinking about writing as a craft.

Reading like a writer: reading for craft

Fortunately, one of the requirements of doctoral research is the necessity to read widely and deeply. Through this reading, doctoral researchers are exposed to a range of texts written in different styles and tones and with various degrees of proficiency and panache. But unless they are directed to read 'for writing', it is likely that students will only focus on the actual content, not its composition. It is therefore important for supervisors to ask doctoral writers to think about the choices other writers have made in order to make their texts writerly.

This means in the first instance recognizing the malleability of language and its constructed nature. As Game and Metcalfe (1996: 109) explain, *everything* about writing is deliberately fabricated:

Writing is a form of travel across the space of the page. A key feature of conventional writing is its linearity. One word comes after another, just as one step comes after another. Readers follow the inkily authorised route of a book and progress from left to right, from top to bottom, and ideally from the first numbered page to the last.

This linearity is of profound significance, because neither experience nor contemplative thought comes naturally in linear form. Contemplation and experience may have no beginning point and no orderly sequence: they can involve simultaneities unavailable on the written line and much more complex patterns of interconnection. Writing, then, is not the report of thought, but the production of a specific type of thought and a specific account of life, distinct from the possibilities offered by painting, dance or speech … It is important not to lose sight of linearity's artifice and cultural specificity. And if this writing is nothing but an invention, a concoction, an illusion, then the choices made in its creation can be located and examined.

We like to ask our doctoral researchers to spend time considering the craft aspects of the texts they use. We suggest that they select a passage which epitomizes the quality of the writing that they find difficult or admire, and then analyse it. We have in mind Bakhtin's (1981) reminder that all writing mobilizes voices from other texts. We hope that by establishing close encounters with well-written texts which students select and admire, they will take these voices into their own writing practices, and make them their own, as they literally rewrite their reading.

It is sometimes helpful to provide structured guidance. We encourage our doctoral researchers to consider a range of technical matters such as sentence construction, syntax and paragraphing. We ask them to think about what kind of opening and closing paragraph sentences are used and whether these adequately sum up what is to come, or has gone before. We suggest that they consider the effort made to tempt the reader into reading the whole passage carefully, and how this is accomplished.

We like to use examples where there are dramatic shifts in sentences to draw attention to the ways in which length and syntax work together. This example is taken from the writings of Zygmunt Bauman (1998: 22).

Ours is a consumer society.

We all know, more or less, what it means to be a consumer. A consumer is a person who consumes, and to be a consumer means using things up: eating them, wearing them, playing with them and otherwise causing them to satisfy one's needs or desires. Since in our part of the world it is money which in most cases 'mediates' between desire and satisfaction, being a consumer also means – normally means – appropriating most of the things destined to be consumed: buying them, paying for them and so making them one's exclusive property, barring everybody else from using them without one's permission.

The first sentence consists of only 5 words, the second of 13, the third of 33 and the final sentence 56. Bauman repeats the same pattern of sentences in his next paragraph:

> To consume also means to destroy. In the course of consumption, the consumed things cease to exist, literally or spiritually. Either they are 'used up' physically to the point of complete annihilation, such as when things are eaten or worn out, or they are stripped of their allure, no longer arouse and attract desire, and forfeit their capacity to satisfy one's needs and wishes – for example, an overused toy or an overplayed record – and so become unfit for consumption.

Here there are only three sentences of 6, 14, and 60 words. We can see that Bauman uses this structure to support a layering of meaning: each sentence is not only longer, but also builds on the previous one. He is literally piling on explanation and example, using short phrases punctuated by commas, colons and dashes: these make clarifications and add emphases. The result is a rhetoric that is both confronting and vivid. This text can be easily read aloud, using Bauman's phrasing. The reader is thus free to focus on the meanings by summoning up other similar or counter examples, connecting the argument to other texts and events, perhaps recalling her view and experiences of consumption and her own worn out toys and overplayed records.

We also think it is important to focus on aesthetic textual features. We ask doctoral researchers to consider how adjectives and adverbs are used to enliven the prose, to consider how 'thick' is the description (Geertz, 1973: Ch. 1).

We also ask them *not* to gloss over what appears to be straightforward writing, but to understand the craft of simplicity and economical detail. This example comes from Ruth Behar (1996) an anthropologist. She is setting the scene for a narrative which discusses race, religion and gender in relation to women's health.

> It is October of 1992, five months after Marta's hysterectomy. With some hesitation I have asked Marta if I can write about her operation for a conference on women's health. I fear that treating her as an anthropological subject will hurt our friendship, but Marta immediately agrees to let me write about her. She considers it an honor, she says, that I am interested.
>
> We sit on her bed with the white lace coverlet. A mirror is behind Marta and I try not to look at my own face as I look at her. Little Eddy is in the living room playing with David, who has accompanied me on this trip because I don't like to drive to Detroit alone. The tape recorder is on the bed and I hold up the microphone toward Marta. We don't know that the tape recorder is not recording anything: only later, when I get home, will I learn that David forgot to put the batteries in the microphone.
>
> On three sheets of lined loose-leaf paper, Marta has begun to write her life story in a few broad strokes. I read her hand-written words and notice how

careful she has been to leave out anything painful; but her sense of solitude is profound and it surfaces, unwillingly, several times in her brief text, which ends in mid-sentence, with the words, 'I have tried not to be an abnegated wife, but a ...'. She has held within herself all the pain of social and cultural displacement, all the tensions of her rite of passage from virgin to wife, and all the anxieties of losing her womb so soon after becoming a mother.

(Behar, 1996: 95)

Instead of simply writing 'I interviewed Marta about her hysterectomy', Behar gives us a word picture of the interview itself. In the first paragraph we find the date on which the interview occurred, the time elapsed since the hysterectomy and a report of gaining informed consent. These details are descriptive, but they also help to establish the veracity of the account. They create a picture of the interview as a research event which occurs between two people in which negotiation and relationship building or breaking can occur.

In the second paragraph we are told the colour of the coverlet on Marta's bed and we see the researcher, Ruth, viewing herself in the mirror, as she struggles to maintain focus on Marta. This is, of course, a wonderful metaphor for the whole research process itself, in which the researcher strives *not* to let her own desires and views dominate. We also learn about the fallibility of the research process. And, without labouring the point, Behar lets us know that she too is a woman who shares some commonalities with her subject.

In the final paragraph Behar offers us three sheets of handwritten paper and we are invited through this small, detailed image to consider the practicalities of putting a life on paper, the option of reading between the offered lines, the ethical dimensions of how the researcher must respond to what she is given in text, and what she can see besides.

This is description not for its own sake, but carefully worked details which say much more than what is on the surface. This text is writerly: it invites the reader to make connections with broader ontological and methodological issues through an eloquent snapshot.

We ask doctoral researchers to find examples in their own work of partial and sparse accounts which do little to help the reader build their own mental picture. We suggest they experiment with the use of metaphor, simile, alliteration and assonance – not for its own sake, but as a means of embroidering possible meanings and fostering an understanding of craft from the 'inside-out'. This strategy goes hand in hand with the next.

Experimenting with writing: practising the craft

Writing is not simply difficult, nor transparent, nor 'work'. It is all these things, but it is also a practice in which technical skills and aesthetic judgments are combined. The production of good doctoral writing depends on having the time, patience, and commitment to practise how to become a better doctoral writer.

As Rose and McClafferty (2003: 29) put it:

> Writing is something you can work on. In very specific ways you can move parts of a sentence around; you can try addressing the reader more directly; you can talk about and try out some of the stylistic things a peer does that appeal to you. ... Writing is craftwork.

To take this seriously means making the space for doctoral researchers to experiment with writing, at the same time that they take methods courses, undertake fieldwork, and engage with the relevant field of knowledge production.

There is no set formula for this, but we think that conversations about writing as an embodied activity can be one place to start. Both of us prefer to work at home and often intersperse writing with housework, which provides space for reflection. We work best in the morning, although we can both work through to the mid-afternoon when the pressure is really on. Both of us have a dictionary and a thesaurus on the table beside the computer, and use them frequently when the same verbs and nouns appear too frequently. We have both separately established this routine for writing, but we do not impose this particularity on our students. Rather, in talking about our own practices, we encourage our students to make explicit how they create a regular time-space-rhythm for writing.

We also set practice exercises for our doctoral writers. Some are able to discipline themselves sufficiently to experiment with different approaches to writing. Others are not. Here we find it is helpful to ask them to go back to questions of nominalization, Theme, and sentence and paragraph construction to deconstruct their own writing. Reworkings of a text in which they vary different elements such as first or third person, passive or active voice, or different orders of moves, can also be helpful.

There is also some mileage in 'cloning the form' of particular admired writers. This requires doctoral writers to analyse the syntactic strategies and language choices of the accomplished and published, and then attempt to reproduce them. But – a caveat here. We have also seen and read some very desperate simulations of high French theory: these are to be avoided at all costs by all but the linguistically accomplished!

We have used our reading groups to create opportunities for reading aloud. We find that it is often very helpful to ask doctoral researchers to read their work aloud – to themselves and to peer postgraduates. Rose and McClafferty (2003: 29) argue that this is an important step in learning to improve the craft of writing, and we agree.

> Reading one's prose animates what is too often a dry, unengaged production and use of text. You hear your writing. And others hear, as well as read it, too.

Hearing the words, distanced on the page, adopting the stance of a reader, allows doctoral writers a different position from which to self-critique. It can help them craft the 'flow of a text', one of the hardest aspects of a text to judge. Reading aloud, for example, makes it clear that the choreography of an argument is neither set to a funereal dirge, nor to a frenetic reel. Dissertation writing must develop a tempo which moves the reader at a regular and pleasing pace through the various points and counterpoints. It is this flow which makes the doctoral argument not only logical, but a good read, and where students can benefit from sharing their work with others.

Throughout this book we have suggested a number of deconstructive tools that can be used in supervision pedagogies. Some of these involve the supervisor and student in cooperative textual analysis. We also suggest that this dialogic approach be continued into joint editing practice. Rather than take a student's work away to make comments, it can be productive for supervisors to combine a responsive reading with cooperative editing. In the first instance, supervisors might talk through the text, pointing out the spots where changes could be made. However, this is not as powerful as supervisor and students working on a set of questions to be asked of a text, as the means to structure a collaborative editing conversation.

We also think it is useful to play with words. In the age of digital articles, the titles and abstracts of academic writing have become even more important. We encourage doctoral researchers to experiment with wordplay: skilful mobilizations of the pun, insertions of a clever double entendre, artful references to seminal texts, the humorous use and abuse of film, book and song titles; the quotable categorization. While none of this is necessary for competent doctoral scholarship, verbal quickstep can, if well executed, lead to work being memorable – and the scholar being remembered. Forming a distinctive writing style is part and parcel of the production of scholarly identity, and supervisors can help by simply spending a little time playing with their words.

We thus establish an ongoing conversation about the purpose of good writing. The real work of writing is not simply getting the ideas down. It is making the text live and sing. It is making an engaging and pleasurable reader-friendly text. As we have suggested in Chapter 6, signposting is part of this process. A dissertation will not by definition be lively if the reader is continually looking around to see where they are up to. The purpose of good doctoral writing is to make the concepts, findings and arguments potent and convincing. A dissertation is not a cemetery of dead ideas!

And complex writing need not use obfuscatory syntax. Difficult ideas and precise language can still be presented in nimble and striking prose. One way to address this challenge is to help doctoral writers find a balance of active and passive voice in their text when they are polishing their writing.

Balancing active and passive voice

Much academic writing is characterized by the use of the passive voice. The passive voice converts the object of the action into the subject of the sentence. The one who is performing the action is not the subject and so disappears from view. If the passive voice carries on regardless, page after page after page, it *can* be tedious to read. It can also create long, over-complicated and awkward sentences that trip the reader up.

Most of the online writing workshops[10] and the academic writing advice books we have seen contain sensible examples of the kinds of passive voice constructions that, when used continually, make for a uniform dullness. The very worst of the writing tips suggests that doctoral writers should avoid the use of the passive voice. While this counters an apparent tacit rule that 'scientific' writing must use the passive voice, we think that this is equally silly advice. The passive voice *is* important in presenting research findings and in conducting discussions – as is the active voice. We suggest that both are required in doctoral writing.

Some decisions about the use of active and passive voice relate to how the writer carries the argument forward. Take for example, these three sentences in which a writer on men's health has chosen to put the issue he is discussing, 'the economics of the family', at the beginning of a short sentence, using the passive voice. This draws the reader's attention at the outset to the topic discussed in the paragraph.

> The economics of the family are adversely affected by male health problems. Illness among men often diminishes work productivity. When men become disabled or die, family income is usually reduced, often in the face of additional health care expenses.
>
> (Bonhomme, 2004: 145)

The first sentence, written in the passive, could be changed to the active voice to make it more powerful.

> *Male health problems* adversely affect the economics of the family. *Illness among men* often diminishes work productivity. When men become disabled or die, family income is usually reduced, often in the face of additional health care expenses.

If we apply our linguistic lens from Chapter 7, we can see that changing from active to passive voice has also changed the Theme of the sentence from 'The economics of the family' to 'Male health problems'. But this shift also creates a new problem of coherence. The first two sentences don't link well and they now have a similar Theme, 'Male health problems' and 'Illness among men'. It would make better reading to put the two short sentences together to make a longer, more complex, but equally readable two-part sentence.

> Male health problems not only diminish work productivity, but also adversely affect the economics of the family. When men become disabled or die, family income is usually reduced, often in the face of additional health care expenses.

This latter construction makes 'Male health problems' the Theme while retaining a balance of active and passive voice. The rewriting reorders the points made (that is, changes what comes first), leaving 'The economics of the family' as the topic to be discussed in the sentence that follows, while providing more logical argumentative flow. The reader is taken from the obvious, the problem with work productivity, to the less obvious and the point of the discussion, the economics of the family. And the rewriting of voice accomplishes this in a way that is unobtrusive and comfortable.

Other decisions about passive or active voice relate to the scholarly requirements for precision. For example, it is less informative to say 'professional training was conducted across the public sector', than to give details of who conducted the training, when, where and how often. To simply say 'the young people were socially excluded' is to deny the reader the opportunity to learn the details of the conditions, decisions, and institutional practices and policies that produced this exclusion. It is important to avoid passive constructions such as these which obscure connections and lack specificity.

However, deciding whether to use the active or passive voice is not just a matter of producing a good read, ensuring the logic of the argument and demonstrating scholarly rectitude. It is also connected to the target readership of the text. Take for example the following passage also discussing men's health.

> [1] Understanding masculinity is crucial for analyzing men's health problems. [2] For instance it is important to appreciate that many men take risks with their health because risk taking is one way men are brought up to prove their maleness to each other and themselves. [3] The long-standing and largely unresolved debate about the extent to which traditional characteristics of masculinity are pre-determined by biology should however be set aside if progress is to be made. [4] The attitude that there is an inherent and thus inevitable relation between maleness and poor health could distract from the chances of changing male attitudes and behaviour to bring about improvements in health.
>
> (Banks, 2004: 156)

The writer here takes an assertive stance using strong modality (see Chapter 5) such as 'is crucial', 'is important' and 'should'. But the use of the passive voice leaves many unanswered questions for the reader. In sentence 1 who should understand men's health problems? In 2 who should appreciate male risk-taking behaviour? In 3 who should set aside preconceived ideas about maleness and biology? And in sentence 4 whose attitude is likely to distract from changing male behaviour and thus bringing about improvements in men's health?

Now this may or may not be a problem if the writer is speaking about general social shifts. If we were to change the sentences to active voice, however, it may narrow the focus more than the writer intended, as in the following rewriting.

[1] It is critical that the medical profession understands masculinity in order to analyze men's health problems. [2] Medical practitioners need to appreciate that many men take risks with their health because risk taking is one way men are brought up to prove their maleness to each other and themselves. [3] Doctors and nurses in particular should set aside the long-standing and largely unresolved debate about the extent to which traditional characteristics of masculinity are pre-determined by biology in order to make progress. [4] If they believe that there is an inherent and thus inevitable relation between maleness and poor health, this attitude could distract from their chances of changing male attitudes and behaviour to bring about improvements in health.

(Reworking of Banks, 2004: 156)

What else has changed here apart from voice? By inserting in each sentence a subject who acts, we have changed the meaning. From a linguistic perspective, changing voice has also changed the pattern of Theme. Across the four sentences, phrases relating to the medical profession now come first: 'It is critical that the medical profession'; 'Medical practitioners'; 'Doctors and nurses in particular'; 'they'. If the writer intended to speak directly about the medical profession, then using the active voice to change the Theme in this way would be a worthwhile move away from generalities in which anyone and no one is required to change. On the other hand, the passage as rewritten now has a critical and vaguely accusatory tone: wagging a finger at the medical profession and telling it what it should do. This may be a more provocative stance than the writer wishes. And, hypothetically, if the intended reader is an examiner, and the writer a doctoral student, then she needs to understand the local textual mores and unwritten rules in order to decide whether the more generalized or specific text is likely to meet the requirements of the examining gaze.

Our point in exploring these examples is to suggest that both active and passive voice have their purposes and their effects. Making these matters the focus of supervisor conversation is a better tactic than blanket rules and prohibitions.

Supervisors can also help students add polish to their writings by looking at the textual features which literally hit the reader in the eye.

Pleasing the eye as well as the ear

A book, even a 'big book' like a doctoral dissertation, is an aesthetic object. It has visual qualities that are generally taken for granted in universities, but which producers of magazines and commercial books attend to closely. Rafts of trained artists debate layout and formatting of newspapers, leaflets, signage, packaging and books. Many of us have not been well served by the visual education we received at school, since school art is largely confined to particular traditions and 'high forms' of representational and abstract art practice (Atkinson and Dash, 2005). Thus, we take the designed nature of our environment and our 'textual tools' as natural and given. Designers know that how a text appears to the eye can be integral to conveying a sense of lightness or heaviness, an impression of impenetrability or invitation, an effect of easy order or of clinical formula.

Many universities have strict regulations about the presentation of doctoral dissertations. They specify the size of page, the width and depth of margins, the size of font, the type of paper, the colour of the cover and the positioning of the title on the spine. However, even within these boundaries, there is room for some decision making.

Citation practices

Academic prose is generally recognizable because of its use of in-text citations. The following example (from Rogers *et al.* 2005: 369) could not be anything but an academic piece of writing!

> Recent developments in Critical Discourse Analysis are rooted in much longer histories of language philosophy (Austin, 1962; Gramsci, 1973; Searle, 1969; Wittgenstein, 1953) ethnomethodology (Garfinkel, 1967; Cicourel, 1974), the functional linguistics tradition in the United States (Gumperz, 1982; Silverstein and Urban, 1996), and Systemic Functional Linguistics in England, Canada and Australia (Halliday and Hasan, 1976). There are many subsections of discourse analysis within the social tradition, including speech act theory (Goffman, 1959, 1971), genre theory (Bakhtin, 1981; Martin, 1985; Hasan and Fries, 1995), intertextuality (Bakhtin, 1981; Kristeva, 1980, 1986, 1989; Lemke, 1992), discursive formations (e.g. Foucault, 1972, 1979, 1981; Lemke, 1992), conversation analysis (Collins, 1986; Gumperz, 1982; Sacks, Schegloff and Jefferson, 1974; Schegloff, Ochs and Thompson, 1996), narrative analysis (Gee, 1992, 1994; Labov, 1972; Michaels, 1981; Propp, 1968; Scollon and Scollon, 1981; Wortham, 2001), discursive psychology (Davies and Harre, 1990; Edwards and Potter, 1992), ethnography of communication (Hymes, 1972), multi-modal analysis (Gee, 2003; Hodge and Kress, 1988; Kress and Van Leeuween, 1996; Scollon and Scollon, 2003), and critical discourse analysis.

This text is an eyeful. It takes effort on the reader's part to get through the citations to work out precisely what is being said. But this kind of citation can't be simply abandoned.

In the context of doctoral research, citations demonstrate that the dissertation writer knows the field. Indeed, if key texts are not referenced and cited, examiners may well query the depth of scholarship involved.

However, many doctoral researchers treat citations as the scholarly equivalent of Imelda Marcos's shoe collection. They like to signal their conspicuous consumption of academic literatures – the more the better. Other doctoral candidates have told us they need to buttress every statement with the appropriated expertise of their betters, because doctoral candidates are regarded as having so little authority. Needless to say, the former view often leads to paragraphs where it is almost impossible for readers to disentangle the sense between the brackets, while the latter more often than not leads to low level cynicism about the purpose of referencing. Neither of these positions is the most useful approach to thinking about citation.

Citations are the scholarly means of correctly attributing the source of particular ideas, theories and findings. They demonstrate that all scholarship is located within a field to and with which it speaks. Citations counter the fallacy that scholarship is the work of a single scholar. Since all of us are always beholden to the efforts of others, the insertion of names and dates in brackets is our way of 'paying our dues'.

While doctoral researchers can't dodge the issue of citation, this doesn't mean that they just have to lie back and bracket. There are still some decisions that can be made about the use of within-text and footnoted citations, for example:

- How many references are needed to acknowledge an idea?
- When is it appropriate to put a few references and say 'for example' or 'as in' or 'see also'?
- If there is a large body of work in the area, is it a good idea to put in references from a range of dates or from a number of locations?

A further decision concerns whether to put all of the references in the text proper or whether to put some in endnotes or footnotes. Some endnotes or footnotes amplify details of points that are germane to the main argument, but not necessarily integral to the main narrative. But endnotes and footnotes can be a way of moving really hefty sets of references out of the way so that they don't affect the flow of the writing. Figure 8.1 shows what a page looks like when a doctoral writer has decided to send a discussion weighed down with citations out of the main frame.

There are no hard-and-fast rules about whether it is a good idea to footnote or endnote citations. And simply moving them doesn't work in all cases. The process of shifting attention from the main text to a footnote or endnote can be distracting for the reader. However, sending brackets off the main page can give the reader the option to read through the main body of the text without too much distraction, if they so choose.

We acknowledge that some universities and some disciplines may place restrictions on the use of citations, footnotes and endnotes. Nevertheless, a discussion about referencing helps doctoral writers focus on questions of readability and can lead to broader questions of the aesthetics of the page.

Texts that are easy on the eye

Aesthetic decisions can also be made about the adoption of numbered sections and subsections. Some disciplines require the use of numbered texts. Chapter 4 may

THESE TIMES

Those who study and comment on society agree that we are living in a time of great change,[1] but they cannot agree about the nature of those changes. Some studies of society centre on the rise of global technologies and communications (Virilio, 1997; Wresch, 1996), the dominance of the image and appearance (Baudrillard, 1988; Baudrillard, 1996; Perry,1998), and propose that there is a change from the dominance of modes of production to those of consumption (Baumam 1998b; Lee & Turner, 1996) although others argue they cannot be separated (LeFebvre, 1971). The importance of cultures – popular, youth, different, everyday, multiple, global, simulated, bricolaged[2] – and spatialities of difference (D. Harvey, 1993; Soja, 1996) dominate our lives.

It is suggested that, in this emerging new world, ethics and democratic politics need to be remade in order to prevent a lapse into fragmentation and relativism[3] and social isolationism.[4] Writers and scholars call this a postmodernist age which coexists with modernist industrial, and pre-modem, feudal social organisations (Gibson-Graham 1996) … a postcolonial age (Bhaha, 1994; Gelder & Jacobs 1998; Jacobs, 1996; Said, 1991; Spivak, 1988) peopled by flaneurs (Benjamin, 1969, Tester, 1994), multiple shifting chimeric subjectivities (Serres, 1997).

Other scholars focus on the changing dimensions of the internationalisation of economies and changes in the organisation of work, using terms such as post Fordism, fast capitalism, and de-industrialisation.[5] Some suggest that the internationalisation of capitalism envisaged by Marx is being brought further into being by the digital flows of international financial exchange (Castells, 1996, 1997, 1998; Lash & Urry, 1994), the growth of world cities that function as nodes of exchange (Sassen, 1994), changes in the regulatory capacity of nation states (Beilharz, 1994; S. Bell, 1997; Hinkson, 1991; Hinkson, 1998; James, 1996; Offe, 1996; Pinch, 1997), the fragmentation of classes (Bradley, 1996; Marshall et al., 1997; Pakulski & Waters, 1996) and the prominence of localised, culturally based political action (Pile & Keith, 1997, Wark, 1997).

---

[1] A point found in many texts (e.g. Bertens, 1995, Crook, Pakulski, & Waters, 1992; Deleuze & Guattari, 1987; Dunant & Porter. 1996; Foucault, 1977; S. Hall & Jacques, 1990; Hassan, 1993; Jameson, 1991, Latour, 1993, Lyotard, 1984, Taylor, l992).
[2] Cultures are now seen as plural and highly fragmented and 'niched' (e g. Andrews, 1997; Aronowitz, Martinsons & Menser, 1996; Davis, 1997; du Gay, Hall, Janes, Mackay, & Negus, 1997; Featherstone, 1995; Fiske, 1993; Giroux, 1996; 1997; A. Hall, 1997; A. Hall & Jefferson, 1976, Hebdige, 1989; Humphery, 1998; Jameson & Miyoshi, 1998; C. Luke, 1996).
[3] There is a growing literature that seeks to put together a normative politics of postmodernity (Bauman, 1993; Fraser, 1997a; Mellucci, 1996; Mouffe, 1993; Soper, 1993; Sunstein, 1997; Szkudlarek, 1993, Touraine, 1997; Young, 1990).
[4] There is an emerging concern with questions of community and social networks (e.g. Davis, 1992; Etzioni, 1993; Farrar & Inglis, 1996; Frazer & Lacey, 1993; Putnam, 1993).
[5] This literature variously looks at organisations, labour process, subjectivity, the availability of work and its transformations (e.g. Burrows & Loader, 1994; C . Casey, 1995; du Gay, 1996; Gee, Hull, & Lankshear. 1996; Grint & Woolgar 1997; Kincheloe, 1999; Probert & Wilson, 1993; Reich, 1991; Rifkin, 1996; Ritzer, 1993).

67

Figure 8.1 Footnoting citations (from Thomson, 1999: 67)

have three major sections, which in turn have subsections and sub-subsections. Readers are strongly steered through the text via 4.3.1.1., 4.3.1.2, etc. We find it surprising that so many doctoral students in our discipline of education choose to write using this structure, even though there is no requirement to do so. This textual configuration certainly gives the impression of linearity, order and logic, but it is not our writerly preference, although we clearly do not eschew the use of bullet points and lists! Our own preference is for a text that appears more open in its conformation. Again, this is a topic for supervisor-student discussion and decision.

Doctoral researchers also need to discuss the play of graphic representations. Many dissertations contain a number of graphic representations of findings in the form of diagrams, models, tables, graphs, flow charts and pie-charts. Such data realization appears to be straightforward. Major decisions focus on what goes into the model, table or graph, rather than the kind of image that is used. But different data visualizations may be better suited for some purposes than others, and doctoral researchers do need to discuss the rationale for their choice and their discarding of other options.

Modern word processing does have the capacity to provide more than the basic data figurative tools, and it may be that some supervisors can encourage interested students to experiment with ways of representing data that are more visually interesting and equally as precise and telling. The incorporation of symbols and pictures, for example, can do much to enhance the impact and meaning of boxes, arrows and numbers.

It is becoming more common across the social sciences for doctoral research to develop a way with images – photographs and other illustrations. But even in disciplines where the use of visual research methods is uncontentious, the most common form of their reproduction in the doctoral text is as a single boxed image with a caption underneath. The use of more design-conscious layout, such as storyboard, collage and montage, superimposed and annotated images is far less frequent (see Figure 8.2). Such moves, of course, are not in the repertoire of all doctoral researchers, but it is likely that many do have the requisite visual knowledge and competence to experiment more effectively with the images they use as methodology or as data representation.

Unfortunately, the visual characteristics of the text, its formatting and layout, are often last minute concerns. Take for instance the deployment of blank space and title pages.

Most supervisors are focused, quite rightly, on what students have to say, and how well they say it. It is not common practice to pay attention to the absence of text in dissertations. But, the use of uncluttered space can be used to punctuate the flow of a text. This might be, for example in the form of chapter title pages, blank spaces at the top of new chapters, or blank pages between major sections (see Figure 8.3).

The expansiveness created by the insertion of blank spaces produces a sensation of navigability. The association of this spatial configuration with that of novels

Figure 8.2   Designed pages (from Thomson, 1999: 138 and 97)

and magazines can be very helpful in inducing a perception that this text is a 'good read', simply because it is a more pleasing design. We are not suggesting here a new visual formula, but rather that this is another area for decision and discussion.

In making this point, we have begun to veer into the territory of artistic skills, and it is with this topic that we conclude the chapter.

Arts-informed dissertations – not the Dead Poets Society!

Some doctoral researchers want to do more than write a lively text. They aspire to a more artistic product, possibly combining art forms. As such, they aspire to that minority part of the academy seeking to move away from a research practice geared to producing generalizable and 'paradigmatic' knowledge, to one where the purpose of research is the creation of meaning (Rorty, 1982). We do not wish, nor have we space, to argue this point here. Suffice it to say, that if one takes the creation of meaning as the point of knowledge production, then there can be multiple ways of producing meaning, including the use of methods found in the arts (e.g. Barone and Eisner, 1997; Diamond and Mullen, 1999; Ellis, 1999; Stronach and MacLure, 1997).

Attempting an arts-informed dissertation is risky ground, but not, we suggest, because it is difficult to find examiners who will treat such experimental forms sympathetically. There are now enough people in universities who can do such examination fairly and well. Those who use poetic forms for data representation

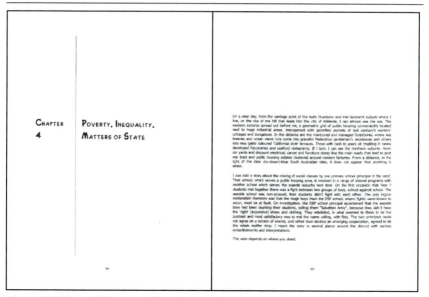

Figure 8.3   Using blank space (from Thomson, 1999: 66–7)

will no longer find the same incredulity and hostility that Laurel Richardson encountered (see Richardson, 1997), although debates about arts-informed research are alive and well within disciplines and among arts-informed researchers themselves. It is risky first of all because working in art forms is a highly skilled activity, and second because judging what constitutes a 'good' piece of art, let alone a good piece of arts-informed research, is contentious.

We must confess at this point that we have ourselves dabbled in arts-informed research, combining data poems with more conventional research prose. We have also supervised students whose dissertations have combined video, theatre, art and music with aspects of the more orthodox doctoral research 'big book'. We are supportive of the desire to move research, as Denzin (2003) has it, to more of a performance base. However, we do have some qualms about the process.

We are concerned about form following function rather than the other way around. Doctoral researchers must start with what they want to say, not with questions of artistic form. They need to look at the argument they wish to make and consider what kind of aesthetic form might best convey the idea. If people are looking to do something interesting, then it is not simply about adopting particular kinds of aesthetic forms because they happen to appeal. Some kinds of research questions and findings lend themselves to particular kinds of artistic media, and some do not. Policy analysis, for example, is not amenable to some artistic forms, although it might well be supported by visual media. Some kinds of ethnographic work, on the other hand, are more amenable to artistic media as a means of conveying multiple perspectives and voices, contextual specificities and researcher reflexivity.

We are also vexed by the question of artistic competence. If the purpose of the artistic dissertation is to provide different modes of meaning making than are afforded by conventional sociological prose, then it is critical that the artistic medium is handled well. It is counterproductive to have a reader distracted from the meaning by gauche and clumsy art. Thus, except in exceptional circumstances, it is not appropriate, we think, to make the doctoral dissertation the occasion to take up painting, to begin to write poetry or to experiment with a novel. Those who work with artistic media as part of their dissertation practice need to have high levels of skill and knowledge with the chosen art form. This is also a question of respect for the form itself. It is one thing to seek to be interesting by adopting alternative forms of representation, it is another to damage the form rather than enhance it.

Furthermore, because the dissertation is a representation not only of the research but also of the scholarly self, it is important that an alternative arts-informed doctoral dissertation is skilful. Getting the coveted doctor title hangs on it. Bad poetry does not achieve the goals of either enhanced meaning making or a successful representation of a scholar on top of their material. On the other hand, a skilful dissertation which combines art forms can be not only convincing, but also stimulating and highly thought and emotion provoking.

But if arts-informed dissertations are out of the question, all supervisors can still support doctoral researchers to write in more lively and interesting ways and can assist them to see how their thesis can be more writerly, pleasurable and meaningful. Individual supervisors, of course, can only do so much. In the next and final chapter we consider what groups of supervisors and students can accomplish together.

Chapter 9

Institutionalizing doctoral writing practices

We have argued in this book that research is writing and that a focus on writing in supervision can support the co-construction of a scholarly identity. We have demonstrated a range of writing and textual strategies that might be used by supervisors in a dialogue-based supervision practice.

Our argument has been that the supervisor embodies and mediates institutional and disciplinary cultures, conditions and conventions. But in this final chapter we want to move beyond the single supervisor. Supervisors, as we suggested in Chapter 1, are now under extreme pressure. It is not reasonable to expect supervisors to take on doctoral writing in the ways we have outlined, without institutional support. By this we do not mean that institutions must start 'training' supervisors about writing. Rather, universities themselves must take up the question of research writing. They must establish institutional writing cultures.

A writing culture is one in which questions of writing are foregrounded and not confined to the realm of a pre-dissertation technical fix. It is one in which writing initiatives are linked to policy priorities and wider institutional aspirations (Lee and Boud, 2003). It is one in which there are faculty-sponsored spaces to talk about writing, to play with writing, and to perform writing. It is one in which writing is not ruthlessly and narrowly connected to productivity, but linked to fostering research capacities, practices and 'know how'. It is a culture in which the hitherto private pleasures and pain of writing are made public through institutionally-resourced writing groups, courses and collectives. In such circumstances we might expect to see doctoral writings shared, writings honed to exact meaning and nuance not sent off before their time, writings discussed not displayed. Here too, we might see language prodded, moulded, and caressed into phrases, tropes and metaphors pleasing to the eye and ear while advancing understanding.

Such a writing culture is not remedial. It recognizes that research practices are writing practices and that all university staff and students benefit from systematic attention to writing. It *is* important to offer individualized services to students who experience real difficulties with writing, because either English is not their first language, or they have learning difficulties or have somehow missed out on 'basics'. But these services do not constitute, or substitute for, an overall institutional writing culture. They are a base level service only. However, staff within such academic units do have particular knowledges, practices and dispositions which make important contributions to the development of a writing culture. (We discuss how these services might support writing cultures further in this chapter.)

In short, a writing culture does not simply happen. It must be consciously produced.

In this chapter, we suggest five sites in and through which writing-oriented practices can be initiated. These are not the only sites for building a writing culture; there are of course many others. But they are sites in which we and our colleagues and peers are active and here we report on some of these activities.

The sites we propose in this chapter are: (1) supervisor-initiated reading/ writing groups; (2) writing-for-publication groups; (3) collaborative work with academic support units; (4) school/faculty-based writing courses; and (5) cross-university projects.

Supervisor-initiated reading/writing groups

Many supervisors initiate and support writing-focused pedagogies without expectations of institutional support or even attention. We have suggested that supervisors who are writing-focused begin from the position that writing is not the attribute of a few clever people, but a focus for discussion with all students. Such dialogue is about the practices of writing as research, of writing during the research, and of how to represent the research in texts, including the dissertation text.

Individual supervisors can foster changes to doctoral writing practices by supporting reading and writing groups. When discussing multiple texts in reading groups, it is not hard to foreground questions of writing or 'reading like a writer' (see our discussion in Chapter 8). This might include a focus on choreography, for example:

- the ways in which the argument is carried between chapters and within each one, or is built up through the sections of a journal article
- the ways in which headings, subheadings and paragraph sentence beginnings and endings carry the argument forward
- the kinds of signposting that are constructed for readers.

Or a focus on the language used, for example:

- searching for the ways in which the writer uses metaphor, trope and simile
- examining the ways in which the writer has brought colour and shade to the writing through the use of vivid language
- debating the wording of titles and headings.

Reading groups can create a motivation for students to read texts outside their usual ambit in order to advance their own and the group's general understandings. Reading that is both wide and deep enriches discussion of research 'findings' as a contribution to the wider field of knowledge production. During her doctoral research, Pat attended a reading group in which she encountered a range of texts that were associated with a quite different field of study. These were not texts she would normally have picked up in her policy analysis research, let alone read thoroughly. However, some of these unlikely books, mostly related to language, linguistics and literacy education, became very important in the process of theorizing her findings.

Reading groups can be lively and supportive places where doctoral researchers can say unfamiliar words out loud, test out ideas, practise taking a 'hands on hips' stance to the work of senior scholars, and enter the dialogue of scholarship. They are spaces in which students learn to question received theory, rather than slavishly follow any set pattern of thinking. They can also be places in which students break from the dominant dependency model of 'apprenticeship' to encompass learning from and with peers and texts.

At their worst, reading groups become routinized, dull events which a few dominate and it is important to sort out the protocols for the group to ensure that this does not happen. These include setting out how books are to be chosen, what contribution members are expected to make (introductory papers, timed responses from each member), and how to resolve conflicts about group process.

Supervisors may also establish writing groups with students. In a writing group, students and supervisor each write papers, singly and together, share them and produce critiques of each other's texts. They discuss the processes of writing as practical and theoretical problems. They bring questions about research ethics, epistemology and representation into meaningful conversation with questions of choice of words, possible structures and convincing arguments.

Some writing groups have produced books that are helpful for other writing-oriented collectives to consider. We think, for example, of Noeleen Garman's narrative and arts-informed writing group (Ceroni *et al.* 1996; Piantanida *et al.* 2003) in which students jointly explored theoretical approaches to writing through extant literature on writing and different forms of texts, and through writing and debating their own theory and exemplars.

Susan Moore Johnson's work provides another example. She has worked with her doctoral students on a long-term research agenda examining the retention and attrition of newly appointed teachers. Their collaborative project, *The Project on the Next Generation of Teachers*, resulted in an award-winning jointly-authored book *Finders and Keepers: Helping New Teachers Survive and Thrive in Our Schools* (Moore Johnson *et al.* 2004). Through the process of joint research and joint writing, Susan has provided a collective space in which students learn not only from her, but also from and with each other.

We are familiar with the work of colleagues who have extended other scholarly writing activities to doctoral researchers. For example, we know of journal editors who ask doctoral students to work as a filtering committee doing a collective first cull of articles, or who have them work in pairs to referee articles. Students then put their refereed work alongside the other referee reports when they are submitted to see the similarities and differences. Students can learn a lot from critically appraising articles written by others for publication, including how to structure an article, the kinds of argument that are convincing and what makes an abstract work.

Such individual supervisor activity is important, but it can be greatly strengthened when supervisors work together on writing projects and programmes. There are, for example, research centres and schools that have gone against the grain of the individualized social sciences model (for example, Malfroy, 2005). In these instances a group of researchers/supervisors declare a common agenda and students are recruited on the basis of their contribution to this agenda. There are joint research projects, shared writing, and ongoing seminars which allow staff and students to share writing in progress, as well as to advance the theoretical and methodological development of the whole group. Taking such action goes against the notion that the doctorate, and indeed scholarship, is an individualized pursuit borne of individual curiosity. The Birmingham Contemporary Cultural Studies[11] group is one such example: staff and students wrote individually and collectively for many years and were known as a productive organizational grouping, as well as individual scholars.

Writing-for-publication groups

Unfortunately, many doctoral students are left to their own devices to sort out how to publish out of their doctorate research (Dinham and Scott, 2001; Engestrom, 1999). Individual supervisors vary in the support they give to writing for publication during and after the doctorate. There are also different disciplinary traditions around the importance of writing for publication. We know of one university in the UK where the school of psychology expects each doctoral candidate to write a paper each year for an international conference and to have it sent to a refereed journal afterwards. In this case, not only are conversations about writing integral to supervision, but students' progress is evaluated in relation to the papers and articles they write.

In her investigation of doctoral writing practices in science and education, Barbara (Kamler, 2005a; Kamler and Rowan, 2004) highlights the crucial role of specific discourse communities in shaping publication output. Her interview-based case study compared the writing experiences of doctoral graduates in education with those in the physical and biological sciences. A key finding of the study was that science graduates were far more successful than education graduates in achieving high quality journal publication: producing 13 international refereed publications, compared to only two in education. In science, where co-authorship with supervisors was accepted practice, students began writing for publication earlier in their candidature and viewed the process as a team effort with supervisors, that is, as a crucial part of learning the ropes of academic publishing.

In education, where co-authorship was perceived more negatively for ethical reasons of ownership, autonomy or self-exploration, students produced significantly fewer publications. They were more reluctant than science graduates to submit to international refereed journals, had fewer strategies for doing so and received less supervisor support in the process. While they did not share any expectation that supervisors should play a key role in assisting them to publish, the only two refereed texts in the sample were also the only texts that were co-authored *with* supervisors. That is, the two education graduates in the study who achieved refereed publication did so *because of* the scaffolding from co-authoring with a more experienced supervisor/mentor. In this study, co-authorship with supervisors produced 'know how'. It helped students move past their anxieties and stay robust through the refereeing and resubmission process that is part of publishing.

Heath's (2002) quantitative study of supervision at The University of Queensland also found significant disciplinary differences in publishing practices. Of the 355 students surveyed, 83 per cent had one or more publications by the time they submitted their thesis. However, students in the sciences published more, and included their supervisor as co-authors more often than did their peers in the humanities and social sciences.

In situations where publishing is the norm, questions of writing are rolled into everyday supervision pedagogy, but they may not go beyond the individually focused supervision to become 'institutionalized' via joint supervisor dialogue or cooperative activity. One way in which the process of institutional support for publication can begin is via writing groups. We discussed the usefulness of writing groups earlier, but here we draw attention to their role in publishing – putting the scholarly identity out in the public arena.

Page-Adams *et al.* (1995) report on a student-sponsored initiative in social work to support doctoral publication through the formation of a writing group.

The group was initiated by two students at Washington University in the US who believed social work doctoral students needed more structured support in writing for publication during candidature. Their impetus was career-oriented; they recognized the low publication productivity of new social work faculty members and wanted to improve the quality of their scholarly writing as future social work educators.

The chairperson of the doctoral programme offered administrative support (photocopying, meeting space), but students worked without supervisory input. Of the 25 enrolled doctoral students, eight joined the group. They set deadlines for written drafts and offered detailed feedback to one another on conceptualization, substantive content and writing style.

> Members pushed to ask the hard questions first. Is this piece worth writing? Does it contribute enough to warrant a publication attempt? Members approached these potentially charged issues by helping one another identify ways to improve the substantive content, or by suggesting alternative conceptual approaches that might yield bigger contributions.
>
> (Page-Adams *et al.* 1995: 403)

An evaluation of the group showed a positive correlation between group membership and scholarly productivity. The eight members wrote, submitted or published nineteen papers during the group's first year, compared to five papers written or submitted for publication by non-members. Page-Adams *et al.* strongly recommend such groups as an effective way to enhance the quality of writing and make a contribution to a professional knowledge base early in academic careers.

While they claim student initiative and administrative support were crucial to the development of the publication group, what was supplied seems an exceedingly modest input from the university community. Certainly it sidesteps the question of supervisors, faculties or institutions supporting such groups as part of a writing culture.

Barbara initiated a form of publication support for early career researchers at her university in Australia; it had greater institutional support than the Page-Adams initiative. Her work became part of her faculty's strategic research planning and was resourced in 2004 by giving Barbara workload allocation to mentor her colleagues on writing for publication. The aim was to foster the capacity of early career researchers in education by fast-tracking publications from their dissertations.

The initiative was undoubtedly shaped by the increasingly performative environment of Australian universities and the need for younger academics to build their research profile in order to be competitive in research grant submission. It also recognized the intense pressures on recent doctoral graduates to deal with heavy teaching workloads at the same time that they 'become known' through publication. While the faculty had been funding a number of initiatives to bring research money into the university (for example, workshops on grant writing, administrative support with research budgets), no assistance was given to the other end of research – publishing findings from research and disseminating new contributions to knowledge.

Since 2004, Barbara has worked individually with six to eight researchers each year, to discuss their thesis and provide assistance with publication. She reads each dissertation and collaboratively develops a publishing plan, outlining four to six articles to be published in academic refereed journals. The plan creates a structure for writing, specifying target journals, titles and abstracts. Writing the plan creates a site of pedagogy, as discussions range from how to write compelling abstract bids to analysing the different genres of journal publication. Once the writing begins, Barbara provides close reading and critique of successive drafts before they are submitted for publication.

The evaluations of this work have been very positive. Early career researchers remark on gaining practical and political 'know how' about journal submission, as well as success in publication. They also talk about learning how they might work differently with their own doctoral students to make writing a more central part of their supervision practice. From Barbara's perspective, the work is about reinvigorating the faculty research culture and developing a pedagogy for post-PhD writing and publication that moves beyond advice and financial incentive. It is not simply editing or a 'remedial intervention', but a strategic interaction about building professional identities through writing. The work has gained sufficient recognition that the faculty is now supporting writing groups for all academics (not just early career) who want to engage in peer review and discussion of their journals articles prior to submission.

One final example of productive writing-for-publication groups is described by Lee and Boud (2003) at another university in Australia. They share a similar commitment to fostering the research potential of university staff and repositioning them as active writers. But their approach is located more firmly in peer learning frameworks and the need to foster academic research development in light of the changing conditions of academic work – including pressures to find new forms of funding for teaching and research, develop research concentrations, increase doctoral research completions, and prepare research students for employment (2003: 189).

In this context, they see writing groups as 'a useful place to do research development work' (p. 187) and research development itself as 'crucially about the making and remaking of academic identities' (p. 189). They discuss two staff groups which were oriented around writing for publication. In the 'new researchers' group, members discussed 'using conferences strategically, analysing key journals and their practices of submission; and … the practices of writing itself' (p. 192). In the 'extended publication' group, members engaged in writing throughout the year and brought their writing to the group. There was greater emphasis on productivity and 'all were successful in producing at least one article or book chapter ready for submission' (p. 193).

Based on these groups, Lee and Boud distil a set of principles which might be generalized to other sites of practice. Their first principle is mutuality, a term they use 'to disrupt the effects of an excessive attachment to notions of academic autonomy' (p. 194). Promoting a group approach to writing development works to break down solitary and private approaches to academic work. It creates new spaces for dialogue, reciprocity, respect for difference and enriched peer relationships.

The second principle views research development as normal university business, built into daily practices and the way 'the organization governs itself, organizes itself and plans for its future' (p. 195). 'Normal business' in the writing groups involved a focus on 'know how', on the practical and procedural measures for playing the publishing game and for developing and supporting the writing goals of all group members. But it was also achieved through policy measures. Writing groups were given funding and workload allocations for the convenors and then for participants, and were thus inscribed into strategic planning and budgeting.

The third principle recognizes that 'questions of desire, identity and emotions are crucial to the sustainability of any developmental activity, yet they are often ignored' (p. 196). Academic writing, not surprisingly, became a focus for major questions concerning identity and change. The desire to become recognized researcher-writers often warred with writers' fears and anxieties about their own competence and inexperience. The confidentiality and mutuality of the groups allowed these issues to surface, be spoken about and worked through. As a consequence, all participants were repositioned as active scholarly writers.

Collaborative work with academic support services

Most universities offer a range of academic support services. These usually include undergraduate workshops and individual and group tutorial assistance. Together with study skills, academic writing is a major concern for those who work in such centres. In recent times, these services have begun to support doctoral students as well. Increasing numbers of students are writing in languages other than their first language, and tighter frames for doctoral completion have created new pressures for the provision of research writing support (Aitchison and Lee, 2006).

But language and academic skills advisers in these centres often operate from a remedial or crisis model of intervention separate from graduate schools. They are often physically and organizationally removed from the faculties with which they work. They may not be seen as academic staff and may be represented differently in employment classifications. They do not 'teach' on university degrees. What they do is discursively positioned as complementary and supplementary to the 'mainstream'. Thus, staff from academic services often find themselves working at a physical, social and cultural distance from faculties.

This structural divide is also constructed by the discourse of 'service' which sees students as 'clients'. The mission of support staff is directed towards the provision of specific 'skills' and remedial assistance to students. Such centres often contain staff who are particularly interested in language and writing as a social practice, and many have completed specific education and have done research in the field. In recent years, staff with doctorates have been appointed and many are pursuing doctoral studies. They have begun to initiate research into aspects of student academic experience and to hold conferences at which student services staff are the major attendees. They have also begun to publish articles and books (e.g. Aitchison, 2003; Leibowitz and Goodman, 1997; Nelson and San Miguel, 2000; Starfield, 2003) and there is now a specific publication, *The Writing Centre Journal*,[12] devoted to the activities of such staff. These university colleagues possess a significant pool of expertise and they are a writing resource with which supervisors can connect.

We suggest that universities need to do more to bring academic support staff and supervisors together – not in supervision training but rather in fruitful partnerships that will benefit students. We report briefly on two such initiatives developed in Australia: thesis writing circles by Claire Aitchison and proposal writing workshops for international students and their supervisors by Kate Cadman.

Aitchison (2003) initiated thesis writing circles in the Learning Skills Unit of a large metropolitan university, where she was employed as a language specialist. Frustrated with urgent calls from supervisors and management for a 'quick fix' to student writing problems, she sought to create a different kind of support that moved

> from a model of writing development as crisis control, to a proactive program that embedded writing with research, acknowledging writing as knowledge-creating rather than merely as knowledge recording.
>
> (Aitchison and Lee, 2006: 70)

The writing circles were structured as peer writing groups to mitigate the isolation experienced by many doctoral candidates. The aim was to foster the development of social, linguistic and academic literacies required of thesis writers. The groups ran for ten consecutive weeks, with six to eight students meeting weekly for three hours to share their own writing and discuss an aspect of thesis writing of common interest. The groups were multidisciplinary and culturally diverse, with students at all stages of candidature.

As facilitator, Aitchison played a key leadership role. She developed protocols for giving and receiving language-focused feedback. She taught linguistic concepts. She developed a meta-language for students to describe and deconstruct language. Over time, group members built up their own repertoire of skills so that peers became the primary resource for learning.

A third of each session was 'teacher-led', where specific features of academic writing were discussed, such as aspects of thesis structure, using evidence in argument and micro-level questions about style and grammar. This set of topics was negotiated ahead of time and modified depending on group needs. The rest of the session was devoted to critiquing new written work and reviewing reworked writing in light of group criticism. Three to five pieces of writing were critiqued at each meeting. Aitchison suggests that this work helped doctoral researchers develop skills to critique and improve writing as well as a meta-language to articulate their understandings.

Student evaluations of thesis writing circles have been very positive. Students valued the sustained feedback from peers and the opportunity to interact with a language expert in a forum that was not assessed. They reported increased self-esteem, writing production and knowledge about how to critique their own writing.

Aitchison and Lee (2006) highlight multiple values of such peer review groups. Peer writing groups, they argue, attend to the sociality of writing and locate it in a network of social, institutional and peer relations; they are explicitly negotiated, evolving and responsive to group needs and they foster community and a pedagogical space for writers to experiment and explore questions of identity, textuality and authority together.

> We propose that research writing groups, with their 'horizontalising' pedagogical frame of peer review (Boud and Lee 2005), address many of the epistemological, experiential and textual dimensions of writing within

research degrees. In the common absence of formal curriculum, such groups provide a learning environment that is antithetical to notions of the all-too-commonly isolated research writer. Writing groups explicitly address the questions of knowledge, textual practice and identity in a context of peer relations.

(Aitchison and Lee, 2006: 266)

Aitchison also recounts a number of institutional challenges in offering thesis writing circles on a larger scale, as the success of the groups is dependent on frequent meetings, small numbers of participants, high levels of self-motivation and an expert facilitator (Aitchison, 2003: 110). Nevertheless, such initiatives highlight the invaluable expertise language advisers can bring to research supervision and how wasteful it is to quarantine their considerable talent.

Kate Cadman's work in a Research Education Programs Unit illustrates the possibilities of fostering more deliberate institutional links between the language specialist, the supervisor and the student. Cadman and her colleagues hold academic tenure-track positions and have expertise in teaching advanced academic literacies. They work only with research students and are assigned to particular faculties (education, engineering or arts) to provide discipline-specific support to native and non-native language students.

Of particular interest to our discussion is the Integrated Bridging Program (IBP), an institutionally mandated semester-long course for international postgraduate students and their supervisors. It runs throughout the first semester of candidature and is a task-based programme which seeks to facilitate international students' academic English language development. Students are mostly from EAL backgrounds in Asia, Africa and South America. Cadman and her colleagues use the acronym REAL, Research English as an Additional Language (Cadman 2005), to locate their work in the university's internationalization programme and capture the political as well as pragmatic hopes they have for their teaching.

> The IBP was structured around a core set of writing and presentation tasks which form the basis of the early stages of the students' candidature ... Students work in small discipline- or paradigm-specific groups, and each student focuses on his/her own research project as the basis for tasks. These comprise a critical review of a single research article from the literature relevant to the student's topic, a draft literature review justifying the student's research and a draft research proposal, presented as both a seminar and a document. Language feedback on each task is provided by IBP lecturers, with content feedback given by the student's research supervisors ... An outcome of this curriculum structure is the establishment of a tripartite collaboration between student, supervisor and IBP lecturer.

(Cargill and Cadman, 2005: 2)

Regular evaluations of the course show that student satisfaction has remained consistently high and that supervisors comment on a range of beneficial outcomes (see Cadman, 2000 for details of this analysis). Cargill and Cadman (2005) have also documented significant changes to the programme during the ten years since it was established – most notably:

- supervisors have been brought more explicitly into class processes and assessment procedures; they double-mark all written work and attend combined student-supervisor workshops
- supervisor involvement is compulsory and it is widely acknowledged that this is why the programme succeeds
- a move from a pragmatic English for Academic Purposes approach to a 'pedagogy of connection' (see Cadman, 2005) that values international students' investments and interests, and fosters greater agency
- a shift in emphasis from language remediation and grammar work to an enhanced focus on the discourse level of research language, including how arguments are developed in discipline- and paradigm-specific varieties of English.

Such institutional moves clearly foster a writing culture, through the provision of funding and time to both academic and study support staff. They foster more than a crude process geared to productivity and doctoral completions. Rather, such interventions produce structures which embed collective conversations about writing and disciplinary conventions in the practices of academic life.

Writing courses

While North American universities have a long tradition of offering compulsory composition classes for first-year undergraduates, there are no comparable institutional structures to support the writing of graduate students. Rose and McClafferty (2001: 27) recently issued 'a call for the explicit and sustained teaching of writing in graduate education' (see also Mullen, 2001). They argue that while the quality of scholarly writing is widely bemoaned inside the academy, little is done 'to address the quality of writing in a systematic way at the very point where scholarly style and identity is being shaped' (p. 28). They describe one such effort at UCLA, where Rose instituted a course on professional writing in 1996.

The course is structured as a writing workshop and is taught by rotating faculty members. It is not framed as a remedial site of intervention but rather as a discursive space to support students to learn scholarly genres. The primary texts for the course are student writing across a range of education disciplines (social science and comparative education, psychological studies, urban schooling, higher education and organizational change). Each week students bring three to five pages of their writing to the workshop, they distribute it to small groups or the group at large, read it aloud, give their assessment of it and then engage in discussion with peers and the instructor about it. Students range from first year to those writing their dissertations. The topics of discussion range widely from issues of grammar and mechanics, to style and audience, to evidence and argumentation, to research design and broad issues of conceptualization.

Rose and McClafferty (2001) cite numerous benefits for students enrolled in the ten-week workshops, including: an increased sense of agency about how to craft writing; a stronger sense of audience and rhetorical stance (how to make writing accessible while honouring the conventions of a discipline); and improved skills as critical readers and co-instructors, 'guiding, prodding, pushing and encouraging each other to write more effectively and more authoritatively (p. 30). Above all, they emphasize the positive effects on student scholarly identities. Workshop spaces encouraged students to establish and refine their relationship to their work and disciplines, and more consciously shape a scholarly identity within their disciplines.

It is important to emphasize, however, that the UCLA course also had long-term institutional effects – generating other courses and the involvement of many academic staff. Over time, a further special topics course in writing and rhetoric was introduced. The faculty experimented with writing tutorials for non-native speakers of English, some students formed writing groups and some faculty began talking more frequently and forcefully about writing, with divisions increasingly giving attention to writing in their newly revised core courses on research practices. Issues of teaching and workload allocation, and finding appropriate instructors and resources were debated, shifting a view of writing as simply a technical or service enterprise and generating 'a heightened attention to writing beyond the boundaries of the course itself' (p. 31).

In Australia, a number of institutionally sanctioned courses for graduate students in a variety of disciplines is also beginning to emerge. Starfield (2003) reports on a faculty-based thesis writing course for postgraduate research students in the arts and social sciences. Initially conceptualized as solely for ESL writers with problems, the course was extended to both first and second language speakers of English in recognition of the fact that thesis writing requires 'a range of contextualised, negotiable literacy practices unfamiliar to many students' (p. 138).

The course uses annotated examples of Australian arts and social sciences theses taken from the Australian digital thesis website and focuses on writing different sections of the thesis genre. Starfield calls on current applied linguistic research on academic writing (Bunton, 2002; Dudley-Evans, 1997; Swales and Feak, 1994) and offers a range of strategies to students for constructing their own theses. She argues that students from other faculties could benefit from such courses, especially if they use rich examples from recent theses in appropriate disciplines.

Paltridge (2003) also describes a course on dissertation writing at a large Australian university: this was designed for TESOL students. Like the example given by Starfield, this course also makes extensive use of models and analysis of actual dissertation texts to build student knowledge. The course meets weekly for an hour over a full semester and is situated in genre-based approaches to writing. The teacher is a faculty member and teaching is generally in small groups of six to ten students. The starting point is a discussion of the social and cultural context of dissertation writing, the effect of novices writing for expert examiners and the roles and responsibilities of student writers. Students then engage in analysing sample dissertations.

As Paltridge explains, this strategy allows students to

> ... carry out an 'on-line genre analysis' (Flowerdew, 1993) of a dissertation with a similar research perspective to their own. This analysis takes them through the major sections of the sample dissertation, considering both the context and organization of the stages of the text as they go. Students then consider the reasons for the various organizational choices the writers of their texts have made. They report on their analyses to the class, and see to what extent the practices of particular research types differ (or not) from each other. Students then use the results of their analyses as a guide for preparing the writing of the dissertations. The use of models not only gives students a guide to conventional forms of texts (Dudley-Evans, 1997) but also provides 'valuable clues to the status of knowledge in the field' (Charney and Carlson, 1995: 116).

(Paltridge, 2003: 12)

On the basis of this work, students propose a table of contents for their own dissertations which they present to the class, explaining their rationale for the way they have organized their text. This leads to sessions on planning individual chapters, using the results of previous genre studies as a framework to guide student writing.

Thus, a very closely guided set of textwork strategies is used to scaffold student writing and increase textual knowledge, genre knowledge and social knowledge. As with other institutional initiatives we've considered,[13] the student evaluations are overwhelmingly positive and point to yet another way for supporting thesis writing outside the supervisory relationship.

International collaborations

The new globalized and networked conditions in which universities operate provide new opportunities for creating writing cultures though international online graduate exchange. There are many benefits for doctoral researchers and their thesis development in building doctoral writing communities across nations. To illustrate the possibilities, we consider one example where supervisors used their international networks and intellectual partnerships to create new spaces for doctoral text work and identity work.

The collaboration between Julie McLeod in the Faculty of Education, Deakin University, Australia, and Mimi Bloch, in the School of Education, University of

Wisconsin-Madison, USA, was based in their research conversations developed during sabbatical. They decided that students in both countries would benefit from a cross-institutional reading group. But it took two years of planning and implementation to make it happen. Below we use excerpts from McLeod's (2004) discussion to outline the nature of this ICT-based doctoral exchange.

> The exchange was conducted through a combination of an online 15 week seminar and discussion of readings and research, video-conferences and synchronous chat, face-to-face meetings and a two-day student research conference held at the University of Wisconsin-Madison. The exchange was conceived as a valuable way for students to extend their research and doctoral studies through cross-national and comparative dialogue, and through the building of new kinds of doctoral communities that spanned time and space. At one level, it was a form of 'research training' and induction into the culture of international networks and collaborations. At another level, it was a learning 'adventure', embraced with enthusiasm, excitement and dedication by all who participated, and which carried with it throughout a sense of the unexpected and uncertain. Indeed, it has been the unexpected learnings, the unpredictable outcomes and 'lines of flight' arising from collisions and conjunctions of ideas and experiences that have provided some of the most powerful insights for participants in their reflections on their own research. (McLeod, 2004: 1)

> The two universities were enthusiastic and supportive of the initiative, and our respective Departments and Faculty provided strong financial support for the program—for example Deakin Education subsidised the travel of its students, and Madison School of Education provided accommodation and meals for the visiting Deakin students. On the one hand, such support can be interpreted as symptomatic of the sector push for markets and internationalisation, but, on the other hand, it also allowed for innovation in learning and cross-cultural collaboration. Students who participated in the exchange did not pay any additional university fees—there was no immediate 'market' or commercial gain, though the exchange very likely contributed to strengthening links between the two institutions. A primary motivating goal for all participants was to learn across and with national differences, to encounter different traditions of graduate education. It was not market-driven, its focus on 'differences' was not subordinated to economic ends, and it was designed as a collaborative exchange, where the 'host' country was neither one institution/country nor the other: the point of reference for 'difference' was constantly shifting. The exchange itself was made possible by the use of ICT, and ongoing reflection on the kind of learning and interactions this created (or inhibited) was a key feature of our learning experiences.
>
> (McLeod, 2004: 3)

McLeod stresses that the mix of 'virtual and actual' communication was crucial to the success of the exchange. Students in the US and Australia had to negotiate the challenge of email online discussions and the vulnerability of showing their scholarly selves in formation on the screen and in teleconferences. The opportunity to meet face-to-face 'in the flesh' at a two-day conference at Madison in 2004, with all the social events and dinners attached to such gatherings, generated enormous excitement and anxiety. Each student presented a research paper, based on their dissertation work, research interactions and the readings from the seminar. But the conference facilitated a wide range of student understandings, some of which were unexpected. These are the reflections of Annelies Kamp, one of the Australian doctoral researchers:

> ... it was not until the entire exchange community met face-to-face in Madison in April 2004, that the influence of our diverse pedagogies struck me. The Madison students impressed all of us as being very well grounded theoretically, no doubt a reflection in part of the depth of the coursework component of their candidatures. In contrast they appeared struck by our mode of independent research, the way we would take theories and apply them to our own studies. Their journey from knowledge transmission to knowledge production was by way of a more structured route, more closely supervised; ours was more fluid, less closely supervised.
>
> (Kamp, 2004: 1)

All the Australian students highlighted the importance of being taken seriously 'overseas'. They returned home energized and re-enthused about the significance of their research. It was as if they had acquired a new vantage point from which to view their work and emerging scholarly identities. There have also been other textual spin-offs. Four Australian students presented a seminar with McLeod and Bloch at the national education research conference in December 2004 and subsequently wrote chapters on their experience for a book on international doctoral collaborations, edited by Bloch and McLeod. Such work offers new opportunities for thinking about the text work/identity work in doctoral research communities and yet another opportunity to think institutionally about how to foster international writing cultures.[14]

Making institutional writing cultures happen

We have argued throughout this book that writing and doctoral research are one and the same, and that thinking of a neutral stage of 'writing up' at the end of doctoral research is profoundly misleading. We have suggested a range of strategies that supervisors can adopt in order to make scholarly writing practices and the formation of a scholarly identity integral to their pedagogy. We noted at the beginning of this final chapter that a reliance on the initiative of individual supervisors was the predominant situation, and that universities needed to do more to support, spread and develop writing-focused supervision practices.

We have outlined five sites in which writing has begun to be taken more seriously. It is important to state that these kinds of initiatives are not cost neutral. Pilot writing projects are often initiated because interested staff have donated time, on top of ordinary workloads, to get them up and running. Or, conversely, it may be that pilot projects are funded, with the expectation that new practices will somehow be absorbed into unchanged workloads. Neither of these scenarios is sustainable in the long term. If thorough evaluations of writing-oriented initiatives are conducted (and in our experience this is often not the case), then the long term costs of such ventures must be part of the evaluation. Changed cultures require changed management systems, including shifts in the ways resources and workloads are managed.

Because most universities now rely heavily on reputation, quality measures, marketing and, in many countries, incomes derived from student fees, they are increasingly vulnerable to evidence which suggests that some are more responsive to student needs than others.[15] Doctoral completions count more than ever in 'image' and 'quality' management technologies, and institutions can ill afford to continue to ignore the connections between writing and doctoral success in examination.

This could be taken to mean more attention to technical writing skills in the undergraduate phases of university education (Avery and Bryan, 2001), and greater provision of student support services for particular students who are seen to be deficient and in need of remediation. However, we suggest that these kinds of approaches are insufficient.

As universities move to ensure that all university teaching staff are cognizant of a range of teaching and learning strategies appropriate to adult learners, and as they begin to experiment with models of group supervision and peer support, it seems to us that it is the right time for them to consider how to provide support for writing-oriented supervision practices. Making doctoral writing a topic of conversation among supervisors would at least be a start.

We hope that this book provides an incentive for such discussions and that it constitutes a resource for those supervisors whose institutions are not yet aware of the importance of text work and identity work.

Notes

1 This is not to suggest that identity is not discursive – it is (Czarniawska, 1997; Du Gay, 1996; Hall, 1996; McDonald, 1999). Nor is it the case that knowing oneself is an unproblematic concept (Britzman, 1994). However we have no time to go into theoretical debates here: those who are interested could start with *Identity: A Reader* (Du Gay *et al.* 2000)

2 It would be fruitful to apply the theorization of pedagogies developed by Basil Bernstein to supervision practices. This is not our project here, but we note that our ideas about writing work at the level of framing, but do potentially challenge the classification of some disciplinary fields.

3 This is not like Foucault who uses discourse to mean much more than text (see Foucault, 1991). But what Foucault calls discourse does appear in and as Fairclough's three boxes.

4 Golden-Biddle and Locke (1997) offer one framework for creating a warrant using scholarly literatures through what they call synthesized coherence (putting together previously unrelated work), progressive coherence (using works already recognized as related in either theory, method or both) or non-coherence (where there are points of disagreement).

5 It is common in many of the advice books to use metaphors to help students better understand aspects of the research process. For the most part, however, students are not asked for their own metaphors for doing research and when they are (e.g. Brause, 2000) these are often attributed to individual differences and approaches to research, rather than examined for the identity issues at stake in becoming a researcher.

6 Metaphors are particularly powerful forms of expression because they position the speaker and that being spoken about. Lakoff and Johnson (1983) for example, in their seminal work, noted the ways in which war metaphors appeared in many different contexts. Arguments for example are often described as 'indefensible' as having 'weak points', as 'providing ammunition' for something, as being 'on target' and as 'attacking'. Lakoff and Johnson suggest that this militarization positions those who argue as combatants, rather than as persons engaged in dialogue, and the argument as something to be won, rather than as an exploration of different points of view. Fairclough (1992) suggests that such metaphors 'structure the way we think and the way we act, and our systems of knowledge and belief in a pervasive and fundamental way' (1992: 194). He proposes that struggles over the metaphors used to describe domains of experience and practice point to significant ideological differences. He cites as an example the ways in which the discourse of consumption has entered higher education, and the ways in which some actively resist using notions such as 'services', 'marketing' and 'packaging'. Like Lakoff and Johnson, he suggests that some metaphors are insidious in their naturalization, and that such taken-for-granted expressions do political and cultural work that goes unrecognized.

7 *Deliverance* (1972) directed by John Boorman and based on James Dickey's novel of the same name (1970) was an action-adventure film about four suburban Atlanta businessmen friends who encountered serial disasters on a summer weekend's river-canoeing trip. It was nominated for three Academy Awards (Best Picture, Best Director, and Best Film Editing), but was awarded nothing.

8 Hyland's claim rests on the distinction made by linguist Michael Halliday between the ideational and the interpersonal functions of language. Halliday (1985) argues that texts are always multifunctional, always serving more than one purpose. They convey information, but they also build social relations at the same time. Language is never ideologically neutral because it inevitably codes for orientation and perspective as well as information. And so it is with dissertation writing and academic writing, more generally.

9 We have some sympathy with Ursula le Guin who wrote about the difficulties of working both with and against literary theory saying, 'Recently, at a three-day long symposium on narrative, I learned that it's unsafe to say anything about narrative, because if a poststructuralist doesn't get you a deconstructionist will. This is a pity, because the subject is an interesting one to those outside the armed camps of literary theory' (Le Guin, 1989: 97).

10 See for example Passive Voice on UNC-CH writing centre: http://www.unc.edu/depts/wcweb. Accessed 12 November 2005. Online Writing Lab: http://owl.english.purdue.edu/handouts/grammar/g_actpass.html. Accessed 12 November 2005.

11 The BCCS group included, for example, Stuart Hall, Dick Hebdidge, Angela McRobbie and Paul Willis: the quality of its alumni is testament to the power of the model.

12 There is also the journal *College Composition and Communication* in which writing support staff publish.

13 Our purpose in presenting these examples of writing courses has been to signal possibilities and positive institutional moves. However, we also want to acknowledge that there are debates that exist amongst those who work in this space: for example, there is concern that writing courses can be too removed from disciplinary particularities. The alternatives offered include: using academic literacies as a basis for course design (Lea, 1994); designing writing feedback into formal courses and programmes (Mullen, 2001); and a writing across the disciplines approach (Anson, 2002; Waldo, 2004). The writing across the disciplines approach is itself critiqued for failing to engage the majority of academic staff (Holstein, 2001).

14 See also cross-country collaboration at masters level between New Zealand and Canada (Robertson and Webber, 2000).

15 See for example Deem and Brehony (2000) who show that research students have different access to research cultures within and between universities.

Bibliography

Aitchison, C. (2003). Thesis writing circles. *Hong Kong Journal of Applied Linguistics*, 8(2), 97–115.

Aitchison, C. and Lee, A. (2006). Research writing: problems and pedagogies. *Teaching in Higher Education*, 11(3), 265–78.

Alcoff, L. and Potter, E. (1993). *Feminist epistemologies*. New York: Routledge.

Anson, C. M. (ed.) (2002). *The WAC casebook: Scenes for faculty reflection and program development*. New York: Oxford University Press.

Atkinson, D. and Dash, P. (eds) (2005). *Social and critical practices in art education*. Stoke on Trent: Trentham.

Atwood, M. (2003). *Negotiating with the dead: A writer on writing*. London: Virago.

Avery, S. and Bryan, C. (2001). Improving spoken and written English: from research to practice. *Teaching in Higher Education*, 6(2), 169–82.

Bakhtin, M. (1981). *The dialogic imagination: Four essays* (C. Emerson and M. Holquist, trans.). Austin, TX: University of Texas Press.

Banks, I. (2004). New models for providing men with health care. *The Journal of Men's Health and Gender*, 1(2–3), 155–8.

Barone, T. (1989). Ways of being at risk: the case of Billy Charles Barnett. *Phi Delta Kappan*, 71(2), 147–51.

Barone, T. and Eisner, E. (1997). Arts-based educational research. In R. Jaeger (ed.), *Complementary methods for research in education* (pp. 73–94). Washington, DC: American Educational Research Association.

Barthes, R. (1970). *S/Z* (R. Miller, Trans. 1974). London: Cape.

Barthes, R. (1986). *The rustle of language* (R. Howard, Trans.). Oxford: Basil Blackwell.

Bartlett, A. and Mercer, G. (eds) (2001). *Postgraduate research supervision: Transforming relations*. New York: Peter Lang.

Bauman, Z. (1998). *Work, consumerism and the new poor*. Buckingham: Open University Press.

Bazerman, C. (1981). What written knowledge does: three examples of academic discourse. *Philosophy of the Social Sciences*, 11(3), 361–87.

Bazerman, C. (1988). *Shaping written knowledge*. Madison, WI: University of Wisconsin Press.

Beck, U. (1992). *Risk society: Towards a new modernity*. London: Sage.

Becker, H. (1986). *Writing for social scientists: How to start and finish your thesis*. Chicago, IL: University of Chicago Press.

Behar, R. (1996). *The vulnerable observer: Anthropology that breaks your heart*. Boston, MA: Beacon Press.

Berkenkotter, C. and Huckin, T. N. (1985). *Genre knowledge in disciplinary communication: Cognition/culture/power*. Hillsdale, NJ: Lawrence Erlbaum.

Bhatia, V. J. (1999, August 1–6). Analysing genre: an applied linguistic perspective. Paper presented at the 12th World Congress of Applied Linguistics, Tokyo.

Bird, S. E. (2002). It makes sense to us: cultural identity in local legends of place. *Journal of Contemporary Ethnography*, 31(5), 519–47.

Bishop, R. and Glynn, T. (1999). *Culture counts: Changing power relations in education*. Palmerston North: Dunmore Press.

Bochner, A. and Ellis, C. (2002). *Ethnographically speaking: Autoethnography, literature and aesthetics*. Walnut Creek, CA: Alta Mira Press.

Boden, R., Epstein, D. and Kenway, J. (2004). *Academic's support kit*. London: Sage.

Bolker, J. (1998). *Writing your dissertation in fifteen minutes a day: A guide to starting, revising and finishing your doctoral thesis*. New York: Henry Holt.

Bonhomme, J. (2004). The health status of African-American men: improving our understanding of men's health, *The Journal of Men's Health and Gender*, 1(2–3), 142–6.

Boote, D. N. and Beile, P. (2005). Scholars before researchers: on the centrality of the dissertation literature review in research preparation. *Educational Researcher*, 34(6), 3–15.

Bourdieu, P. (1984). *Distinction: A social critique of the judgement of taste* (R. Nice, trans.). Boston, MA: Harvard University Press.

Bourdieu, P. (1988). *Homo academicus* (P. Collier, trans.). Stanford, CA: Stanford University Press.

Brause, R. (2000). *Writing your doctoral dissertation: Invisible rules for success*. London: RoutledgeFalmer.

Britzman, D. (1994). Is there a problem with knowing thyself? Towards a poststructuralist view of teacher identity. In T. Shanahan (ed.), *Teachers thinking, teachers knowing* (pp. 53–75). Urbana, IL: National Council of Teachers of English.

Bruner, J. (1986). Life as narrative. *Social Research*, 54(1), 11–32.

Bunton, D. (2002). Generic moves in PhD thesis introductions. In J. Flowerdew (ed.), *Academic discourse* (pp. 55–75). London: Longman.

Burdell, P. and Swadener, B. B. (1999). Critical personal narrative and autoethnography in education: reflection on a genre. *Educational Researcher*, 28(6), 21–6.

Burton, S. and Steane, P. (eds) (2004). *Surviving your thesis*. London: RoutledgeFalmer.

Burton-Jones, A. (2003). Knowledge capitalism: the new learning economy. *Policy Futures in Education*, 1(1), 143–59.

Butler, J. (1990). *Gender trouble: Feminism and the subversion of identity*. London: Routledge.

Cadman, K. (2000). 'Voices in the air': evaluations of the learning experiences of international postgraduates and their supervisors. *Teaching in Higher Education*, 5(4), 475–91.

Cadman, K. (2005). Towards a 'pedagogy of connection' in research education: a 'REAL' story. *Journal of English for Academic Purposes*. Special Edition on Advanced Academic Literacies, 4(4), 353–67

Cargill, M. and Cadman, K. (2005, July 6–8). Revisiting quality for international research education: towards an engagement model. Paper presented at the Australian Universities Quality Forum, Sydney.

Ceroni, K., Garman, N., Haggerson, N., MacMahon, P., Piantanida, M. and Spore, M. (1996, April). Disturbing our universe: the dissertation as personal narrative. Paper presented at the American Educational Research Association Annual Meeting, New York.

Charney, D. and Carlson, R. (1995). Learning to write in a genre: what student writers take from model texts. *Research in the Teaching of Writing*, 29, 88–125.

Cixous, H. and Calle-Gruber, M. (1997). *Rootprints: Memory and life writing*. New York: Routledge.

Clark, R. and Ivanic, R. (1997). *The politics of writing*. London: Routledge.

Clements, P. (1999). Autobiographical research and the emergence of the fictive voice. *Cambridge Journal of Education*, 29(1), 21–32.

Clough, P. (2002). *Narratives and fictions in educational research*. Buckingham: Open University Press.

Connelly, F. M. and Clandinin, D. J. (eds) (1999). *Shaping a professional identity: Stories of educational practice*. New York: Teachers College Press.

Convery, A. (1999). Listening to teachers' stories: are we sitting too comfortably? *Qualitative Studies in Education*, 12(2), 131–46.

Cotterill, P. and Letherby, G. (1993). Weaving stories: personal auto/biographies in feminist research. *Sociology*, 27(1), 67–80.

Cryer, P. (2001). *The research student's guide to success* (2nd edn). Buckingham: Open University Press.

Czarniawska, B. (1997). *Narrating the organisation: Dramas of institutional identity*. Chicago: University of Chicago Press.

Deem, R. and Brehony, J. (2000). Doctoral students' access to research cultures – are some more equal than others? *Studies in Higher Education*, 25(2), 149–65.

Delamont, S. and Atkinson, P. (1995). *Fighting familiarity. Essays on education and ethnography*. Cresskill, NJ: Hampton Press.

Delamont, S., Atkinson, P. and Parry, O. (1997). *Supervising the PhD: A guide to success*. Buckingham: Open University Press.

Delamont, S., Atkinson, P. and Parry, O. (2000). *The doctoral experience: Success and failure in graduate school*. London: Falmer Press.

Delanty, G. (2001). The university in the knowledge age. *Organization*, 8(2), 149–53.

Delbridge, A., Bernard, J. R. L., Blair, D., Peters, P. and Butler, S. (1991). *The Macquarie Dictionary* (2nd edn). Sydney, Australia: Macquarie University.

Denzin, N. K. (1997). *Interpretive ethnography: Ethnographic practices for the 21st century*. London: Sage.

Denzin, N. K. (ed.) (2003). *Performance ethnography: Critical pedagogy and the politics of culture*. Thousand Oaks, CA: Sage.

Derewianka, B. (1990). *Exploring how texts work*. Newtown, NSW: Primary English Teaching Association.

Derewianka, B. (1995). Taking it for granted. *Idiom*, 30(1), 28–34.

Derrida, J. (1976). *Of grammatology*. Baltimore, MD: Johns Hopkins University Press.

Derrida, J. (1978). *Writing and difference* (A. Bass, trans. 1995). London: Routledge.

Dewey, J. (1897). My pedagogic creed. *The School Journal*, LIV(3), 77–80.

Dewey, J. (1916). *Democracy and education: An introduction to the philosophy of education* (1996 edn). New York: Free Press. http://www.itl.columbia.edu/academic/texts/dewey/d_e/contents.html. Accessed 20 March 2000.

Dewey, J. (1934). *Art as experience* (1980 edn). New York: Perigee.

Dewey, J. (1938). *Experience and education* (1963 edn). New York: Collier Books.

Diamond, C. P. and Mullen, C. (1999). *The postmodern educator: Arts based inquiries and teacher development*. New York: Peter Lang.

Dias, P. and Paré, A. (2000). *Transitions: Writing in academic and workplace settings*. Cresskill, NJ: Hampton Press.

Dickey, J. (1970). *Deliverance*. New York: Dell.

Dingwall, R. (2000). Language, law, and power: ethnomethodology, conversation analysis and the politics of law and society studies. *Law and Social Inquiry*, 25(3), 885–911.

Dinham, S. and Scott, C. (2001). The experience of disseminating the results of doctoral research. *Journal of Further and Higher Education*, 25(1), 45–55.

Du Gay, P. (1996). *Consumption and identity at work*. London: Sage.

Du Gay, P., Evans, J. and Redman, P. (eds) (2000). *Identity: A reader*. London: Sage.

Dudley-Evans, T. (1997). Genre: how far can we, should we go? *World Englishes*, 16(3), 351–8.

Dunleavy, P. (2003). *Authoring a PhD: How to plan, draft, write and finish a doctoral dissertation or thesis*. London: Palgrave.

Dunsmire, P. (1997). Naturalizing the future in factual discourse: a critical linguistic analysis of a projected event. *Written Communication*, 14(2), 221–64.

Edwards, T. (2000). 'All the evidence shows ...': reasonable expectations of educational research. *Oxford Review of Education*, 26(3&4), 299–311.

Eggins, S. (2004). *An introduction to systemic functional linguistics* (2nd edn). New York: Continuum.

Ellis, C. (1999). He*art*ful autoethnography. *Qualitative Health Research*, 9(5), 669–83.

Ellis, C. and Flaherty, M. (eds) (1992). *Investigating subjectivity: Research on lived experience*. London: Sage.

Ellsworth, E. (2005). *Places of learning: Media, architecture, pedagogy*. New York: RoutledgeFalmer.

Ely, M., Vinz, R., Downing, M. and Anzul, M. (eds) (1997). *On writing qualitative research: Living by words*. London: Falmer Press.

Engestrom, C. M. (1999). Promoting the scholarly writing of female doctoral students in higher education and student affairs programs. *NASPA Journal*, 36(4), 264–77.

Evans, T. D. (2002). Part-time research students: are they producing knowledge where it counts? *Higher Education Research and Development*, 21(2), 155–65.

Evans, T. D. and Pearson, M. (1999). Off-campus doctoral research in Australia: emerging issues and practices. In A. Holbrook and S. Johnston (eds), *Supervision of postgraduate research in education* (pp. 185–206). Coldstream, Victoria: Australian Association for Research in Education.

Fairclough, N. (1989). *Language and power* (1994 edn). Singapore: Longman.

Fairclough, N. (1992). *Discourse and social change*. London: Polity.

Flowerdew, J. (1993). An educational, or process approach, to the teaching of professional genres. *ELT Journal*, 47, 305–17.

Foucault, M. (1991). Politics and the study of discourse. In G. Burchell, C. Gordon and P. Miller (eds), *The Foucault effect: Studies in governmentality* (pp. 53–72). Chicago, IL: University of Chicago Press.

Foucault, M. (1994). The birth of social medicine. In J. D. Faubion (ed.), *Power: The essential works of Foucault, 1954–1984. Volume 3* (pp. 134–56). New York: The New Press.

Franklin, B. (ed.) (1999). *Social policy, the media and misrepresentation*. London: Routledge.

Game, A. and Metcalfe, A. (1996). *Passionate sociology*. London: Sage Publications.

Geertz, C. (1973). *The interpretation of cultures*. New York: Basic Books.

Gibbons, M., Limoges, C., Nowtowny, H., Schwartzman, S., Scott, P. and Trow, M. (1994). *The new production of knowledge: The dynamics of science and research*. London: Sage.

Giddens, A. (1991). *Modernity and self identity*. Stanford, CA: Stanford University Press.

Giltrow, J. (1995). *Academic writing: Writing and reading across the disciplines*. Ontario: Broadview Press.

Glatthorn, A. (1998). *Writing the winning dissertation: A step by step guide*. London: Corwin Press.

Golden-Biddle, K. and Locke, K. (1997). *Composing qualitative research*. Thousand Oaks, CA: Sage.

Graves, D. (1983). *Writing: Teachers and children at work*. Portsmouth, NH: Heinemann.

Hall, S. (1996). Who needs 'identity'? In S. Hall and P. du Gay (eds), *Questions of cultural identity* (pp. 1–17). London: Sage.

Halliday, M. (1985). *An introduction to functional grammar*. London: Edward Arnold.

Halliday, M. and Matthiessen, C. M. I. M. (2004). *An introduction to functional grammar* (3rd ed., revised by C. Matthiessen). London: Edward Arnold.

Hammond, J. (1990). Is learning to read and write the same as learning to speak? In F. Christie (ed.), *Literacy for a changing world* (pp. 79–117). Melbourne, Victoria: Australian Council for Educational Research.

Haraway, D. (1988). Situated knowledges: the science question in feminism and the privilege of partial perspective. *Feminist Studies*, 14(3), 575–99.

Hart, C. (1998). *Doing a literature review*. Thousand Oaks, CA: Sage.

Hart, C. (2001). *Doing a literature search*. Thousand Oaks, CA: Sage.

Haug, F. (1987). *Female sexualisation* (E. Carter, trans.). London: Verso.

Heath, T. (2002). A quantitative analysis of PhD students' views of supervision. *Higher Education Research and Development*, 21(1), 41–53.

Hendricks, M. and Quinn, L. (2000). Teaching referencing as an introduction to epistemological empowerment. *Teaching in Higher Education*, 5(4), 447–57.

Hogan, C. (2005). Professional learning through narratives of practice. Unpublished PhD, Deakin University, Geelong, Victoria.

Holstein, D. H. (2001). 'Writing across the curriculum' and the paradoxes of institutional initiatives. *Pedagogy*, 1(1), 37–52.

Hyland, K. (1999). Disciplinary discourses: writer stance in research articles. In C. N. Candlin and K. Hyland (eds), *Writing: Texts, processes and practices* (pp. 99–121). London: Longman.

Hyland, K. (2000). *Disciplinary discourses: Social interactions in academic writing*. London: Longman.

Hyland, K. (2002). Options of identity in academic writing. *ELT Journal*, 56(4), 351–8.

Ivanic, R. (1998). *Writing and identity: The discoursal construction of identity in academic writing*. Amsterdam: John Benjamins.

Janks, H. (2002). Critical discourse analysis as a research tool. In M. Toolan (ed.), *Critical discourse analysis: Critical concepts in linguistics, Volume IV* (pp. 26–42). London: Routledge.

Jones, A. (1992). Writing feminist educational research: am 'I' in the text? In S. Middleton and A. Jones (eds), *Women and education in Aotearoa* (pp. 18–32, 224). Wellington: Bridget Williams Books.

Jones, K. (2003). *Education in Britain: 1944 to the present.* Oxford: Polity Press.

Kamler, B. (2001). *Relocating the personal. A critical writing pedagogy.* New York: State University of New York Press.

Kamler, B. (2005a, September 14–17). Learning the ropes of academic publishing: doctoral writing output in education and science. Paper presented at the British Educational Research Association Annual Conference, University of Glamorgan, Wales.

Kamler, B. (2005b). Research writing: doctoral studies in education seminar. http://dse. moodle.com (closed website). Melbourne, Victoria: Deakin University.

Kamler, B. and Maclean, R. (1997). 'You can't just go to court and move your body': first year students learn how to write and speak the law. *Law/Text/Culture*, 3, 176–209.

Kamler, B. and Rowan, L. (2004, December 14–16). Quality learning and quality education: new times, new relationships, new pathways. Paper presented at the International Symposium on Quality Education, National Normal University of Taiwan, Taipei.

Kamler, B. and Thomson, P. (2004). Driven to abstraction: doctoral supervision and writing pedagogies. *Teaching in Higher Education*, 9(2), 195–209.

Kamp, A. (2004, November 28–December 7). The disembodied apprentice: reflections on a doctoral exchange. Paper presented at the Australian Association for Research in Education Annual Conference, Melbourne.

Kilbourn, B. (2001). The art and structure of the first paragraph. *Teachers College Record*. http://www.tcrecord.org. ID number 10707. Accessed 19 May 2003.

King, T. (2003). *The truth about stories.* Toronto: House of Anansi.

Lakoff, G. and Johnson, M. (1983). *Metaphors we live by.* Chicago, IL: University of Chicago Press.

Lather, P. (1992). Critical frames in educational research: feminist and poststructural perspectives. *Theory into Practice*, 31(2), 87–99.

Le Guin, U. (1989). *Dancing at the edge of the world: Thoughts on words, women, places.* New York: Harper and Rowe.

Lea, M. R. (1994). Academic literacies: a pedagogy for course design. *Studies in Higher Education*, 29(6), 739–56.

Lea, M. R. and Stierer, B. (eds) (2000). *Student writing in higher education: New contexts.* Buckingham: Open University Press.

Lea, M. R. and Street, B. (1998). Student writing in higher education: an academic literacies approach. *Studies in Higher Education*, 23(2), 157–72.

Lea, M. R. and Street, B. (2000). Student writing and staff feedback in higher education: an academic literacies approach. In M. R. Lea and B. Stierer (eds), *Student writing in higher education: New contexts* (pp. 32–46). Buckingham: Open University Press.

Lee, A. (1998). Doctoral research as writing. In J. Higgs (ed.), *Writing qualitative research* (pp. 121–36). Five Dock, NSW: Hampden Press.

Lee, A. and Boud, D. (2003). Writing groups, change and academic identity: research development as local practice. *Studies in Higher Education*, 28(2), 187–200.

Leibowitz, B. and Goodman, K. (1997). The role of a writing centre in increasing access to academic discourse in a multilingual university. *Teaching in Higher Education*, 2(1), 5–19.

Lemke, J. (2003). *Multimedia semiotic analysis: Focal questions.* http://www.personal. umich.edu/~jaylemke/guides/multimedia_semiotic_analysis_questions.html. Accessed on 6 May 2004.

Leonard, D. (2001). *A woman's guide to doctoral studies.* Buckingham: Open University Press.

Leonard, D., Becker, R. and Coate, K. (2004). 'To prove myself at the highest level': the benefits of doctoral study. *Higher Education Research and Development*, 24(2), 135–49.

Lillis, T. (2001). *Student writing: Access, regulation, desire.* London and New York: Routledge.

Lillis, T. and Turner, J. (2001). Student writing in higher education: contemporary confusion, traditional concerns. *Teaching in Higher Education*, 6(1), 57–68.

Lynn, M. (2004). Inserting the 'race' into critical pedagogy: an analysis of race-based epistemologies. *Educational Philosophy and Theory*, 36(2), 153–65.

Maclean, R. (2003). Learning literacies in the law: constructing legal subjectivities. Unpublished PhD, Monash University, Melbourne, Victoria.

Malfroy, J. (2005). Doctoral supervision, workplace research and changing pedagogic practice. *Higher Education Research and Development*, 24(2), 165–78.

Martin, J. R. and Rose, D. (2003). *Working with discourse.* London: Continuum.

McDonald, K. (1999). *Struggles for subjectivity. Identity, action and youth experience.* Cambridge: Cambridge University Press.

McDowell, L. (1997). *Capital culture: Gender at work in the city.* Oxford: Blackwell.

McLeod, J. (2004, Dec 14–16). Rethinking quality doctoral learning: reflections on and from an international doctoral student exchange. Paper presented at the International Symposium on Quality Education, National Normal University of Taiwan, Taipei.

McLeod, J. (2005). *Writing literature reviews: Online course materials.* Melbourne: Deakin University.

McWilliam, E., Taylor, P., Thomson, P., Green, B., Maxwell, T., Wildy, H. and Simon, D. (2002). *Research training in doctoral programs: What can we learn from professional doctorates?* Canberra: Evaluations and Investigations Branch, Department of Education, Science and Training.

Moore Johnson, S., Birkeland, S., Donaldson, M., Kardos, S., Kauffman, D., Liu, E. and Peske, H. (2004). *Finders and keepers: Helping new teachers survive and thrive in our schools.* New York: Teachers College Press.

Mullen, C. (2001). The need for a curricular writing model for graduate students. *Journal of Further and Higher Education*, 25(1), 117–26.

Murray, D. M. (1982). *Learning by teaching: Selected articles on writing and teaching.* Montclair, NJ: Boynton Cook.

Murray, E. (2002). *How to write a thesis.* Maidenhead: Open University Press.

Myers, G. (1985). The social construction of two biologists' proposals. *Written Communication*, 2(3), 219–455.

Nelson, C. and San Miguel, C. (2000, May). Writing a professional doctorate. Paper presented at the Professional Doctorates Conference, Adelaide, South Australia.

Neumann, A. and Peterson, P. (eds) (1997). *Learning from our lives: Women, research, and autobiography in education.* New York: Teachers College Press.

Ogden, E. H. (1993). *Completing your doctoral dissertation or master's thesis in two semesters or less.* Lancaster, PA: Technomic Publications.

Page-Adams, D., Cheng, L. C., Gogineni, A. and Shen, C. Y. (1995). Establishing a group to encourage writing for publication among doctoral students. *Journal of Social Work Education*, 31(3), 402–7.

Paltridge, B. (2003). Teaching thesis and dissertation writing. *Hong Kong Journal of Applied Linguistics*, 8(2), 78–96.

Paltridge, B. (2004). Academic writing: review article. *Language Teaching*, (37), 87–105.

Parker, L. (1998). 'Race is … race ain't': an exploration of the utility of critical race theory in qualitative research in education. *Qualitative Studies in Education*, 11(1), 43–55.

Pearson, M. (1999). The changing environment for doctoral education in Australia: implications for quality management, improvement and innovation. *Higher Education Research and Development*, 18(3), 269–87.

Phillips, E. and Pugh, D. S. (1987). *How to get a PhD: A handbook for students and their supervisors*. Milton Keynes: Open University Press.

Piantanida, M., McMahon, P. and Garman, N. (2003). Sculpting the contours of arts-based educational research within a discourse community. *Qualitative Inquiry*, 9(2), 182–91.

Prain, V. (1997). Textualising yourself in research writing: some current challenges. *Journal of Curriculum Studies*, 29(1), 71–85.

Prior, P. (1998). *Writing/disciplinarity: A sociohistoric account of literate activity in the academy*. Mahwah, NJ: Lawrence Erlbaum.

Reed-Danahay, D. (ed.) (1997). *Auto/ethnography: Rewriting the self and the social*. Oxford: Berg.

Richardson, L. (1990). *Writing strategies: Reaching diverse audiences*. Thousand Oaks, CA: Sage.

Richardson, L. (1994). Writing. A method of inquiry. In N. Denzin and Y. Lincoln (eds), *The handbook of qualitative research* (pp. 516–29). Thousand Oaks, CA: Sage Publications.

Richardson, L. (1997). *Fields of play. Constructing an academic life*. New Brunswick, NJ: Rutgers University Press.

Robertson, J. and Webber, C. (2000). Boundary breaking: an emergent model for leadership development. *Educational Policy Analysis Archives*, 6(21). http://epaa.asu.edu/epaa/ v6n21.html. Accessed 21 July 2002.

Rogers, R., Malanchuraruvil-Berkes, M. M., Hui, D. and O'Garro Joseph, G. (2005). Critical discourse analysis in education: a review of the literature. *Review of Educational Research*, 75(3), 365–416.

Rorty, R. (1982). *The consequences of pragmatism*. Minneapolis, MN: University of Minnesota Press.

Rose, M. and McClafferty, K. (2001). A call for the teaching of writing in graduate education. *Educational Researcher*, 30(2), 27–33.

Sanderson, I. (2002). Evaluation, policy learning and evidence-based policy making. *Public Administration*, 80(1), 1–22.

Schleppegrell, M. (2004). *The language of schooling: A functional linguistics perspective*. Mahwah, NJ: Lawrence Erlbaum.

Schultz, K. (2001). Stretching the boundaries of participatory research: insights from conducting research with urban adolescents, *Australian Educational Researcher*, 28(2), 1–28.

Seaton, J. (ed.) (1998). *Politics and the media: Harlots and prerogatives at the turn of the millennium*. Oxford: Blackwell.

Smith, L. T. (1999). *Decolonising methodologies: Research and indigenous peoples.* London: Zed Books.

Smyth, E., Allen, C. and Wahlstrom, M. (2001). Changing educational environments for professional doctorates at the Ontario Institute for Studies in Education at the University of Toronto (OISE/UT). In B. Green, T. Maxwell and P. Shanahan (eds), *Doctoral education and professional practice: The next generation?* (pp. 69–84). Armidale, NSW: Kardoorair Press.

St Pierre, E. and Pillow, W. (eds) (2000). *Working the ruins: Feminist poststructuralist theory and method in education.* New York: Routledge.

Starfield, S. (2003). The evolution of a thesis-writing course for Arts and Sciences students: what can applied linguistics offer? *Hong Kong Journal of Applied Linguistics*, 8(2), 137–54.

Stronach, I. and MacLure, M. (1997). *Educational research undone: The postmodern embrace.* Buckingham: Open University Press.

Swales, J. M. and Feak, C. B. (1994). *Academic writing for graduate students: Essential tasks and skills.* Ann Arbor, MI: University of Michigan Press.

Taylor, S., Rivzi, F., Lingard, B. and Henry, M. (1997). *Educational policy and the politics of change.* London: Routledge.

Thomson, P. (1999). Doing justice: Stories of everyday life in disadvantaged schools and neighbourhoods. Unpublished PhD, Deakin University. Accessible on http://tux.lib/ deakin.edu.au/adt-VDU/public/adt-VDU20031119.101136/.

Threadgold, T. (1997). *Feminist poetics: Poiesis, performance, histories.* London: Routledge.

Torrance, M. and Thomas, G. (1994). The development of writing skills in doctoral research students, in R. G. Burgess (ed.) *Postgraduate education and training in the social sciences* (pp. 105–24). London: Jessica Kingsley.

Tripp, D. (1993). *Critical incidents in teaching: Developing professional judgement.* London: Routledge.

Wagner, J. (1993). Ignorance in educational research: or, how can you not know that? *Educational Researcher*, 22(5), 15–23.

Waldo, M. L. (2004). *Demythologising language differences in the academy: Establishing discipline based writing programs.* Mahwah, NJ: Lawrence Erlbaum.

Walker, C. (1999). Practitioner of a dangerous profession: a conversation with Frederick Busch. *Poets and Writers*, May/June, 33–7.

Winnicott, D. W. (1989). *Playing and reality.* New York: Routledge.

Wisker, G. (2004). *The good supervisor.* London: Palgrave Macmillan.

Wolcott, H. (2001). *Writing up qualitative research* (2nd edn). Thousand Oaks, CA: Sage.

Index

Lightning Source UK Ltd.
Milton Keynes UK
UKOW051822261112

202814UK00003B/18/P

9 780415 346849